THE SMALL BUSINESS SURVIVAL GUIDE

THE
SMALL BUSINESS
SURVIVAL GUIDE
A Handbook

by Bob Coleman

W.W. NORTON & COMPANY
New York London

Published simultaneously in Canada by Penguin Books Canada Ltd.,
2801 John Street, Markham, Ontario L3R 1B4.
Printed in the United States of America.

The text of this book is composed in 10/12 Compano, with display type set in
Craw Modern Bold. Composition by Haddon Manufacturing.
Book design by Nancy Dale Muldoon.

This book contains many case histories drawn from my own experience. In
retelling these personal anecdotes, I have, naturally, altered many details to protect
client confidentiality. As a result, these stories should be read solely for the business principles they illustrate.

First published as a Norton paperback 1987

Library of Congress Cataloging in Publication Data
Coleman, Bob.
   The small business survival guide.
   Bibliography: p.
   Includes index.
   1. Small business—Management.   I. Title.
HD62.7.C64   1984   658'.022   83–17228

ISBN 0-393-30418-3

W. W. Norton & Company, Inc., 500 Fifth Avenue, New York, N. Y. 10110
W. W. Norton & Company Ltd., 37 Great Russell Street, London WC1B 3NU

   5 6 7 8 9 0

TO MY FATHER, WHO TAUGHT ME MOST OF WHAT FOLLOWS.

CONTENTS

ACKNOWLEDGMENTS

It would be impossible to thank by name all the people—clients, colleagues, teachers, friends—who have helped to show me both the importance of small business in American life, and the many ways small businesses can be successfully organized and run. Yet I am indebted to them all, and here offer them collectively my sincere thanks.

The people who helped turn that information into a book are, happily, easier to name individually. Thanks to George Nicholson, Ruth Milliman Pollack, and Markham Harris, who early encouraged me to try my hand at writing. Sincere thanks to my agents, Steven Axelrod and Peter Ginsberg. Above all, a very special thanks to my editor, Starling Lawrence, who showed patience, good humor, and technical skill all the months this book was a-writing.

Introduction

WHY BUSINESS FOR YOURSELF, AND WHY THIS BOOK

Let's talk about investments. Suppose you had bought gold at its decontrol price—about $40 an ounce. When the price peaked in 1980, you could have sold out for around $840 an ounce. That's a twenty-one-fold increase in value. Not bad. If you had unluckily held the gold another year and a half, it would have brought only about $400, but that's still respectable. Again, suppose you'd bought Southern California real estate. A run-of-the mill house bought in 1975 for about $40,000 might have been worth $100,000 in 1980, a two-and-one-half-fold increase in five years. If you'd picked very wisely—perhaps a run-down beach house in Del Mar—your $40,000 might have grown to $200,000. Another sound investment.

But suppose—for the sake of discussion—that in 1960, you'd put up $150,000 for a half interest in a new meatpacking firm called Iowa Beef Processors. By 1980, when that company sold out to Occidental Petroleum, your undiluted half interest would have been worth . . . $400,000,000. That's *four hundred million dollars.* And that's only part of the story, since the young men who actually started the firm didn't use their own money; they got a federally-backed loan from the Small Business Administration. They ran up the original investment from $300,000 to $800 million, and the original investment was someone else's money.

Now, obviously, IBP is not a typical case. Still, it *did* happen, and so did Atari, Apple Computers, Genentech, and a host of other companies that began in back yards, garages, and laboratories, and ultimately made it to the big board.

Small businesses, then, can be superb investments. But the money is only a starting point, because small businesses also form a cornerstone of American personal freedoms. For some of us, that means freedom from rigid corporate life. For others, it means the freedom to experiment with new products or ideas, or to find new outlets for our talents and energies. And for many of us, it simply means a freedom which, if not grand, is still terribly important: freedom from economic worry, the chance to secure our own futures while making the world a bit better for others.

In that regard, I think of a young client of ours. Shortly after the Arab Oil Embargo of 1973, Walt, then fresh out of college, became convinced that the hardships of soaring energy prices would create a growing need for someone who could build and sell basic solar-powered heating systems. He began with $50 and the loan of his parents' garage, and by the time he contracted us in early 1980, his company was set to sell for about $400,000—a conservative figure, but, at age 28, he was anxious to retire. Beyond that, he was able to keep about $100,000 in accounts receivable, money from goods he had already sold. Whether you consider that a 10,000-fold return on investment ($500,000 from $50), or a college graduate with a BA pulling down $100,000 a year his first five years out of school, our young client Walter had done extremely well.

And those are only the figures from the sale of the business. They say nothing about the $42,500 in salary Walt regularly drew, or the fringe benefits like expense accounts and company cars, or the infinite satisfaction of having been his own boss at an age when most young people are either still in school or else just reaching the bottom rung of some corporate ladder. Add to that the fact that his products helped several thousand people achieve a measure of energy independence at a time when this country was in trouble, and you have an idea of what even a modest small business can achieve.

So from the smash hits of an Atari or an Apple, down to the more modest triumphs of our young client Walt, success in business is possible these days—eminently possible. Yet business has its hazards, mostly of a sort never mentioned in economics courses, or even in business schools. Anyone hoping to succeed in business must find a way to deal with the dangers, the difficulties, which are part of free enterprise.

That's the "why" of this book. I'm not here—except in passing —to teach you accounting, or tell you what business to enter. I'm here to explain the sixty or so most common trouble spots faced by people going into business, and the ways to meet and beat them. I want to help you cope with both the traditional small business problems, and the newer challenges posed by low-cost and aggressive foreign competitors. I want to teach the tactics of modern small business, the tricks which will let you survive and prosper in the '8os and beyond.

Between us, my father and I have a combined nearly fifty years in the business brokerage field. It would be presumptuous in the extreme to say we've seen every way a business can go wrong, or learned every way one can be righted, but we've seen more than the average person—even the average business person—could see in several lifetimes. The best of all we've learned has gone into what follows.

THE SMALL BUSINESS SURVIVAL GUIDE

1

PREBUSINESS PREPARATION

SITUATION:
Too many businesses fail because their owners neglected pre-business preparations
OBJECTIVE:
Setting goals, determining resources, and making key choices before *starting into business*

In this chapter, we'll discuss the three key decisions (or calculations) you need to make before even looking at your first business. We'll consider them in the order most likely to make you both a *happy* and a *financially successful* buyer. Remember, please, that these two goals are not automatically the same.

The First Decision.

The first decision is a subjective or psychological one, and for that reason many nominally hard-nosed people pay it scant attention. They're making a mistake.

Begin by deciding your private priorities. Never mind what the world expects. What do *you* want from life? Is there one single line of work that will make you happy, whether or not you become rich, or are you interested solely in the independence of a large income, and willing to undertake almost any business so long as it makes big money? Obviously, everyone would like both, and a fair number of us get it,—but if your situation comes down to a choice, you've got to know which way you'll jump.

This is an issue which has to be settled at the outset, and settled so there is accord among all partners (if partners there be). If two partners decide to build sailboats, one because she wants to make the best sailboats the world's ever seen, and the other because he wants two Mercedes and a home in Newport Beach, they're dead before they've started.

A concrete example? Certainly. A client of ours, a dentist, discovered that his line of work had begun to disgust him. He wanted into any other business at all, so long as it approximated what he earned as a professional. We found a construction-related concern which suited him perfectly. As an owner/officer he could expect about the same income he had enjoyed as a dentist—just over $100,000 a year. The operation was first-rate, the hours reasonable. In fact, the business was a "cash cow"—you could milk it forever. The more he looked, the more he liked. Finally, happy, he signed the preliminary papers, thanked us and left.

The next day, early, he called again. The deal was off; he would pay any forfeiture to be released. His wife, who previously had given her approval to any career change necessary for his peace of mind, now said she would leave him if he completed the purchase. The reason? The company installed chemical toilets at construction sites, and no matter how much money it made, she was not about to have to tell everyone at the country club that her husband was into "crappers."

Can we laugh? Yes, now. But the misery she felt, and the expense and pain to which she subjected her husband and herself, weren't funny at all. Moreover, the same fundamental feelings— perhaps more artistically expressed—exist within us all. If nothing in life will make you happy but owning a book store, or an art gallery, or a tackle shop on a pier, then recognize that, and don't devote your life to an infinite set of deferrals and disappointments.

You'll pay a price for not understanding yourself. Most likely, when you finally come to signing the papers for that high-profit chemical toilet business, you'll find some ground for backing out. Do that a couple of times, and you'll begin to despise yourself, never knowing why. Or worse, you'll buy the firm, and then suffer painfully all the years you own it.

If, on the other hand, you are the type of person who can be pleased with any business at all, so long as it is profitable, you are simply saying that business itself is your great love, or that your happiness is unconnected with your line of work. Then you are fortunate; and your range of opportunities is likely to be very wide.

Either personality is respectable; either can succeed. But it is crucial at the outset to understand what precisely is motivating you. That understanding makes partnerships workable, and individuals happy. Remember, too, that business salesmen are paid in part to determine your motivation. If they figure it out before you do, they're likely to use it against you.

The Second Decision.

The second decision is the *way* you will get into business. There are three basic options: 1) acquiring a franchise, 2) buying or taking over an existing operation, or 3) starting from scratch. In choosing, keep in mind that *the freedom of action of any endeavor is likely to be inversely proportioned to its security.* In that way, your choice is again partly psychological—you have to decide how much freedom you're willing to trade off for how much security.

FRANCHISES. At the top of the security ladder (and so, at the bottom in terms of freedom) is the franchise. For the last fifteen years or so franchising has been probably the hottest (that is, most popular) way of getting into business in the US, and there are few signs of its cooling. You can buy a franchise to put you in any business from fast food to roller skating, from computers to car repair. At its worst, the franchise is nothing but a fly-by-night scheme selling second-rate knowledge at a high price. At its best, it takes you step-by-step through every aspect of running your chosen business, teaching you the most efficient operating methods, and assuming some of the risk by providing land and buildings. It also provides the muscle for advertising (and in a few cases, lobbying) on a massive scale. Those unending TV and radio ads urging us to "Midasize" or "have it better at the box" are all funded by monthly "marketing fund" assessments of 3–4% of the franchise holder's gross sales.

The money, certainly, is good. According to *Fortune* magazine, the average Burger King outlet, for example, does a bit over $700,000 volume per year, and nets around $70,000 before taxes—a good if not staggering return on an average investment of $179,000 per store.

Recognize though, that the investment is not small by any means, and that with potential franchisees lining up in droves, the big franchisers aren't going to want to hear about "creative financing". To even bother to apply for a Burger King franchise, for example, requires at least $110,000 in cash or other highly liquid assets.

Even more to the point, bear in mind what *Fortune* (June 16, 1980) has to say about people who apply for those franchises:

> In this rigorous competition, knowledge of, or even interest in, food counts for little; the candidates could as well be prospective Midas Muffler dealers. What Burger King is mainly looking for is people who have management ability, enthusiasm, (and) . . . *willingness to follow orders to the letter.*

I've underscored that last point myself, and I'd like to do it again. We've never handled Burger King, but we've handled any number of other franchises (and turned down as many more),* and found that strict systemizing common to them all—and the better the franchise is, the more they insist upon it. The best franchises can be very good investments indeed, but they all have one thing in common: you do things the company way or you don't do them at all. If a burger in Bismark is going to taste like one in Baton Rouge, it's got to be made just like it—from salt to sauce to seeds

---

*Americans are supposed to be the great advocates of franchising, but it was not always so. In the early '50s, our firm was the original agent for Jack-in-the-Box stores. The first three franchises we offered for $500 apiece (entirely our broker's fee) for stores already in operation, and had not a single taker. People were very clever in those days, and *knew* that a company would not be selling off stores it could run itself unless there was something wrong with them. So much for the early, golden days of franchising!

on the bun. Standardization is the essence of franchising: it's what a franchise has to sell, both to the public and to the franchisee. If following orders and working by the book don't appeal to you, you'd better look elsewhere.

STARTING FROM SCRATCH. At the other end of the freedom/risk scale is starting from scratch. It's the best way to go after an entirely new market, or a market where demand has far outstripped supply. Examples are the mini-computer market of five years ago, or the computer software market today. When clients or customers are going begging, it's not necessary to pay for good will, and when nobody knows yet what the best products will be, you have as good a chance of figuring them out as anybody else.

Again, if your imagination and desire for independence are very strong, or your resources are very limited, you may do best this way no matter how the market looks. You'll be responsible for everything from product lines to the soap in the restrooms, but also find an independence equal to the effort required.

The risks of starting from scratch are obvious. The two huge benefits of it are, first, you can do whatever the law and your resources will allow, and second, you can begin on a very small scale. Sadly, people with money too often make the two benefits work against each other. They launch elaborate, expensive businesses for which they have little or no training, and usually end up in terrible straits. If starting from scratch appeals to you, fine but even before going on to read the appropriate chapter, please bear in mind its suggestion to begin on a modest scale. If you succeed, you can always expand, or sell out and then begin a grander venture. Spend six months or a year learning the ropes—you'll not regret it. Otherwise, you're begging for trouble.

BUYING A GOING CONCERN. Lying in the middle ground between the high-risk, high freedom starting-from-scratch approach, and the low-risk, low-freedom franchise, is the purchase of an existing business. From my point of view, it is the way for the first-time businessperson to go. Other things being equal, a carefully chosen existing business blends the safety of a workable franchise with much of the flexibility of a from-scratch operation.

In buying an established business, you'll be getting at least *a* method of doing things, but it will be one which you are free to alter at your discretion. Normally, the old owner will train you (for thirty days, at a minimum) or even stay on as an employee. You'll inherit a clientele. At least in theory, you'll be able to begin work the day you sign the papers, and often there's great flexibility in the financing, since the seller will normally accept your note for at least some part of the purchase price. Buying existing businesses —under the names of mergers and acquisitions—is a beloved tactic of big businesses. But it makes sense for the small businessperson too, for the reasons listed above, and for reasons that will become clearer as we consider the third prebuying decision.

The Third Decision.

The third decision is entirely practical. You must decide how much money you have free to invest—not only going in, but over the months of operating before the business first turns a significant profit. Remember that you may spend many early months supporting the business, rather than the other way around.

Your financial strength is encapsulated in your *Personal Financial Statement.* This can be either a formal document drawn by your bank or accountant, or a simple sheet you prepare yourself. In fact, some people simply appropriate a bank credit application, since it normally covers the same ground as a PFS, and has the key categories already labelled.

A PFS will really have two separate functions: early on, it helps you decide how much you have to invest, and later it will establish for sellers, brokers, and lenders, your ability to afford business ownership. For those later uses, a formal PFS may be required, but just now—especially if you are doing this on a shoestring—a homegrown version will work fine.

Take a sheet of paper—ledger paper, if you like. On the top half of the page list any assets for which a plausible market value can be established. *Liquid Assets* are assets in cash or immediately convertible into cash, including demand notes, bonds, savings bonds, term accounts, and demand-loan assets such as whole life insurance. *Equity* is your owned share in any significant fixed assets, especially real estate—that is, the market value of any saleable real or personal asset minus any money owed on it.

Most of these values are easily calculated. You know what your bonds and savings are worth; your insurance agent can tell you how much you can borrow and at what rate. Your personal property must be estimated according to *low* current secondary (used or antique) market prices; real estate can be roughly evaluated by pricing similar properties in the neighborhood, or more accurately, can be judged by an appraiser—try borrowing one from your bank. (Mistrust the estimates of ordinary real estate salesmen, who, after all, will usually quote a high figure to induce you to list the property with them.)

Beneath these assets, list all your major *liabilities*—any monies you owe, for taxes, mortgages, other borrowings against property, personal loans, etc. Minor charges, such as credit card balances (assuming you are approximately current) are generally not included. (If you are just beginning, however, and seeking a fairly small business, you might mention any uncommonly high credit card limits, as a way of showing at least the beginnings of a credit reputation.) The difference between your assets and your liabilities is your *net worth.*

Finally, your PFS should include the names and phone numbers of your primary financial references—bank, savings and loan, or whatever. If it is professionally prepared, it will automatically carry the name and number of its preparer; a name well-known in the community is itself a powerful recommendation. Remember that when the time comes to actually start looking at businesses, you will need a separate PFS for each (nonspouse) backer or partner. Anyone who offers to back you in a venture should be willing to furnish such a document early on. A "backer" who refuses to do so is probably insincere.

While you are preparing your PFS (or having it prepared), check with any people you intend to use for financial references. There are times when no PFS—however well prepared—will serve the function of a strong personal endorsement. We had a buyer whose credentials were incessantly challenged by the seller, until the deal verged on collapse. Finally, in desperation, he gave the seller the name of a Bank of America official in Los Angeles, and offered to pay for the phone call. About two minutes into the phone conversation, the Bank of America executive, who had handled the buyer's earlier commercial accounts, asked the seller, "You'll take good care of him, won't you? He's one of our better customers." That was all the seller wanted to hear. At last he trusted the buyer, and after a lengthy, chastened silence, the deal closed on a note of sweetness and light.

How much you have to spend. Both your PFS and your financial references will only come into play when you are ready to discuss specific businesses. More immediately, though, you want to use your PFS to determine approximately how much you can afford to spend on a business.

While the "net worth" figure from your PFS may tell you how much you could *theoretically* raise if you sold or mortgaged your every earthly possession, it's unlikely you'll want to go so far. So your first task is to subtract (on a piece of scratch paper—this is for your personal consumption only) those assets you consider untouchable. If your net worth is $200,000, but you won't risk the equity in your home (say $90,000) or a life insurance policy to protect your spouse (another $25,000), then your true available funds are more like $85,000—still quite a respectable sum.

Now you need to allow for those months before the business becomes profitable. For that, you must calculate your personal "nut"—the money (including house payments) you intend to live on each month. *Be realistic.* People—especially young people—imagine themselves making heroic sacrifices while getting their firms off the ground. Many really make them, including a young man I know who lived on one large sandwich a day for nine months while launching a construction firm. But you must decide honestly how long you will be willing to sacrifice: "Sweet are the uses of adversity," Shakespeare tells us, but the sweetest adversity grows tiring after a while. Be sensible when you calculate.

Note that we are only discussing personal expenses, not any

operating losses from the firm itself. Operating losses obviously cannot be judged until you have a particular business in mind. Neither can the number of months those losses will continue be accurately forecast, but a good *minimum* figure is three months. If your personal expenses run around $3000 a month, then you have to budget at least $9000 to cover them. Call that $10,000 for safety's sake, and your available capital is now down to $75,000.

OK—after adjustments, you have $75,000 to invest. Does that mean you can walk into a business broker's office and say, "Show me some $75,000 businesses"?

No! In fact, this is one of the main reasons people buying without brokers—or with disreputable brokers—so often manage to sink themselves before they ever see the open water. There are people who only want to get a hold on your purchase money, and who could not care less what happens to you thereafter. With such people, you must make your own calculations of the hidden costs of getting into business. From an honest broker you should receive sufficient help. Here, for example, is the checklist we provide for anyone considering buying a restaurant:

CASH NEEDED (THIS IS APPROXIMATE)

Rent Current	$ 600
Rent Deposit	$ 1200
Gas & Electric Deposit	$ 0
Water Deposit	$ 80
Sales Tax Deposit	$_____
Telephone Deposit	$_____
License Transfer	$_____
City License	$_____
Federal Stamps	$_____
Sales Tax on Fixtures	$_____
Prorate Insurance & Taxes	$_____

Cash for Register	$_____
Sanitation Training	$_____
Sanitation Permit Premises	$_____
Stock	$_____
Miscellaneous	$_____
Escrow Fee	$_____
Publish Notice to Engage	$_____
Fictitious Name	$_____
Total	$_____

Each type of business will, of course, require its own list, and even here the cost of each item will depend upon the size of the restaurant. One without alcohol would require neither federal stamps nor the "notice to engage" publication.

Some of these cost are minor. Filing for a fictitious name (which gives you the exclusive rights to the name of your business in your area) will normally run $50 or so. Still, taking only the larger items, a nice medium-sized restaurant might owe $2500 for the first month's rent, another $2500 rent deposit, $1200 for a month's sales tax deposit, $1500 for sales tax on the fixtures, $2000 for prorated insurance and taxes, and so on—easily $10,000 or more in "hidden" initial costs. Neglect these (as some unscrupulous dealers would have you do), and you are going to be in hot water from the day you open.

Such necessary expenses further reduce your (hypothetical) purchase capital to about $65,000. This beginning figure usefully indicates your capacities without friends, allies, or elaborate financing schemes. We'll discuss those shortly, but remember that backers often lose heart, and financing schemes often crumble. Too many would-be owners build dreams on promises of support, and then find themselves deserted when the time comes to close a deal. When that happens, be prepared to go it alone, with whatever capital you yourself can raise. (For more details, see RAISING MONEY, but meanwhile, remember this: mistrust the person who offers to back you in any business you choose; the chances of his coming through are one in a hundred. The serious backer will discuss financing only with a specific, factual proposal in hand. The rest is mere conversation.)

How Far You Can Go on What You Have.

OK—you've determined how much capital you have to invest. How do you get the most business for your money? Are all courses equal, or is one better than others?

Remember that one of the major drains on your capital is going to be the time that passes before your business begins paying off. Every month's "nut" that you need to hold in reserve is that much less to invest in plants and tools and merchandise. The question, then, is which type of business begins paying soonest—franchised, existing, or from-scratch?

If you apply for a major franchise, you're going to fill out forms, have your credit checked, and then (if lucky) go on a waiting list running a year or more. When your number comes up (and assuming you can live with the location the company assigns you), you'll be sent to school to learn to work "by the book." Pass that, and you'll return home to begin hiring and training your staff. If everything goes right, you should have your crew shaken down about the time the company-built building is ready to open, and you can then take in your first dollar—as much as eighteen months after you started. Of course, you can hold down another job for part of the time you're on the waiting list—but if holding down a job was what you wanted, you wouldn't be reading this book.

Starting from scratch means slightly different problems. You will have to support yourself while signing leases, finding suppliers (and waiting for their shipments to start), manufacturing or designing your products, and so on. You'll also have to expect the business to grow more slowly than would a name franchise.

The lack of reputation will drain your capital another way. Everybody from landlords to suppliers is going to want their money up front, and delivery will be very slow until your checks clear. That's a problem two ways—your dollars buy no leverage, and your business loses valuable time.

I'm not saying you can't win with a franchise or a from-scratch operation. Almost by definition, people seeking big-name franchises can afford to wait for returns (remember that $110,000 in liquid assets that Burger King requires). And if you're starting from scratch, you'll either learn the tricks of expediting and economizing (which we'll cover later), or be content with relatively slow initial growth.

I *am* saying, though, that in the majority of cases, the fastest, most efficient way of getting into business is to buy a going concern. In California, you can complete a purchase by an escrowed bulk sale in as little as ten days. Special considerations can extend that somewhat, but rarely will you wait as long as two months to take possession. You may need on-the-job training, but while getting that, you'll also be earning the profits of a running business.

The sooner your business begins paying, the less money you're going to have to hold out from your capital to invest to cover your monthly "nut." That in turn means greater effective capital, and so a higher real rate of return. That means an edge to buying an existing firm.

Existing businesses have another edge. We've been assuming that buying a dollar's worth of business means putting down a dollar's worth of money. If you're starting from scratch, that's absolutely true, but with a going concern, it's generally not. In fact, until quite recently, an owner who took more than 29% down on the sale of his business paid a very stiff tax penalty. Tax law changes have eliminated the penalty, but 29% down remains a kind of informal guideline figure for the sale of a going firm. In other words, by going after an existing firm, *you can afford* (on average) *a business worth about two to two-and-a-half times your capital to invest.*

(That figure assumes your paying 29% down, plus full wholesale cost of stock. It also allows for operating capital, and such mandatory costs as insurance prorates and license transfers.)

IMPROVING THE RATIO. Alright, a two-and-one-half to one leverage on the purchase of a going firm isn't bad, but can you improve it?

Often, yes. Remember that all of this is negotiable, even to the license and escrow fees, since often a seller will split costs—or a broker shave a commission—to keep a deal alive.

Note, too, that bargains exist. You might have to pay all cash for a business that's making money hand-over-fist. But for a business in trouble, or where death or illness forces sale, you might be allowed in for *little or nothing more than your willingness to take charge.* Businesses, which require much owner involvement, are difficult for an estate or relative to run successfully. With the loss of an owner, a business will often enter a tailspin. A buyer competent to reverse the dive can often name his or her own terms.

I'm not suggesting that you become a professional ghoul (the business world has plenty already), but if the situation is handled right, the sellers get a solution, the employees get their jobs saved, and you get a bargain—no small achievement, overall.

Even more tempting (and less morally suspect) is taking over a mismanaged, money-losing operation. Assuming you have the aptitude for working twenty-six hours a day, plus the talent for stalling creditors, the dollar-stretching opportunities can be incredible.

TAKING OVER: AN EXAMPLE. However a business came to be troubled, you want to avoid the psychological complexities, about which you can do nothing. Instead, devote your energies to a workable proposal, and you will do far more good.

Some very wealthy people bought their son-in-law a wholesale nursery with several retail outlets. This son-in-law was an intelligent fellow, but knew absolutely nothing about the business, and in a series of arguments lost all of his key people. The business staggered, losing $270,000 in two years. The family wanted out on any terms better than simply closing the doors.

We found them a buyer, who had in fact been one of those fired key people. He was certain he could quickly rescue the firm, but had only about $50,000 of the $400,000 asking price, far short of even the usual 29% down.

What we devised was a modified takeover proposition, which means simply that the family financed *100%* of the cost of their being bought out. The buyer owed $400,000, of which $40,000 was our brokerage commission, a fee normally not defferable. This time, however, we accepted $25,000 immediately, and the balance in 180 days. The family, the sellers, signed the note guaranteeing our commission. Beyond that, they agreed to postpone the first payment on the $360,000 owed to them for the same six months.

Our buyer was into a potentially hugely profitable $400,000 business for a $25,000 payment plus $25,000 in operating capital. True, he's taking a risk comparable to the benefits—if he can't stabilize the business in six months or less, there's a real danger of his losing everything. But if he can (and after three months, he's ahead of schedule), then four years from now, he'll have converted his $50,000 into whatever the business is worth at normal profitability—probably about three-quarters of a million dollars. Taking over a losing proposition requires guts, expertise, and careful planning, but there is no finer way to increase your business leverage. If you have the taste for wild territory, and your energy suffices, there's no way known to travel farther, or faster, on a dollar.

INCREASING LEVERAGE: INVENTORY. While existing businesses can offer tremendous bargains as takeover prospects, they also hold a potential danger in the form of inventory. First-time business buyers love inventory. It's real, substantial; you're getting something solid for your money.

But inventory is a capital sponge, soaking up dollars you can use better elsewhere. You must buy some, surely, but don't buy more than you need.

Inventory, unlike the rest of a business, must be paid for in full at the closing of a sale. Otherwise, an unscrupulous buyer might simply sell the inventory off, pocket the profits (one hundred cents on the dollar), and then disappear. For the honest buyer, though, a big inventory is a big problem. Buying a $50,000 business should take only about $14,500 down, while buying a $50,000 inventory requires the whole $50,000 at once.

The problem can be managed. First, if you have no strong preferences about type of business, seek one tending to small inventories. A $400,000 bakery might carry $10,000 worth of flour and syrups, while a $400,000 lumber yard will probably be stocking $250,000 in boards and nails. The bakery will take *half* the cash of the lumber yard.

But if your heart is set on a lumber yard, try asking the seller (once you are close to a deal) to draw down the stock by selling oversupplied inventory items without reordering. It won't help to acquire a business *devoid* of stock, but a reduction from, say, $250,000 to $215,000 or $185,000 might put you over the top at the outset. It reduces your cash-out-of-hand remarkably and lets you reorder items according to your own judgment. The chances of getting stuck with unsaleable merchandise are likewise reduced: in the smaller inventory, it's much easier to see what's good and what isn't. If the final inventory does contain unsaleable goods, you are entitled to demand a major price adjustment, or even to refuse them outright.

There are many other workable tactics for stretching your business buying dollars. We'll discuss them in detail in Chapter 11: PRICING AND NEGOTIATING. For now, let's keep our priorities straight, and concentrate on the pre-business decisions. Before worrying too much about leveraging your business-buying dollars, after all, you need to calculate the number of free dollars you have. So let's pause here and review what's gone before.

Summing Up.

In this chapter, we've discussed the basic prebusiness decisions, the key calculations and choices you need to make before looking at particular business opportunities. We've also covered briefly the three basic ways of getting into business (starting from scratch, franchising, buying a going concern), and discussed a few of the ways for converting your resources into business purchasing power. Now let's recap briefly the basic steps you want to take before hitting the business trail in earnest:

1. Decide your priorities. Know what you want from the business you're seeking.

2. Determine your assets, your liabilities, and your personal "nut." Decide what you can safely invest. Remember leverage.

3. Find your allies. Approach potential backers; line up an accountant and a lawyer. *Get business specialists,* especially in a lawyer. Using a lawyer who doesn't know business will sink you faster than nearly any other error. He'll run up fees, blow your deal, and possibly involve you in litigation over negotiations, a terrible fate.*

4. Shop for a broker. Find one you trust; ask your accountant or bank for a recommendation. You may ultimately deal privately, but a good broker can still teach you quite a lot.

5. Doing all the above will prepare you psychologically and financially to act on your business when you find it. A swift, strong first proposal will often quickly succeed. If you stall, you risk a more jaded, less accomodating seller. You also miss the panic seller—the fellow who wants out because of one bad month. He's often a plum.

Those are five points to keep in mind, to attend to before looking at your first business. In the next few chapters, we'll move on to specific issues—the pros and cons of partnerships, the dangers of existing corporations—but please don't slight these faintly "abstract" early matters. To succeed in business you need a big dose of forceful determination, and that force is only possible when you have your fundamental goals clearly in mind at all times.

---

*Except where you anticipate special problems, however, avoid paying any large retainer fees. In a normal business sale, your lawyer will only examine the escrow instructions plus one or two ancillary documents. A lawyer who wants one or two thousand dollars up front for "services" either doesn't know what he's doing, or is ripping you off. Remember, too, that, with a lawyer glut rapidly developing, legal fees (including hourly rates) are increasingly negotiable. Often, by shopping around and dealing firmly, you can save as much as 50% and still get fine service.

2
PERMITS AND LICENSES

SITUATION:

In this well-regulated country of ours, nearly every form of business activity requires one or more permits or licenses. Some of these are technicalities; others can be real stumbling blocks

OBJECTIVE:

Determining early on what licenses are required, what they cost, and how long they take to receive

The Situation.

Before you move too far along in seeking a business, it's a good idea to take a half-day or so and assemble a list of the various permits, licenses, bonds, and such that you will need before starting operation.

Permits and licenses are rarely a problem, but advance preparation will help you in two ways. First, it will smooth out potential snags. Some permits can be had on request, but others take as long as sixty or ninety days to receive. Ideally, you want all your permits ready on the same day, so that nothing delays your starting business.

Second, a knowledge of permits will help you look for a competent broker or advisor. Play dumb! Walk in snapping your suspenders, and ask what kind of cash reserves it takes to open a travel agency. If the broker says, "none," you walk right out. (The ATC, the regulating conference for air travellers, requires at least two months' operating cash or line-of-credit, with a usual minimum of $20,000. The idea is to keep travel agencies from issuing airline tickets they can't afford to pay for.)

More generally, helpfulness about permits is a mark of a broker's overall quality. A good broker will take you around personally for every permit you need, from water and sanitation to alcohol and general business. He or she should know the ropes and the shortcuts through the bureaucratic forest; a good broker can help you accomplish in one busy morning what would take you two or three frustrating weeks to accomplish on your own. Unless you have a taste for standing in the wrong lines at government offices, you'd be wise to ask at the outset how much personalized help your broker gives with licenses and permits.

The Nature of Our Problem.

It would be very nice if I could list here all the permits and licenses you might need for any type of business. I would if I could, but unfortunately, these requirements vary from business to business, from city to city, state to state, and (even with the more uniform federal practice), day to day. For any given business, you'll need to check with city, state, and federal agencies. One way is to sit down with the "Government Agencies" section of your phone book. More conveniently, ask your lawyer or broker, the Small Business Administration (SBA), or, better still, someone already in the business that interests you. Meanwhile, here are a few standard requirements:

1. Federal: To report employees' earnings, you'll need an IRS Employer Number. For alcohol, a Federal Tax Stamp.

2. State: States with sales taxes will require a Sales Tax Permit and a resale number. The state may also ask for a deposit based on your expected sales volume. The usual agency for this is the State Board of Equalization. Plan to open a Benefits Account to hold your contributions to unemployment insurance. This usually must be done within ten days of start of business and is generally handled by your accountant.

If you intend to sell alcohol, the state may demand a more

rigorous check on your past. Your never having committed a felony is a standard requirement. The check will include FBI fingerprints, and takes the longest of any ordinary license—up to ninety days or more.

3. City: For business license, fictitious name filing,* cabaret and games, and Amusement Licenses. Usually at the City Treasurer's, or County Recorder's, office. When you go down to register or transfer the business name, ask whether you need to publish a fictitious name notice in a local financial paper.

The city or county will probably also have responsibility for any health or sanitation permits, either for your place of business or (if appropriate) for any food handlers you might employ. Anyone working around food will probably need at least a TB and (if there's been a recent outbreak), a hepatitis test. These initial tests can be done quickly at a public clinic; later, a complete doctor's report may be required.

MORE SPECIALIZED PERMITS AND LICENSES. Those are general controls. You'll need more specific licenses and permits to undertake, for example:

· Contracting or Construction
· Firearms Sales
· Food Manufacturing
· Anything involving toxic or chemical wastes
· Anything with significant environmental impact
· Anything involving aircraft safety or aircraft mechanics
· Sale of Drugs or Pharmaceuticals
· Practice of Law, Medicine, or Certified Accounting
· And on, and on . . .

WAYS AROUND LICENSING PROBLEMS. Some of these licenses—one to practice medicine, for example—take years to acquire. Even where strictly controlled licenses are required, though, it's rarely essential

---

*Again, a fictitious name filing simply registers your right to exclusive use of a particular business name. Some cities require that you publish such a filing, so that anyone with a pre-existing complaint can find you under your new business name.

that you hold them yourself. As long as you observe a few simple rules, there's no reason you can't invest in any business you choose.

First, never hide your involvement in any regulated business. You have a right to invest, so don't create the impression you're some kind of organized-crime figure. (Organized crime *does* favor silent investments in high-profit professional groups like hospitals; that's one reason why silent investing has a bad name.) Second, *stay* legal by keeping strictly on the fiscal side of the business. Leave the surgery and bridge-designing to the people with the licenses. Third, be sure that the deal you design makes simple financial sense.

Above all, don't pay so much for your licensed talent that you end up working for them. We had a client who owned a medical testing laboratory. He started by running a few simple tests which could be legally done by a medical technician, and he made a lot of money. Then he expanded into a fancier laboratory with greater capacity. That required a pathologist, and pathologists are near the top of even the MD pay scale. The one he hired drew nearly a six-figure salary, *plus* a cut of every test run. There went the profits, and shortly after, there went our client, wisely selling out to his erstwhile "employee."

Sometimes you can find a highly skilled person with more moderate demands. If our client had discovered a semiretired pathologist willing to oversee the laboratory a few hours a day just to keep his hand in, perhaps the arrangement would have lasted. In general, though, riding on someone else's license only makes sense where a) your own license will be coming through in a short time, or b) where the business is big enough (as with a hospital, a nursing home, or a good-sized engineering practice) to afford the paying of numbers of large professional salaries.

If that's beyond your present means, then either spend the time to put yourself through school, or choose some related field—like our friend's first lab tests—which requires no special licenses. For some hints on getting into business on a shoestring, please see STARTING FROM SCRATCH. Meanwhile, just bear in mind the need to check about licenses and permits before you spend much time planning a particular type of business.

3
CHOOSING A BUSINESS STRUCTURE

SITUATION:
A business can be operated as a sole proprietorship, a partnership, a pseudocorporation, or a true corporation
OBJECTIVE:
Choosing the business structure best suited to your needs and goals

Choosing a Structure.

Even before you have a particular business in mind, it's worthwhile to think a moment about business structures.

The first thing to recognize is that none of these structures are immutable. You can begin your business as a sole proprietorship, take on (and later, buy out) one or more partners, form a Subchapter S pseudocorporation, dissolve that, create a true corporation which then goes public, buy back the stock and revert to a sole proprietorship, and so on, forever. You would never make such changes frivolously, but it's reassuring to know that few moves are irreversible. Now let's consider some of your basic options.

THE SOLE PROPRIETORSHIP. About 90% of all American small businesses are sole proprietorships—the simplest of business structures. To become a sole proprietor requires only a standard business license and (usually) the registration of a fictitious name for the firm. As sole proprietor, you have the greatest possible freedom of action. As long as you obey the law and pay your bills, you can do whatever you want. If you want to paint the store purple and sell nothing but apes, that's your business; you answer to no one else. Your tax situation is similarly clear. Whatever the business earns is passed directly on to you for reporting as ordinary income.

Of course, sole proprietorships have their limitations. It's unlikely any one person will have all the skills necessary to run a very complex firm. Credit, and true security will be hard to come by, because the entire business rests on your shoulders alone. If you get sick, or even want to take a vacation, who will keep the business running?

PARTNERSHIPS. Those problems suggest some of the reasons for considering taking a partner. There are basically four reasons why people seek business partners. Three of the reasons are economic or practical, one is emotional:

1. To receive moral support.
2. To divide work in an undifferentiated fashion
3. To combine specialties
4. To raise capital

I haven't separated number one because it's unworthy, but because it too often leads to unnecessary and harmful partnerships. What often happens is something like this: you get a good idea, discover you need a change of pace, or are about to lose a job, and decide to go into business for yourself. A business is found, plans are made, and then, at the last minute, you get cold feet. Instead of bailing out, you decide to hedge your bet by taking on a partner.

For a while, everything's fine. Then, one day, you find you *can* handle all the work. Suddenly your old reasons for wanting to be a sole owner resurface, only now you've got a partner. Resentments arise. It was your idea originally, and here's someone trying to impose his or her own ideas—and taking home half the profits.

Often these ill-planned partnerships have to be dissolved. On the other hand, since moral-support partnerships are usually started between friends, you might try to see whether you can expand the business enough to 1) justify the presence of another partner, and 2) put some additional distance between the two of you. Is it time, perhaps, for a second branch? If you're going to expand shortly anyway, it might be worth hanging on for a while longer, and trying to save the partnership—and keep a friend.

The truth, though, is that lack of self-confidence is a dubious reason for taking a partner. If your problem is only temporary self-doubt, try finding someone to give you a *temporary* boost. Here are some possibilities:

1. *A spouse.* Can your husband or wife, or some very good friend, help you out for the first month or so? I knew a woman who had a wonderful idea for a restaurant, and assembled a fine operation, but then decided she needed someone to stand up beside her temporarily. Her husband took a month's vacation and served as a (slightly intimidating) maitre d'. Once the restaurant was rolling, she assumed full charge, and he went back to his regular job as a policeman. The restaurant was a roaring success.

2. *The former owner.* If you're buying an existing establishment, often the old owner will be willing to stay on. He should remain a minimum of thirty days to train you in any case. Often you can sign him to a work contract for a period of some months more. You won't find anyone who knows the operation better.

3. SCORE. The Service Corps of Retired Executives will often be able to provide you with a former businessperson widely experienced in your field. The quality of the help will vary greatly, from poor to superb, but with luck this can provide you with many of the benefits of partnership *at no charge.*

It may be that all you need is a friend to chuck you under the chin and tell you to buck up. In any case, these three possibilities all have the advantage of being easily terminated. Above all, remember that the best confidence builder is success.

SUBSTANTIVE PARTNERSHIPS COME NEXT. *One: Dividing Undifferentiated Work.* This is the simplest kind of partnership—suitable for very small businesses. Two or more people pool their money to open a business together. They share the profits equally, and agree to divide the work up the same way, each turning a hand to whatever needs to be done. These partnerships work best where the business itself is quite simple, and, perhaps because they rarely ever face severe challenges, they seem remarkably durable. On the other hand, if they are to grow, a measure of specialization is inevitable—and that means a different sort of partnership altogether.

Two: The Combined Specialties. As the business grows larger, or if it operates in more complex and demanding fields from the outset, the best partnerships will combine particular skills. Thus, what is now the largest solar installation firm in San Francisco began as a group of Fred Harris campaign workers who decided to promote their social goals by forming an undifferentiated partnership (they called it a co-op) to provide clean energy sources. That worked fine until 1) business began to zoom and 2) well-organized competitors appeared. At that point, they had to use their individual talents more effectively by differentiating specialties. Once, everybody took a turn at every job; today, some are installers, others sell systems or keep the books, and so on. Bending the original social ideal became a practical necessity. The company evolved successfully. (From Los Angeles *Times,* 9 March 1981)

The basic organization for this type of partnership is for one partner to handle the financial operations and the other, the products. Note that the financial partner is not silent. He is salary-drawing and present at the firm every day. He deals with the banks, the insurance companies, clients, and so on. Partner number two takes charge of designing products, choosing new equipment, etc.

Such a partnership might similarly unite a product engineer with a production designer, allowing the company not only to introduce a new product, but to get it efficiently into production. Any combination which makes practical sense will probably produce a durable partnership. The main proviso is that the two partners have mutual respect for each other's skills. One partner cannot be convinced that he's the sole brains of the operation.

Neither can you expect the work, in fixed hours, always to divide equally. We often see problems when, for example, the inside partner can't understand why the outside partner spends half his time entertaining clients at fancy restaurants. Once you've chosen a partner for expertise in a field outside your own, let him work in his own way. You can always listen for feed-back from your employees or customers, but mostly you must act upon faith—and the bottom line.

Expertise partners are fine—indeed, most of the best high-performance partnerships are of this sort. They let you share burdens, concentrating on the things you do best. They also provide for continuity of leadership, and help you attract additional investment capital. Just make certain that any expertise partner you choose has 1) true competence in his field and 2) a truly complementary skill, so that he won't be simply duplicating abilities you already have.

Three: The Silent Partner. "Silent Partner" is simply a popular term for a partner who invests money in your venture but (normally) remains "silent" about its day-to-day operations. He differs from a creditor because he takes an equity position in the company and is repaid, not according to some fixed schedule, but from his share of the firm's profits. His investment is protected only by the company's assets; like other general partners, moreover, he can be held personally liable for business debts. (Be careful of anyone who offers to become your "partner" and then wants you to put up outside collateral for his protection. He's not offering a partnership, he's offering a loan—and an expensive one.)

The formal, legally-recognized version of a "silent" partner is called a "limited" partnership, in which the investor is guaranteed limited liability for any company losses or misdoings, but is prohibited from any involvement in the actual running of the firm. Such arrangements have long been popular for real estate investments, but are less common in ordinary business.

In theory, you have every reason for seeking a silent partner. Anyone with loose money to invest should be financially astute, and able to make useful operating suggestions, while generally staying out of your hair. As long as you can keep the business showing reasonable growth and profits, you should have operational freedom—without the pressure of monthly loan payments.

Still, there are questions. What if the firm hits hard times? Will the silent partner put in more money? How deep are his pockets? What are to be the maximum acceptable losses in a year? Will additional money be in the form of increased equity participation (meaning, in exchange for a bigger chunk of the firm), or as loans? If as loans, with what kind of security?

Remember, too, that a silent partner will never let you draw off an unreasonable wage, leaving him no profits to share. Your wages will have to be justified. Neither is a silent partner likely to share your emotional attachment to the firm. If it starts showing losses, or if you get an advantageous buyout offer, he's likely to pressure you to dish out. Lastly, remember you'll be in the trenches daily, while your silent partner will only be making occasional trips to the front pick up a check and review the books.

Despite the hazards, silent partnerships often work very well, especially if you choose your partner not only for financial strength, but for enthusiasm. If you can't find an enthusiast, make one. A backer who cares about the company—as opposed to just his investment—will be not only a more pleasant, but a far more reliable, ally.

Structuring a Partnership.

How elaborate an agreement do partners need? Albert Lowry, in *How to Become Financially Successful By Owning Your Own Business,* lists fifteen specifics he feels each agreement should have, from "how the business will be managed" to each partner's "functions and duties and powers." Lowry's points are all sensible, and if you feel you can work in a highly-structured system, you should certainly consider them.

In my experience though, most small businesspeople resist such agreements, because too many rules sap a company's flexibility and initiative. To ensure honesty, most of us would rather rely, first, on a partner we know well and trust, and, second, on a careful system of checks and balances. In most states, after all, the Uniform Partnership Act is supposed to prevent such crimes as having one partner liquidate the firm without the knowledge of the other: a second legal document, drawn up by your attorney, isn't likely to deter a dishonest partner. A relatively simple agreement can provide both safety *and* flexibility—if you need more rules later, you can add them:

1. The partnership should protect both partners, both by key-man insurance (to prevent the company's going down if one partner suffers death or incapacitation), and by a set of counterchecks to ensure that both partners remain honest. Eliminate undue temptations. If your partner oversees the books, and if you can't interpret them, require that they be checked periodically by an outside accountant. Also reserve your right to call for a certified audit at reasonable intervals, to be paid for by the company. Meanwhile, get yourself an accounting handbook, and start studying!

2. *All partnerships should be founded with the expectation that someday they'll be dissolved.* A partnership can be amicably ended by *buyout,* by *partial liquidation* or *spin-off,* or by *sale* of the partnership. Each method has merits and drawbacks.

In a buyout, one partner buys the other's share at an agreed-upon price. Where the partnership is new—say, less than a year old—the buyout is often made at the original investment amount. if the partner put up $50,000 for his share, he now sells it back for $50,000, or a token increase. He's had a year's share of the profits; otherwise he breaks even on the deal. A one-year buyout clause is wise in any partnership agreement.

Where the partners have been in business longer, or where the firm has grown greatly in a short time, setting a price will be harder. You can go to an outside appraiser (bank, broker, or business attorney), or use a much older method—you flip a coin; the loser names a price for half the business, and the winner chooses to either buy or sell at that price. It sounds unimpressive, but the method has been used to sell properties as large as the Empire State Building. As a means of last resort, it far beats litigation, which will almost certainly wreck the business.

Remember: when partnerships break up, the partner who has lived more cautiously is likely going to end up being the buyer, while his less provident friend ends up selling. If you're in a desirable business, and have a partner with a taste for the high life, hang onto your money, and sooner or later, you'll be offered a chance to buy increased (or even complete) control. You may as well be ready. If you are not, the firm will be sold to an outsider, partially liquidated, or run down. Stipulate at the outset that the partners are to have first chance at any shares or interests offered for sale.

In a spin-off or a partial liquidation, you reduce the size of the company so it can be run by one person. *Spin-off* here means splitting the business into separately-owned units. If the company has two stores, you arrange each to keep one, assuming (as should be the case) that they are far enough apart that you won't become instant competitors. Sometimes reorganization will produce separable companies, as when you've done sales and service for a product, and volume in each is large enough to be self-supporting. Some cash may have to change hands to equalize the transaction, but the amount will be less than would be needed for a complete buyout.

Where neither partner has the cash to replace the other, it may be necessary to *liquidate* part of the business, raising money to pay off your partner by selling off assets such as real estate, a branch store, or excess inventory. Your partner keeps the profits from the sale, and you are left sole owner of whatever remains. It's a workable solution—just don't let a partner in a hurry sell the wrong things at the wrong price, or give the impression that the business itself is unsound because it is closing offices or selling off merchandise.

The same problems limit the *sale of the partnership,* and are compounded by the fact that if your partner takes an unrealistically low price for his or her share, your share is likewise depressed in value. To prevent that, it may be worthwhile to strain your resources to buy out a troubled partner, even if you'll have to put the partnership back on the market in a very short time—at, of course, a substantially higher price. At the very least, your initial partnership agreement should guarantee your right to approve the buyer of any other partnership share.

Summarizing Partnerships.

None of this is meant to discourage you from seeking partners, but only to demonstrate the main hazards and precautions. Perhaps the most important of all precautions is one most frequently neglected—choosing your partners carefully. The last thing you want is to have a couple of drinks with old George at the club and decide to go into business together. Before striking a deal with old George or anyone else, make sure you and your potential partner share:

1. Similar goals and motivations.
2. Compatible personalities.
3. Comparable ethics.

In short, while screening partners, never forget the importance, and the closeness, of the relationship. They say no man's a hero to his valet; well, that's doubly true of partners. Not long ago an acquaintance (*not* a client) of mine was loudly lamenting that his partner (and brother-in-law) had relieved the company safe of $100,000 they had skimmed from their janitorial supply firm. As far as I was concerned, he got just what he deserved (let him go tell the police, "Help! My partner just stole the money we were stealing from Uncle Sam!")—but a more common situation does deserve pity. That's where an honest partner can do nothing against a dishonest one for fear of destroying the whole business. So choose your partner with care, because a mistake can be ruinous.

Corporations: True vs. Subchapter S.

Such dangers suggest why successful partnerships rarely go on long without evolving into corporations. In a moment, we'll see how corporations can simplify partner's disputes, but first let's make a few general remarks.

Because of their flexibility, tax advantages, and inherent pres-

tige, corporations are often considered the finest of business structures. A corporation (as shown more clearly in DANGERS OF AN
EXISTING CORPORATION) is a legal entity distinct from its owners or
shareholders. It can sue and be sued, and perhaps more importantly, it can borrow money without endangering the noncorporate assets of its shareholders. When a debt-ridden corporation
files bankruptcy, creditors lose their shot at the personal wealth of
the stockholders. Corporations can provide tax-free benefits like
medical insurance, can retain large amounts of cash for various
purposes, and can distribute earnings widely among stock-holding
members of an owner's family through dividends, directors' fees,
or company services. Corporations can provide key executives
with pension plans far more generous than the Keogh retirement
programs allowed to ordinary proprietors. Moreover, since a block
of stock in a corporation is easier than a partnership to sell, corporations tend to have longer and smoother lives than partnerships,
and so, are generally better able to attract loans and investment
capital.

On the other hand, true corporations have some clear liabilities.
If you choose incorporation, expect to be more tightly regulated
than you would be as a partner or sole proprietor. Expect that your
competitors and suppliers will know more about your financial
situation than you may wish; most of the papers you file with the
regulators will become matters of public record. Lastly, expect to
encounter a more complex situation with taxes.

Suppose you have a high personal income, but an investment in
a losing business. If the business is a partnership or sole proprietorship, you can transfer its loses directly to your own personal tax
calculations—in other words, take a fat deduction. Corporate
losses, on the other hand, stay strictly within the corporation—
they can shelter its future profits over the next five years, but
otherwise vanish. Moreover, corporate *income* is taxed twice—once
at the corporate rate, and again as personal income for whatever
you take as dividends. Only when the business becomes significantly profitable—$50,000 a year for at least two consecutive
years is a fair minimum figure—do the benefits of incorporation
begin clearly to outweigh the double-taxation penalty.

To help ease the complexity of your choice, there exists an

intermediate state between partnership and true corporation, called a *Subchapter S*, or pseudocorporation. This very sensible compromise allows for small domestic companies (those having fewer than thirty-five shareholders) to gain the legal structure of a corporation, but the *tax* situation of a partnership. A few types of business activity are off limit to Sub-S firms, so check with your accountant. In most cases, though, the Sub-S corporation can own property, sue and be sued, and so on, while still passing its profits and losses directly onto the income statements of its shareholders.

Many CPAs recommend starting new firms on a cash accounting basis—almost guaranteeing early losses, since whatever the firm spends is taken as an immediate expense. A Subchapter S will then hustle those losses right onto your personal income statement, where they can shelter other earnings. Fine, but as Laventhol and Horwath warn, you can deduct expenses only for a *going* concern. Money spent before the doors open must be capitalized, then depreciated over *five* years—be careful! (*Tax Reporter*, April '83)

Remember, too: while a corporation chooses its own fiscal year, *you* personally must use a calendar tax year. To capture the largest chunk of these Subchapter S startup losses early on, start the firm in, say, August or September. That way, you'll have four or five months of heavy losses to set against your income. (A company started in January, on the other hand, will almost certainly show a net profit by the time the year ends the following December 31. You lose your advantage.)

How CORPORATIONS HELP. I said we'd discuss how corporations simplify partner's disputes. Here's an example from my very recent experience.

A wealthy young woman married for love, and her mother established her and her husband in a carpet and ceramic importing business which, by catching a particular boom, shot quickly up to net around $250,000 a year. Meanwhile, unfortunately, the marriage soured as the young man showed himself to be both uncaring and ferocious. Not only was he impossible to live with, but in a fit of vindictiveness, he set out to destroy the business as the marriage began to crumble. For example, the ceramics were made abroad but repainted in the US. At the peak of the season, the company employed about twenty-four painters, but in a burst of domestic pique, one morning (a month before the annual buyer's fair), he fired them all. When his wife burst into tears at the news, he hired back two of them. And on, and on—one low stunt after another.

A divorce, obviously, was pending. Still, that hardly solved the problems of the business partnership. As I say, the young man intended to bankrupt the firm purely for vengeance. Deciding they wanted no more of the business however the divorce came out, the young woman and her mother decided to put the business up for sale, and the young man, with his usual unpredictability, temporarily agreed. We found a buyer, but her offer was contingent on the firm's showing well at the upcoming fair. The young man, meanwhile, had reverted to his old tricks—sometimes slamming down the phone in the middle of conversations, once even locking himself inside the plant and refusing to come out. With him bent on sabotage—he was, after all, the president of the company— there seemed to be little hope.

Except that this was a corporation, not a partnership. If it *had* been a partnership, the young woman and her mother could have found an attorney, asked for a court date, waited some months for a hearing, and then tried to convince a judge with lengthy arguments that the husband's business decisions were unsound, and then—perhaps—have gotten a restraining order.

Fortunately, the young woman's mother had been down the business trail many a time before. When setting the two lovebirds up in business, she had demanded a corporate structure, giving each of them 45% of the stock, and keeping 10% for herself. That meant that between them, she and her daughter voted a majority of the shares. Once the young man proved himself to be completely unredeemable, the mother and daughter simply gave notice of a board of directors' meeting. Then they voted the young troublemaker out on his backside, and five minutes later, voted to accept the offer to purchase the firm. The young man would get his 45% of the proceeds of the sale, but otherwise he was gone.

A corporation is one way to take on partners of any sort, share work and profits, even surrender day-to-day administrative power, and still maintain absolute control over your own fate.

The one key to this, of course, is that you must retain 51% of the voting stock. Depending upon your faith in human nature, this may mean 51% in your own hands, or 51% combined in your own and your family's possession. Just be careful you don't wind up like a friendly competitor of ours, who dispersed too many shares among close family members. Everything went fine until the firm hit a rough patch, and he was accused of having missed opportunities. The directors notified him of a directors' meeting, and when he walked in, they took a vote to bounce him as president. His family was all there, and stood 100% firm—against him. He was out of there faster than a pitcher who'd just walked four straight in the World Series—and was about the saddest, most surprised man I'd ever seen. So even if it slows expansion, try to hold that 51%.

GOING PUBLIC. While incorporation allows more efficient operation, provides personal protection against business failure, and (above a certain income level) offers great tax advantages, it also carries the drawbacks of increased governmental scrutiny and wider public access to your records. That's especially true if you decide to take a corporation public.

The corporations we've discussed so far have been closely-held —that is, the stock is owned by only a few people, and is bought or old at a price privately set. Publicly-held corporations, on the other hand, have many shareholders and prices determined by public trading. Going public is the ideal of many small businesspeople, despite a recent counter-trend to take public companies private to avoid governmental scrutiny and the pressures of paying dividends.

To take a business public, you will likely need the aid of a stock underwriter. Since these firms accept, on average, only about one of every hundred companies which approach them, you should hardly expect instant attention—unless, perhaps, you represent a play in a particularly hot field. If they do take you on, it will be only after a rigorous screening of your financial strength, your management team (you can forget going public with a one-man show), and your competition. Even after they agree to manage your issue, you still have around six months of rigorous examination ahead of you—which is likely to continue even while the prospectus sheets are at the printers.

The grilling will have two purposes. First, both the SEC (Securities and Exchange Commission) and the NASD (National Association of Securities Dealers, an underwriters' self-policing board established, like the SEC, in the aftermath of the market collapse of 1929), demand full disclosure of *anything* likely to affect the value of offered shares. Second, because the underwriter (usually joined with an underwriting group) guarantees the sale of the shares offered, it wants to set a price which will ensure a sold-out offering. (Actually, underwriters will agree to either a *firm,* or a *best* effort. In a firm offering, they agree to buy any shares not publicly sold; in a best effort, they simply agree to try to place every share. If a legitimate underwriter makes you a firm offer, congratulations —you've got an absolutely prime company.)

Small businesses have traditionally found their first attempts at issuing stock to be costly, time-consuming, and frustrating. In 1978, though, the SEC established its Office for Small Business Policy, and since then, a number of programs—some more successful than others—have been tested to help ease the pain. Companies with modest goals (currently, those planning a first-time offering of under $5 million) are now eligible to use shortened disclosure forms, regional processing centers, and less-costly accounting procedures. By some accounts, the short forms alone have shaved as much as 60 days from the time needed for SEC approval.

The system is still far from perfect. Before raging against the regulators, though, it might help to bear in mind the words of Mary Beach, the woman responsible for the Office of Small Business Policy:

> I think it is very important for small businesses to realize that confidence in the market is very important to them too. The fact that we are concerned that we don't go too far in granting exemptions is to their

own good. If we were to move too far too fast, resulting in serious abuses by small businesses in the marketplace, it could hurt legitimate small businesses very much. (LAVENTHOL & HORWATH's *Perspective,* 1982)

Everyone would like to see governmental procedures simplified, but in this case, I think Ms. Beach is entirely correct.

Even more to the point, issuing stock is worth the trouble. One great virtue of a public offering is that it allows the original investors to cash out a large part of their capital gains: in a typical offering, about one-quarter of the shares offered might be those issued by the company, and three-quarters those held by company officers. Still, the process is not exactly cheap; a stock offering which raises, say, $6,000,000 in new capital might cost as much as $600,000 in various fees to a top-rank firm like Merrill Lynch or Dean Witter—money, however, which successful issuers usually consider very well spent.

In this overview, I've tried to avoid giving advice which is likely to be made obsolete by IRS, tax law, or SEC changes, or which might involve particular dangers or require particular situations or its use. You might want to ask your accountant about an occasionally useful device known as Section 1244 stock (which allows certain corporate losses from corporate bankruptcy to be passed through directly to the shareholder's personal income statement, providing a measure of investment insurance for upper-income individuals). But there's one gambit I'd urge you to avoid: the so-called "thin" corporation.

In theory, "thin" is a clever idea: you capitalize your new company, say, 25% by buying its stock, and 75% by making it a personal loan. As the company prospers, it can take its loan interest as a tax deduction, while you receive your capital back from the company mostly tax free. (The interest earned is, of course, taxable.) Some business advisors consider this a fine idea, but I'd argue against it for three reasons: 1. the IRS challenges these deals almost automatically 2. a corporation created with an inborn debt burden will have a hard time raising money from traditional lenders 3. so many potential buyers know about these risks that "thin" corporations often prove unsaleable.

As it happens, the very week I began this chapter, I saw a "thin" incorporation blow the sale of a very promising construction-related business. The buyer (an attorney with a strong tax background) had travelled 120 miles on the strength of a brief telephone description, and been absolutely delighted with his tour of the plant. Then he took one look at the details of incorporation, muttered, "thin" under his breath, and bid us good day.

Think long and hard before creating a "thin" corporation. You often are only trading a few early (potential) tax savings for a larger long-term loss in flexibility. If later on, you need to make a personal loan to the corporation, that's another issue entirely.

Ultimately, the business structure you choose will depend upon the size and complexity of your firm. The choice should always be made in consultation with your accountant and/or lawyer. For now, simply recognize that each structure has its uses, and that changes, when necessary, are not impossible. Here are a few other general rules:

1. Switching among business structures usually means trading off independence for security and access to capital. A sole proprietorship gives maximum independence, and minimum security and capital access; a publicly-held firm provides just the opposite.

2. Changes in business structure become increasingly costly as the structures become more complex. You can start a sole proprietorship for less than $100; having an attorney form a closely-held corporation for you will cost $500–$3000 or so. And taking a firm public can require anywhere from, say, $10,000 for help filing SEC forms, to $500,000 or more for a fully-managed, underwritten offering.

3. Whatever structure you choose, as soon as you take on one or more co-owners, you need to cover your backside. This can mean a formal buyout agreement with partners, or holding onto 51% of the stock of a closely-held corporation. Once a public offering dilutes your control, about the best solution is to wangle yourself a contract as president that makes it prohibitively expensive for the company to fire you.

4. Again, remember that the particular advantages of each business structure vary with every new tax law, and every IRS or SEC ruling. This chapter is only a rough introduction. For specific advice, rely upon your accountant and a good tax attorney. Be certain the ones you use are aware of the latest laws and rulings, and don't be afraid to ask tough questions before hiring *any* consultant or advisor.

4

RAISING MONEY

SITUATION:
Raising affordable money is perhaps the greatest single hurdle faced by small businesses
OBJECTIVE:
Going after the most affordable money first

John B. Schnapp, the distinguished business writer, tells a fine story about the remarkable Soichiro Honda, founder of Honda Motor Company (HMC). In the early days of HMC, after a period of rapid growth, the time came to borrow expansion capital for the first time. Honda, who is known for his wild sense of humor as much as his engineering genius, arranged a meeting with some august Mitsubishi bankers. When the meeting came around, Honda and his partner showed up semismashed and launched into a freeform show, featuring bawdy stories and geisha tunes. The bankers stomped and cheered and had themselves a wild time, but next day, they turned Honda Motors down. "Thanks very much, boys," they are reported to have said, "but we don't loan money to clowns." (*Wall Street Journal*, Feb. 1, 1982)

If borrowing money—an unfortunate but common necessity for successful and unsuccessful companies alike—can cause problems for a human dynamo like Soichiro Honda, it can cause problems for you. So even if it seems a dull matter, you'd better consider it carefully.

The first thing to realize is that, while many institutions will loan you money to buy or expand a business, few will help you start one. With the possible exception of recognized experts in high-tech fields, those of us wanting to start small firms of our own will have to rely on ourselves, our friends, or our families.

The second thing to recognize is that there are some people from whom you do not want to borrow. Loan sharks top the list, but just as importantly, you want to avoid (or at least use with extreme care) loan "finders" of the sort who want a large flat fee to "find" you potential lenders. There *are* loan brokers who charge three to five "points" (that is, percentage points) of any loan they actually deliver and, if necessary, you may want to use them, but watch out for the guys who want $5000 or 10,000 up front to "put you in touch" with lenders—they're almost always running a scam. The currently fashionable variant on this is to claim connections with Arab oil money. Be that as it may, *always* watch out for anyone asking expense or advance money to secure you loans.

The third thing to remember is that money—like any other commodity—has a price. The price of money—stated in points above the prime customer rate charged by major banks—will vary according to the source you choose and the risk of the use you propose. That means you want to shop for your money, and to look for the cheapest money first.

Basically, you can borrow money from almost anyone, but the most common sources, in order of increasing cost, are:

1. Customers/Goods-repayment loans
2. Yourself
3. Your family or friends
4. The Seller of an existing business
5. A bank, with SBA backing
6. A bank, without SBA backing
7. A venture capital, commercial credit, or Small Business Investment company.

Goods-Repayment Loans.

Goods-repayment loans work in only a few situations, and few people ever think to try them, but they are so cheap and sensible that they deserve mentioning.

These loans only work where you propose a product not availa-

ble elsewhere. The theory is that you persuade your future customers to loan you start-up money, to be paid back in product
once you are in business. It has sometimes been done in technical
fields, where a key supplier goes bankrupt, and the people needing
his product back one of his employees to go into the business
himself.

But here's a simpler example. Not too long ago, the Japanese
food product tofu became quite a health food hit. Here in Southern California a young man knew how to make the stuff, but
lacked the capital to start business for himself. Instead he persuaded fifty tofu fanatics each to loan him $100 to buy his initial
equipment and supplies. He repaid the entire $5,000 not in cash,
but in tofu at an agreed-upon rate of so much per pound, on
contract over a period of months. It was a good deal all around—
the young man got his loan interest-free, the community got a new
small business, and the tofu fans (at the cost of a few months'
interest on their money) got the product they desired.

If you're starting small, at least consider goods-repayment. Not
only do you avoid banks and their paperwork, but you get your
money fast. Too, you spread your risk so wide no one can get
seriously hurt, and borrow at the cheapest possible rate—not only
interest free, but at a big discount. Your payback product, after all,
has a retail mark-up of at least 50%. One proviso—don't commit
so much of your production to the payback that you can't take a
living out of the business.

Putting Up Your Own Money.

The next cheapest source of credit can be investing your own
money. Certain shrewd operators will tell you never to put your
own money in a business venture. Perhaps during times when
money is extremely free, that is reasonable advice, but these days
it isn't very realistic. Using your own money makes sense when
1) there's no alternative 2) your money is currently earning very
low yields 3) you need to provide at least some of your funding
to secure another type of loan.

When you do use your own money, you normally face little
immediate pressure to repay it, and your cost of borrowing is equal

only to the income you lose by not having it in some other investment. Since T-bills, for example, usually pay something around 3½% *below* prime, this is cheap money. Especially where you set up a corporation to buy a business, there is no legal problem with making a loan of your own money. If you hold any low-return investments—cash-value life insurance being the classic example —you'd probably be wise to consider liquidating them to give yourself some cheap money with which to work.

That's especially true because banks mistrust people who don't plan to commit any of their own money to a project, especially a new business. Banks recognize a dozen or more good reasons for making loans, ranging from plant construction to inventory expansion. Even so, they are far more receptive to *participation* in a project than to financing it entirely. If necessary, be prepared to liquidate a certain percentage of your fixed assets before requesting a loan. Not long ago, we had a customer with a net worth of about $800,000 who was discourage to find he could not get a loan of $200,000 to buy a highly-profitable clothing chain no matter how much collateral he offered. We simply called his bank and asked what would happen if he converted $100,000 of his assets into cash, and then applied for a matching loan to buy the business. The bank's answer? "That's a whole new ballgame. Tell him to come back in." So always assume there will be more and cheaper money if you're backing the venture partly with your own cash.

One more point: even if you are starting a small business with money from your own savings account, don't just withdraw the money. Instead, get the bank to *loan* you the money against your passbook. These loans are dirt cheap—usually around two points above the passbook rate. The interest will qualify as a business expense, and, even better, by repaying the loan, you'll build yourself a credit rating.

Loans from Friends and Family.

Along with the less formal financial support mentioned earlier, you can sometimes get friends and family to put money into a project purely because you write them an attractive proposition and they have venture money available. A friendship loan of this sort might go for, say, 1% or 1½% below prime—a better rate than you'll get anywhere else, and a yield a bit better than T-bill interest for your backer. Friends in these propositions are entitled to the same kind of collateral as anyone else, and frankly, you had better realize you are risking a friendship in any such proposition. On the other hand, these can work superbly. Sikorsky Aircraft (now part of United Technologies) was started by a $5000 loan to General Sikorsky from his friend, the composer Sergei Rachmaninov.

Loans from the Seller.

When you are buying a going business, your largest single loan may well be in the form of a note held by the seller. The amount of the note, and its terms, are both largely dictated, of course, by his eagerness to sell. In some cases, this can produce a complete inversion of the usual rules of finance. The worse shape a business is in—the riskier an investment it would be for you—the more likely a desperate seller is to let you in cheaply. Even if his pride won't let him cut his price much, he may still carry a tremendous amount of paper—perhaps 80% of the total consideration—at a very low rate just to get out from under. It's by no means uncommon for a desperate owner to let you owe him the balance of the purchase price at as much as four or five points below prime—about as cheap money as you'll find anywhere. When the note is secured by the business assets, moreover, you'll face very little payment pressure, because the last thing the old owner wants to do is take the firm back. If you're willing to gamble on a troubled firm, seller financing is a natural way to proceed.

With seller financing, you have about exhausted the list of easy, informal credit sources. After that, you need to deal with institutions, and the careful preparation of your loan "package" becomes a good deal more important.

Bank Loans/SBA-Backed.

Each year, the Small Business Administration is given money by Congress for the purpose of backing (not making) loans to small business. In fiscal 1980, the SBA backed some 24,000 loans worth nearly 3 billion dollars. Because the SBA backs—that is, insures—these loans to 90% of their value, banks are willing to write them relatively cheaply: the standard rate is 2¾ points above prime. (Note that these are still scarcely free. If the prime's running 12¼%, you'll be paying 15%; in recent years, the prime has often topped 16%.) The average SBA loan is around $100,000, but can go to five times that amount, with repayment stretched over as long as ten years—an excellent arrangement.

There are, however, certain hidden problems with SBA loans. First, you have to be approved twice—once by the bank, and once by the SBA. Since the SBA is a federal agency, it is not exactly quick; in fact, its performance is so variable that I can scarcely suggest an average time-frame. One of the worst examples of SBA trouble I know of involved a client of ours who happened to be a minority member, and who had started a very successful firm supplying well-designed drug-education kits to public schools. To maintain the firm's rapid growth, he needed several hundred thousand dollars in expansion capital. The SBA loan advisor/packager he got happened to be a member of the same minority, and promised him speedy attention. Thirty days went by, and our client called the SBA. The papers were "in the mill." Sixty days, same answer. Finally, after a full ninety days had passed, our client went back in person and his "friend" told him blandly that the papers were still on his desk, and he'd get to them when he could. Our client lost his chance at the one contract that would have made him a rich man, and his company went downhill from there, never to recover.

As I say, that *was* the worst example of bureaucratic arrogance I've seen—and the SBA has some superb people—but it is one of the hazards you face when dealing with government.

Second, remember that the SBA has its own particular requirements for the loan package or presentation. Nominally, the SBA is happy to provide you with a "packager" who will help shape your loan application for bank presentation. In practice, these packagers are often fresh out of college—well meaning, but woefully untrained. You may need an outside consultant. As noted in STARTING FROM SCRATCH, though, avoid those big-bucks packagers, whose fees can run into the thousands, and whose work is often dismissed out of hand by professional loan officers. Technically, no finder's fees are allowed for SBA loans, but the rule is widely circumvented. If you do pursue an SBA loan—and they can be real bargains—remember to provide plenty of lead time (4–6 months is reasonable), and to be ready to push matters along by yourself.

BANK LOANS WITHOUT SBA BACKING. Without SBA guarantees, dealing with a bank will be harder. The interest rates will be higher (as much as 4 or even 5% over prime, and perhaps even up near the legal limit for your state), the repayment periods will be shorter (many short-term in the strict sense: repayable in one year or less, with no guarantee of renewal), and the collateral demands will be stiffer. As with any loan, you want to shop these. All the terms of the loan—even the definition of the prime rate—may vary from bank to bank. Some banks will offer variable interest rates, some fixed; your choice depends upon your guess about the way interest rates are tending, although most people favor long-term, fixed rate loans simply because they aid long-range planning.

When choosing a bank, begin by making a list of at least half a dozen prospects. The usual rule has been to approach mostly local banks for less than $100,000; mostly large banks (Citibank, Security Pacific, Bank of America, etc.) if you need $100,000 or more. Smaller banks, the theory goes, are more willing to invest time in small firms, while large bank can offer not only bigger loans, but more complex financial services needed by bigger firms. That's true in general, but remember that bank branches have individual characters determined by their managers or local VP's. If there's a bank nearby—big or small—with a reputation for being helpful to small businesses, then put it on your list.

You are looking for two things in a loan officer, personal chemistry—a person who takes an interest in you and your business—

and "quality of initial," which is the size of loan that person can approve. If you need two million dollars and walk into a backwater branch where they need board approval for an auto loan, you're in the wrong place.

Your loan presentation or package, of course, will vary according to the size of your business. A small firm should keep things simple. Don't worry unduly about form or style—the point is to get your financial situation clearly and favorably across. For some suggestions about form (and one is pretty much like another), ask your bank or accountant, or perhaps consider the model given in Albert Lowry's well-written *How to Become Financially Successful by Owning Your Own Business.* Here's the format I like best—it's direct, covers the essentials, and can be easily varied to suit your own taste:

I. The Proposal

A. COMPANY REQUESTING LOAN. Company's name, address, principle business(es), and (if helpful) date of founding.

B. PURPOSE OF LOAN. If purpose of the loan is to start a new firm —a difficult proposition—this must be fairly long (say, one to two pages), and must give the sorts of details (proposed products, likely markets, potential competition, etc.) discussed under "Writing A Business Plan" in the next chapter. In describing a proposed firm, keep your language simple and realistic. When I get a forty-page proposal promising to restore the economy and end unemployment, I don't read past the first page. The danger for you is in being mistaken for one of those flakes. So be concise, modest, and matter-of-fact.

If the loan is for an existing firm, then purpose can be brief as a single line: "To write a radio advertising campaign," "To relocate our main manufacturing plant, and to buy new high-speed equipment."

C. AMOUNT REQUESTED. Show the whole amount you want to borrow, and then itemize the *major* ways the money will be put to use.

D. Protection. The collateral by which the loan will secured. Collateral can include current business assets, assets to be acquired with proceeds of the loan, and/or personal assets. A mixture of two or more types is generally preferred. Lenders will also be looking at the firm's "coverage ratios," which show how many dollars of assets you have to cover each dollar of debt. (See Chapter 9, looking at the books)

E. Terms of loan. What rate you expect to pay; how long you want the loan to run (six years is average; try for five to ten); and how you expect to repay it from earnings. (If you're dealing with a bank, it's wise to state your willingness to keep a part of the loan on deposit there. Known as "compensating balance," this is really the small-business equivalent of a "sinking fund debenture," by which big businesses are allowed access to the total value of a loan only over a period of years. It's a reasonable protection for lenders, and many banks insist upon it.) The proposal should be brief, simple, and unromantic. Except where you are trying to borrow money for a new business, you should be able to fit it on one or two typewritten pages. Even a new-business proposal should not exceed three or four pages.

II. Income Projection

With the aid of your accountant, try to show, as conservatively as possible, how growth made possible by the loan will allow you comfortably to repay the loan, including interest, in the period specified. Your projection should detail, and take into account, potential problems and downturns; lenders are automatically suspicious of vast stretches of "blue sky."

The projection will do two things. First, it will show you have a realistic business plan to put the money to work. Too, it will simplify the bank's job of monitoring the loan: if they grant the loan, they'll simply match your subsequent progress against your projections. If you're in trouble, they'll know it early on; if you're ahead of schedule, they'll look kindly on requests for further loans.

III. Supporting Documents

A. Profit and Loss Statements, and Balance Sheets—or the equivalent Spread Sheets—going back about three years. (See LOOKING AT THE BOOKS)
If the business is less than three years old, include whatever you have.

B. A Personal Financial Statement (PFS) for each proposed signer or cosigner of the note.

C. Lease(s) signed or proposed.

D. Supporting photographs, catalogues, etc, of plant or products—especially anything with strong visual appeal.

E. Technical specifications, lab reports, etc, for any proposed product.

F. Any favorable press clippings, letters from major customers, or significant awards—testimonies to your professionalism. (Include photocopies, not the originals).

G. Personal résumés for the major players in your organization. Remember that lenders won't go far with a one-man organization. They much prefer to back a *team,* both for its wider range of skills and for its higher degree of protection against illness or incapacitation.

H. Personal and financial recommendations, names of attorney and CPA, etc. These are of particular importance for smaller organizations.

You have wide latitude in your choice of supporting documents. A, B, and C are probably essential, but after that, choose what you feel is important and helpful. Try not to overload the package—banks will ask for anything else they want, including a look at all your books going back several years—but do put your best foot forward. *Don't* hold back any material weakness, because that could constitute fraud. *All* businesses have weaknesses and risks involved—that's inevitable.

You are within your rights to ask that any of these items—technical diagrams, PFS's, or whatever—be kept confidential. On the other hand, the bank will likely want *independent* confirmation —via lab tests, outside appraisals, etc.—of your claims and estimates. Be prepared to compromise.

You need to use the "sensible and sane" rule when approaching lending institutions. In matters of dress, hosting luncheons, and so on, don't worry about impressing people with $500 suits or $100 lunches—if anything, you would impress them unfavorably with your extravagance. Make it clear early on that they are welcome to visit the plant, but don't insist upon it. Answer all question as precisely and briefly as you can—and don't be afraid to say you don't know something, but will try to get the answer.

It's hard to say how long loan acceptance should take. Firms with solid balance sheets and established credit records can get approval in a day or so, but you should not be discouraged if a couple of weeks pass—especially if it's your first time out. Above all, don't get upset if they come back with a second set of really tough questions—as long as they're asking questions, they're still interested. It's when they start talking about how tough the economy is that you had better start worrying. If the first meeting seems to go fairly well, there's no reason not to ask—in a general way—how long the average loan of your sort usually takes for approval.

Again, you want to shop the loans as far as you can, and whatever the best rate is, you still want to go back and refigure your business plan. If the money's too costly, then either keep looking, or postpone your plans until interest rates come down. Don't end up like the many small-firm owners we saw during the early '80's, who borrowed money at 21% because that was all they could find, and then found themselves working overtime for the bank until they dropped.

One free tip: Put at least one or two newly-opened banks or branches on your list. Whether because they tend to feel rather entrepreneural themselves, or (more likely) because they are anxious to get their loan portfolios rolling, new banks often are particularly receptive to new ventures. During the '70s, for example, we made several useful contacts among the recently-established Japanese banks in California. They frequently came through for our clients when the better-known US banks declined.

Beyond Banks.

Once you move beyond banks, you enter the most expensive realms of money, including finance companies and Small Business Investment Corporations. Finance or commercial credit companies raise money from public offerings as well as banks and insurance firms, and then loan the money to small businesses or larger businesses in trouble. The loans generally are secured by business assets—often equipment—but the collateral can also be passbooks, certificates of deposit, or other cash equivalents.

Again, this is expensive money, but it *is* loaned at high-risk money: these companies will loan when banks will not. Finance companies used to charge 18% back when bank business loans cost 10%; nowadays, many of these loans are up against state usury limits, or at least the limits of what a business can afford to pay while still staying afloat. As a result, most of these companies seek complex arrangements by which to secure the high rates of return they feel their risks justify. Often, for example, they will structure the loans so that they not only get the maximum legal interest rate, but also keep any tax advantages from the deal, such as the 10% investment credits for capital purchases. These companies range in size from a few private investors banded together, to giants like Walter E. Heller International, with assets of some $6 billion.

A variation on the finance company is the small business investment company, a relatively recent innovation meant to help small firms raise money while the markets are tight. SBIC's get SBA money at rates near (or, for minority-group lending, below) the government's own cost, and then relend that money to risky ventures at high rates. Their common tactic is to demand a piece of the business—usually 10%—as their "management" or "consulting" fee along with the loan. Sometimes you *will* get some management aid from these groups, but other groups you'll hear from only about twice—once when they loan you the money, and once when they sue to attach your assets. We've worked successfully with SBIC's before, but in general they're pretty tough customers. Speaking only for myself, if I had to give up a chunk of the business to outsiders, I'd rather go the full distance and take on a true partner, one with a stronger personal commitment. Still, these SBIC loans do deserve consideration, having helped firms like Federal Express and Apple early on.

Once you get much beyond SBIC's, you are nearing the realm of interest rates quoted in percents-per-week, and of "loan offices" in the back seats of Lincoln Continentals. For heaven's sake, remember that when the legal money sources turn you down, the last thing you need is a loan shark. If you wanted the money to start from scratch, you simply need to go back to work and build up your savings. If your business is in trouble, you need a rescue plan: (See ROUGH WEATHER.) Even bankruptcy is better than dealing with the sharks.

The General Goal: Building a Credit Rating.

Some businesses go from inception to final sale without ever tapping formal credit at all. They start out privately funded and generate all their expansion capital internally. Other businesses borrow only rarely—perhaps only once or twice, to buy commercial real estate. However little borrowing you may intend though, you are still well advised to build your credit reputation or rating carefully.

In the first place, no one can accurately foresee every possible emergency or opportunity. When the occasion to borrow does arrive, the availability and cost of the money you need will depend upon your credit rating. The differences can be critical. In mid-1982, after it had already received federal guarantees and put the worst of its losses behind it, Chrysler Corporation was still paying 3 points more than GM for its finance-unit money—at a time when the difference between a sale and no sale was often less than a point or two. So, no matter how little borrowing you may plan to do, you ought to prepare by attending to that all-important rating—a matter easily accomplished.

Remember that you are informally tapping—and so, either damaging or improving—your credit rating whenever you lease equipment, rent property, or place an order for supplies without paying for it in advance. Indeed, if you are starting absolutely from scratch, most suppliers will put you on a "COD", or a three-day, payment schedule. Once you pay reliably over a reasonable period (which can be as short as thirty days, depending upon the generosity of their credit arrangements) you'll be able to receive bills at more extended intervals, and even to use their payment schedule as a source of credit. Meanwhile, if one of those suppliers belongs to a credit reporting bureau, it may already have had occasion to file a report on you—either good or bad. In a short time, you'll have established a credit record, which will largely determine your ability to borrow from suppliers—and subsequently, from banks.

That in turn means you must carefully monitor your standing with the credit services. Such organizations are numerous, ranging from people who simply list bad checks, through local merchant-men's credit services, to the big names like Standard & Poor and Dun & Bradstreet. If you are *ever* denied credit, you are entitled by law to know what credit service down-rated you, and then to demand from that service a copy of your credit file. If there's a false mark against you—and that happens with even the best and biggest companies—you have to get it removed, even if that means suing.

We were once down-checked by a credit bureau belonging to one of the country's bigger conglomerates. The (slightly idiotic) reason turned out to be a big department store's failure to credit us with a returned item of clothing. They kept billing us, and we kept writing letters explaining. Probably we would have eventually paid the foolish bill for nuisance value, but then the department store filed a bad credit report against us, and the rating bureau refused to remove it. We finally had to sue both firms. Since we had all our records, it was a very short case, and we won some thousands in damages as well as the retraction. Ninety-nine times out of 100, I'd say a small business is better off walking away from small disputes. But credit is the lifesblood of business. If you have to go to the mat to protect yours, then do it.

On the other hand, you can also take positive steps to build your credit rating. Along with paying all bills promptly, and keeping alert for harmful reports, you can arrange to have yourself listed with one of the major bureaus like Dun & Bradstreet. Once you have been actively engaged in business for at least one year, you are eligible to be listed with most of these firms. Simply request one of their small-firm profile forms. Once you have become a known quantity in the community, indeed, they'll come to you for information. After all, selling business data is how they make their money. (When it comes time for *you* to extend credit to others you'll turn to the reports of these same companies. If you cannot afford their services—though the local ones are not generally expensive—you can usually arrange to work through your bank's subscription, either as a courtesy, or for a small, per-report fee.)

One argument against being listed in these public ratings is that they advertise to people who might want to sue you—say for negligence or malpractice—just how much you are worth. The argument makes some sense, if you are unlikely to need credit. If you are asset-heavy and intend no borrowing, you might politely decline to be listed by the public credit raters.

If you rarely deal with suppliers, but might need credit for such things as real-estate or going-business purchases, you can ask your bank to formalize its opinion of your credit-worthiness by extending you a line of credit, which is a promise to loan you anything up to a preset maximum simply on your demand, and without further investigation. In general, you will need to use this line to keep it intact and growing. Our firm always generated nearly all of its funds internally, but for many years regularly took out a year's-end loan equal to our line of credit, and then repaid it three days later. The interest cost was small (and tax-deductible); the loan met the bank's requirements; and we kept our credit line operational. When the time came to buy our own office building, our credit line was there and waiting.

In sum, then, remember:

1. Very few businesses work without credit of some kind
2. You should begin building your credit ranking as early as possible
3. You want to shop for the lowest rates among *types* of lenders
4. You want to find a bank that will be sympathetic to your particular needs and plans
5. You need to guard your credit ranking jealously, and to challenge any harmful reports
6. You probably want to establish a formal line of credit as soon as your time-in-business and your balance sheet will permit it.

Lastly, remember that you need to keep in frequent touch with your lenders, when things are going well as much as when they are going ill. Openness breeds confidence—and confidence is the human basis of financial credit.

5

STARTING FROM SCRATCH

SITUATION:
Starting a business from scratch combines maximum freedom with maximum risk
OBJECTIVE:
Designing a business plan allowing for minimum outlay and coherent growth

Into the Cool Blue.

Every year, California papers carry one or more stories of a particular kind of tragedy. Over-eager visitors to the state get their first sight of the cool blue waters of the Pacific, and dive in recklessly from the nearest cliff. They neglect to check the safety of the water below, and they split their heads on the submerged rocks.

That's not only a sad story, it's an uncomfortably apt metaphor for the way too many people try going into business for themselves. They forget that, while buying an existing business gets you a known quantity, starting from scratch means facing a host of unforeseeable risks. They simply dive in head first, and too often, they come to grief.

How Not to Go into Business.

Some years ago, a formerly-successful stock broker came to us looking for a job. In roughly fifteen years of selling stocks, he had built himself a net worth of about two million dollars. He had then put all of that money into his long-standing dream of becoming a restauranteur. Having sunk his entire wealth into not one but three restaurants, he had within four years gone entirely broke. Now, some two decades into his career, he was on the street again, owning nothing and working on commissions.

Starting a business from scratch, as opposed to buying one already in operation, offers the ultimate in personal expression and (potentially) the minimum in initial costs. In his fiscal version of a leap off a California cliff, though, our poor stockbroker violated the three cardinal rules of self-starting: 1) Choose a field you understand 2) Start smaller rather than larger, and 3) Always begin with a clear business plan.

All those rules seem simple, even trivial, but the evidence suggests that they are widely ignored. For example, Control Data Business Centers, which counsel small businesses seeking commercial credit, once noted that of the first 2000 businesses seeking their aid, fewer than 5% had ever prepared a written business plan of any sort. That strikes me as a recipe for disaster.

I know that the great appeal of starting a business entirely on your own is that you can do it exactly the way you choose. If I tried to dictate methods to you entirely, you probably wouldn't listen; if you wanted a strict formula, you'd buy a franchise, and if you wanted an absence of risk, you'd buy a going concern. Still, I hope you'll at least consider the three cardinal rules, as shown in the following examples:

STARTING SMALL. When I say start small, I mean two things: start with a small operation, and with a small, preferably low-cost, product. Nibble at the edges of the market, and build your reputation while you learn the trade—then work up in easy stages.

Consider the postwar Japanese. Unlike the Germans and the English, they began with few products bearing international reputations. In automotive markets, instead of competing with Mercedes or Rolls Royce, they started at the very bottom. Honda, which some people are now calling the "Japanese BMW" began by making two-stroke motorized bicycles, then motorcycles, then micro-cars, and so on. In electronics, Sony began as a radio repair shop, then built simple AM radios, and then more complicated radios. Today Sony ranks as a world leader in consumer electronics, industrial video-taping, some elements of office automation, and a host of other activities.

Even though Honda, Sony, and other Japanese multinationals began as back-shop operations only a few decades ago, they may appear rather abstract or distant. Let's take a simpler example from a business I saw a few years back, and then again recently.

Some years ago, a young fellow, watching the beginnings of office computer automation, decided it was the business for him. Since he had only been a librarian (with a few administrative tasks) up to that time, his resources were slim—especially for a business where the big dollars were beginning to fly. He had little training, few assets, and no credit. All he had was a small bank account.

What he did was, first, to work out a plan describing where he wanted to be in ten years, and second, to look and keep looking for a tiny spot where he could work in the field which interested him—without tying up any capital.

He discovered the IBM typewriter. Seven or eight years ago, IBM still held exclusive patents for its "golf ball" element typewriters. Because of its manufacturing policies which mystify all mortals outside of Armonck, New York, IBM would never make the machines without a firm order in hand. At the peak of demand, small customers ordering one or two machines could end up waiting six months or more for delivery.

Bingo! Our friend had his business. He simply began placing placing regular orders with IBM. In those days, the company wasn't even asking for deposits. After five months of placing orders, he began quietly advertising, by phone and letter, that he had perfectly legal, factory-crated IBM Correcting Selectrics ready for pickup in under a month, cash on delivery. Because other small businesses didn't plan ahead, he had a ready stream of customers, who could either pay his premium ($200 on a $750 typewriter), or wait six months for delivery. All he had to do was to take delivery of his machines, run them over to a customer, clear the customer's check for $950, and write one of his own to IBM for

$750—pocketing the $200 himself. He didn't advertise, except through a few secretarial contacts at the outset, but the business boomed by word of mouth.

Our friend was simply "position selling"; acquiring a spot in line and then unloading it at a premium. Many people have done the same thing with, say, a place on a waiting list for a popular car. It's still widespread practice in industries with long delivery times, like corporate aircraft, for example. Most manufacturers resist the practice—which at the least suggests they don't know how to price their own products—and the truth is our friend probably slipped in under IBM's radar. On the other hand, giants like IBM have to be extremely careful about blasting off tiny competitors. In any case, they never complained, though what they thought a single person was doing with six, eight, or a dozen Correcting Selectrics a week is beyond me.

That Correcting Selectric market gradually dried up, but by then our friend had accomplished three very useful things: 1) he had fattened his bankroll, 2) he had built a reputation among small businesspeople for delivering scarce goods on time, and 3) he had acquired (at no risk) a solid education in the pragmatics of running a small business. In short, he had acquired all the things you nominally are buying when you pay for "goodwill" value of an existing firm.

From that point, he was ready to move into his long-range plan of dealing supplies to small-computer users. Long before, however, he had begun preparing himself, not only by garnering capital and client contacts, but by attending every computer course, fair, or demonstration he could reach. He worked with the people who would be offering alternatives to OEM (original equipment manufacturers') automation supplies—cheaper daisy wheels, diskettes and ribbons. He had already seen how OEM's like Xerox, Wang, and IBM tended to pursue the big users, and gave scant attention (and fewer discounts) to small business accounts.

Our friend decided to fill the gap by bulk-buying high-quality alternatives, and then providing both counseling and personalized, discount-priced supplies, to small users. He began business just as the Apple II's and early TRS computers were coming on-stream, and he trained his salespeople carefully in the philosophy of personal attention. To customers, they represented an alternative to the mysteries of computers and the costliness of the big computer vendors. Once again, with only some direct mailing, he was able to capture much of his local market. He not only had affordable supplies, but had all those contacts laboriously acquired when he was reselling typewriters.

Today, after less than five years in the new line, his firm is netting between $150,000 and 200,000 a year. It carries no debt, is growing rapidly and steadily, and is still 100% owned by him. Of all the businesses I've seen in, say, the last five years, this is the one I'd be most tempted to own myself. Yet his original idea, selling positions on a production schedule, while clever enough, was scarcely beyond the reach of ordinary intelligence. He succeeded because he started small, grew only when he understood his markets, and worked according to a plan. Other businesses may have grown faster, but never with his blend of speed and security.

Above all, I cannot overstate the importance of testing the waters, and beginning cautiously—unless you're just looking for some fat tax losses to set against other income. Here's one last example of the rule:

Testing the Waters.

Two women had husbands who were partners in a prosperous business chain we were attempting to sell. These two women had created a recipe for a condiment made from all natural ingredients. It was a tasty concoction, and they were often urged to sell it commercially. With husbands already prosperous in business, they might easily have started by sinking money into large-scale production, trying to create a Famous Amos operation overnight.

Starting a small commercial kitchen can easily require $250,000 or more. Even without automated canning equipment, you need sterilizers, jars, industrial stainless-steel vats, ovens, and sinks, plus workers, inventory, insurance, property, and so on. Plenty of people try it, and plenty fail.

These two women took a different approach. First they marketed the stuff at charity fundraisers for a local playhouse, and found they could sell more cases than they could provide—so they took orders, and filled them slowly. Then they chose one commercial outlet at a fancy department store, while still donating the proceeds to charity. When sales stayed high, they wanted one final test before deciding to go commercial, so they went to a food trade fair 600 miles away, where they would not benefit from either existing friendships or their image as nonprofit operators. At the trade fair, they both triumphed with their product, and secured several friendships among other small businesswomen, from whom they learned much about the food preparation business.

It was only then that they decided to go into business for themselves. When they did, their first step was to prepare a plan for their first year. Before considering their plan, note that if they had fallen on their faces at the food fair, they could have walked away cleanly, their only loss having been the $500 or so they had invested in the trip. As it was, they were ready for the next step.

Now they could prepare for their first year in actual business. They divided duties, deciding who would keep books, who would make salescalls, and so on. They budgeted their time, and made allowance for the help they could expect from their husbands and children. They contacted suppliers, arranging for both the small lots (difficult to come by) they would need early on, and the larger, truckload orders (much easier to find) they would want later. They set their prices and made up a list of potential outlets. They wrote up a formal agreement dividing financial authority and future profits.

Best of all, they searched until they found a way to rent, rather than buy, the kitchen they needed. They found one owned by a successful local pastry-maker, who was trying to cut his own (excessive) overhead by renting his facilities out evenings and weekends. The kitchen featured all the right equipment, and meant tying up not one cent in capital improvements. Even though they had money available, they went in as low-budget as possible. That does not mean a cheap product (they were using the most expensive all-organic ingredients available), but rather a lean, efficient organization.

I don't pretend that going in low-end is an inviolable rule. A counter-approach is sometimes proper. Cray Computers commenced by making a single product—the world's best-known super computers, with prices starting around $20 million. Remember, though, that Dr. Cray began his company only after many years leading research at the world's only other super-computer manufacturers, Control Data. He was hardly a beginner.

So, those rare exceptions aside, let's talk about the basic rules for succeeding at start-from-scratch business.

1. *Research the Market.* Learn the ins and outs of any business which interests you, and make contacts among people already in the field. If feasible, take a job (even for a few months) with the best-rated firm in the field. At least take any relevant college, or even night school, courses in the field. Attend trade fairs and conventions, even if it means long drives on weekends. (Note: If you want to talk serious business with people in some fields at conventions, you'd better plan to be there during the morning. A lot of people at these things start getting rather plastered around lunchtime.)

Study those expensive one-day seminars. Some are rip-offs, consisting of over-packaged compendia of general financial advice. You might try listening to one or more franchise salespitches, though. You might get some tips, or even find a package that suits you.

Don't neglect the library, the SBA pamphlets (free from your local office—request their mailing list), SCORE, trade organizations (again, listed at your library), or bank or major CPA firms' publications. For some other hints, see the BIBLIOGRAPHY of this book.

2. Aim low rather than high; pick the inexpensive end of a market or, if you favor luxury items, choose a small one. More people make money on top-dollar chocolate chip cookies than on custom-built sports cars.

If possible, avoid the capital-intensive parts of the business. There is not an absolute hierarchy, but a good approximation, in order of increasing capital demands, would be:

A. Services: Consulting, software design, position resales, etc.
B. Retail sales
C. Wholesale sales
D. Manufacture

The higher up the list, the lower the (usual) demands for initial capital. Consider these first if your funds are limited and your ambitions fairly high. Several of my college classmates have already sold out as millionaires from computer software firms they started in dorm rooms while they were in school.

3. Work from a well-structured plan.

Writing a Business Plan.

Of the three steps, the writing of a business plan seems most to annoy the American entrepreneur. It constrains, and, worse, it seems self-contradictory. How can you decide in detail what you want to do with a business which does not yet exist?

The chicken-or-egg quality of business planning does mean your plans will need frequent—perhaps weekly, perhaps even daily—revision during your initial period. Still, even these early plans will indicate your preparedness for entering business. If you cannot write one, you are not ready for the next step, that of seeking venture financing. Your first "plan" may consist of little more than a set of questions. If that's the case, fine—just keep looking for answers until you can provide at least the following:

1. BUSINESS NAME. What are you going to call it? Try for something informative and evocative, something that will stand out. If you want your name in it, remember that last names have more prestige than first names: Cantrell Automotive sounds ritzier than Al's Radiators. The more generalized the name, the more prestigious, but the less likely it is to be associated with your particular product. What does "Allied Enterprises" do for a living?

Make up at least half a dozen names you like. You'll need to make sure that no one else has taken out a business license using the same name. Check with whoever keeps the the fictitious names records for your area. Some names, of course, have already been secured state or nation-wide by copyright or trademark registration. The big firms jealously defend these. Try calling yourself Xerox Corporation—or using an unlicensed "Peanuts" figure in your advertising—and you'll be hearing from their lawyers about two hours after you open your doors.

2. LICENSES, PERMITS, CONFERENCES, ETC. List the special training, licenses, and permits you will need. Include minor items like water and business permits, and major items like construction permits and conference memberships. Specify what they cost, how they are obtained, and how long they take to arrive. (Please refer back to LICENSES AND PERMITS)

3. CONSULTANTS AND PROFESSIONAL AIDS. List the names of the lawyer and accountant you intend to use, and their fee schedules. They should be business specialists, and (ideally) they should have handled businesses like yours before. Decide whether you need high-powered people at the outset, or whether you can use someone less exotic. If you begin modestly, also start searching for hotshots for future application.

Decide what other consultants you may need, and see which you can line up for free. Start with SCORE, the Service Corps of Retired Executives. SCORE is a part of the SBA, which can also direct you to any number of other useful government-sponsored services. You can also try the Center for Small Business of the US Chamber of Commerce in Washington, DC. There are limits to what large organizations can do for you, but do give them a try.

4. CAPITAL EXPENDITURES. Estimate what you are going to need to spend out of pocket for fixtures and equipment, including both office and shop. One look at this figure, and you'll probably begin taking seriously what I said about aiming for the low-capital segment of any market.

Check leasing costs as well as buying. See whether good used equipment is available. Look around to find whether there's a going plant you can use part-time. (Remember our friends the condiment makers.) Shop industrial auctions, garage sales, and the equipment-resale points of major companies. At the Boeing resale center south of Seattle, for example, you can find everything from engineering manuals to workmen's gloves, from machine tools to desks to aircraft seats, all at bargain prices. Just call around to big —or even medium—companies nearby.

5. ADDITIONAL OVERHEAD. List what you expect to pay for rent, insurance, gas and electric, automobiles, and so on. Don't forget advertising. The SBA's "Checklist for Going into Business" can help here, but so can common sense.

6. PERSONNEL. How many people do you expect to employ, and where will you find them? What are the approximate going wages in their fields? If there is heavy physical labor involved for you, are you up to it? (Remember that even people with genteel little bookshops end up lugging forty- and fifty-pound boxes of books.)

7. THE MARKET. Who are your likely competitors, where are they located, how well financed are they, and how good a job are they doing? If they are direct competitors, how are you going to get an edge on them, given that they're already in business?

One market tip on fads: watch for early signs of a softening in prices. When I first began writing this book, one of the hottest small retail markets was for video arcades; the people who owned the first ones had made money hand over fist. But smart operators were noticing that more and more arcades were offering cut prices —six, eight, and then ten games for a dollar. That was the clue to them that the market was oversaturated.

Never be the last guy on the bandwagon. If you miss the start of a fad, let it go by. There'll be another one along shortly.

8. PRODUCTS. What exactly are your products or services, brand-by-brand? What are they going to cost you, and what are you likely to be able to charge for them? How many can you expect to sell?

You need to list not only your initial products (or services), but your follow-on items; what will you be selling when your current products turn obsolete? Funding product development is one of the real crunch-points for small business. If you cannot do it yourself, be sure to tie yourself to suppliers with well-funded research and development (R & D) programs. If, moreover, you have access to a desirable line (Buck knives or Bentley autos), be sure to list it.

As already mentioned in RAISING MONEY, it's hard to get investors interested in launching a new business. Your business plan may not actually become part of a loan proposal until many months after you've gotten the business underway with your own capital. Still, it can be extremely useful to you at the outset. Although starting from scratch offers the maximum degree of freedom, and can be the cheapest possible way to begin, you need to carefully select a section of the market you can handle, and to work methodically to build your enterprise. A business plan will stabilize you, and keep the freedom of a from-scratch operation from becoming a ruinous anarchy.

Once you have your plan, set it aside for several days, and then reread it, paying careful attention to its accuracy. Have you overstated revenues? Understated rent? Does the idea still sound appealing—even when you imagine yourself not only paying the bills, but working Saturdays and nights, lifting heavy crates, meeting deadlines, dealing with nasty customers? If so, then you're a serious potential owner. If the proposal looks good enough, you may even want to see whether you can convince someone to invest in it with you.

Even before that, though, please note that business planning should be a permanent part of your firm. Instead of tossing your plan away once you've gotten the business underway, you should work continually to refine it, incorporating annual sales targets, future expansion, tax planning, and so on. The more you learn about your business, the more sophisticated your planning should become.

The next seven chapters are all devoted to ways of finding and acquiring existing businesses. Even if your preference now is for starting a business from scratch, you might be wise to invest the hour or so needed to read those chapters. In the first place, you might be persuaded to change your mind—at least you'll be acting with full information. In the second, someday you're likely to become a business seller, and it's always wise to understand a transaction from every point of view.

6

BUYING A CORPORATE LOSER

SITUATION:
*Some major corporations cannot profitably maintain minor
acquisitions*
OBJECTIVE:
Locating and acquiring the desirable minor subsidiary

You probably already know the obvious ways to begin seeking an
existing business: you check the "Business Opportunities" section
of your newspaper's classified ads, register your name and interests with reputable local brokers, ask your accountant or tax attorney for possible leads, approach individual owners, or even (if you
have experience rescuing trouble companies) follow the bankruptcy calender of your Federal courthouse. But here's an opportunity you don't want to overlook while conducting your business
search. It'll require some effort, and some luck, but if successful,
it'll give you a bargain and a quick leg-up on your competition.
And its one main hazard is easy to avoid.

As a recent issue of *Fortune* magazine will attest, there is big
money to be made in buying and turning around losing divisions
of major companies. Among the better-known examples of this
approach in recent years are Remington electric shavers, Helena
Rubinstein cosmetics, and American Safety Razor—all of which
were quickly turned into money-makers.

As losing divisions of major companies, all of those had one
major advantage other losing businesses often lack. The big companies which owned them had generally spent plenty of money on

them. When a small business begins losing money, cash flow problems generally force all sorts of budget cuts, many of which harm the corporate structure. Too often key people are let go (or inferior ones hired), plants and products are allowed to age, and so on. When a division of a larger corporation begins to lose money, on the other hand, the reverse is often true. The home office will begin pouring in money to turn things around. In fact, in the case of Remington razors, the hypereffort to show a profit was a part of the problem—the company was bringing out new products so fast it was obsoleting its own merchandise every six months.

What that means, in short, is that normally when you buy a division or subsidiary of a money-making firm, you won't be getting junk. Except in the case where the market absolutely doesn't exist, you'll be getting an operation with potential, and real value.

The problem, of course, is that all those examples discussed by *Fortune* are themselves major concerns, with price tags up in the tens of millions and higher. Buying a losing division might make sense if you've got twenty million to spend, but does it fit anywhere in our scheme?

Yes. It absolutely does, and here's why. Few people realize how often major companies end up, through acquisition or reorganization, with divisions which are simply too small for them to hang onto. Even big-board companies often find themselves with divisions employing as few as half a dozen people. For big companies these small divisions present particular problems. If a division makes $100,000 a year but requires four people at corporate level (each drawing a big salary) just to keep track of it, the company's going to be disappointed. If that division is *losing* $100,000 a year or more, the company is going to have to make an eventual choice between pouring in a lot of money to make it pay big, or either writing or selling it off. That's when your opportunity arises. Since, as we've said, it's likely to offer an excellent plant with only some fine-tuning needed to make it a money-maker, it's likely to be a tremendous bargain for you—if you know how to find it.

There are two basic ways to finding such a bargain—the insider approach and the outsider approach. Each has its own separate problems. However, since in either case you'll be dealing with the big boys when you go after a corporate holding, perhaps our first example ought to be a cautionary tale. There is one classic mistake in this kind of dealing, a mistake made over and over. Make this mistake and you're out of business.

How Film Companies Fry Fish: A Warning Example.

Here's an example of precisely the sort of business you want to look out for, and how *not* to get it.

One of this country's better-known entertainment firms went on a diversifying binge, and as one of its acquisitions, bought a chain of theme amusement parks. Shortly before it was acquired, this chain of parks had been trying a little expansion of its own. At one of its base cities, it had launched a set of fast-food restaurants featuring meals appropriate to its general theme. At the time of the takeover, there were sixteen of these restaurants, and they were losing money at the rate of $200,000 a year.

As is fairly typical of companies making acquisitions, the film makers assumed they would quickly have the fast-food joints turning a profit. But food is quite a specialized line of work, and executives who had successfully taken over insurance companies for example, found themselves stymied by the intricacies of french-frying zucchini. As so often happens when there is a take-over, the fast-food joints went on corporate life-support: enough money was poured in to keep them bright and shiny but still running at a loss.

By chance, pretty far down the corporate ladder, there was one junior executive who *did* know fast food, and who was sure he could turn the restaurants around. Since it was clear that the parent media conglomerate was looking for a way out of fish and chips, he decided to take a gamble. He went to the corporate higher-ups and announced he wanted to take the restaurants private. He would get together a group of backers and buy them from the company. He would run the restaurants as a new, privately-held corporation.

This came across to the parent company like music across an alpine meadow. They had a business they didn't want—one which was not only unsuited to the corporate skills but which was losing money steadily. Here, without their having made a single move—without their even having to pay a broker a fee, or advertise to the world that they had acquired a money-loser they needed to dump—was a ready-made buyer with known skills. They gave him the go-ahead to put together his group of backers.

This young executive, seeing the opportunity of his life, brought together the investors. It was a fairly easy task, and no wonder. The company was talking in terms of $450,000 for the sixteen restaurants. Compare that with the roughly $175,000 average start-up for a *single* Burger King, and you'll have an idea of the bargains to be had in losing divisions. True, the stores *were* all losing money, but our young executive (who, unfortunately, did not become our client until it was too late), knew the operation inside and out, and had a clearly detailed plan for turning the stores around.

Well, negotiations moved along steadily over the course of the next three months. With every meeting, our young executive became more confident and more exuberant. And, as is sadly also human nature, he became less cautious.

One day, when it had begun to seem that the sale was a sure thing (everyone had begun speaking of it as such), one of the other executives asked our friend, in a chummy manner, what specifically he planned to do to turn the restaurants around.

Our friend made *the* classic mistake. He told him.

He told him everything—how the company was overpaying for supplies, and which distributor would provide them cheaper; how they were using too expensive a grade of fish, and which cheaper grade would taste even better; even how their signs were poorly placed at about half the locations and costing them business. He forgot who he was talking to, and he told everything, and what happened next was inevitable.

What happened was that the company informed him, "thank you very much, but the deal's off—and by the way, you're fired." Then they went ahead and instituted every one of his changes. He finally came to us to see whether we could put the deal back together, but the company wasn't interested. Why would they sell off sixteen profitable restaurants that fit so well with their theme parks? Maybe at a much higher price, but probably not even then. The film producers had learned how to fry fish.

PROCEEDING SAFELY: OK—that's rule number one. When dealing with a major company, never tell them what they have no right to know. They have a right to know your background and your financial position—anything to assure themselves they're likely to get paid for whatever they sell you. But that's it. If you want to buy their restaurants and dress your waitresses in mackerel suits, that's *your* business. Make it clear at the beginning (politely but forcefully) that you feel that way: you'll gain respect and avoid a lot of attempts to pump you for free information—attempts known as "fishing expeditions" in the business world.

If people didn't continually succumb to these attempts, which sometimes take the form of intimidation, but more often that of winning one's confidence and then abusing it, we wouldn't be stressing it here. But people *do* succumb on an almost daily basis. Remember, too, that you can sink yourself any time up to the actual completion of the sale and that no matter how sleazy the deception, your chances of proving it in court are not only extremely slight but certain to prove extremely costly in terms of both time and money. If you get into the situation of negotiating with a big company, you might try rereading the "tale of the tuna" every few days, just for safety's sake.

All right. Assuming you feel you can handle the pressure of dealing with a major company, how do you go about approaching one?

As mentioned earlier, insider and outsider approaches involve different circumstances. Since they present slightly different problems, we'll discuss them separately.

The Insider Sale. An insider sale is simply one in which you, or one of your buying partners, is already an employee of the corporation with the losing division. (Do note, of course, that you need not work *in* the losing division to qualify as an insider). At least two factors favor the insider—he is likely to know the troubled division very well, including its major problems, and he is in turn well known by the corporation. As an insider, you won't have the problem of documenting your track record for the company. They are likely to have confidence in you from the beginning.

Many insiders are afraid to raise the issue of buying out a losing operation. They worry about jeopardizing their position with the company. In our experience, however, that's a false concern. In the first place, you're offering to solve a problem for the company. In the second, you're advancing yourself without either threatening your superiors or becoming a direct competitor to the firm. In fact, these spun-off companies often retain excellent, mutually-profitable relations with their former parent companies.

Not only that, but an insider has by far the best chance of managing a highly-leveraged sale. When Burroughs Wellcome sold its animal health products division (with its five employees) to one of its own sales managers, the company took back a note for 90% of the selling price, and later extended still more credit to let the new firm take on some new lines Burroughs Wellcome labs had developed. The buyer, Mr. Bowman, was in business with $50,000 on a $500,000 business; the seller, Burroughs, had turned over an unprofitable concern to a person it knew and trusted. (*Wall Street Journal,* December 29, 1980)

By and large, then, you can expect at least a sympathetic hearing from your company whenever you raise the possibility of the buyout of an unprofitable line. As long as your presentation is well worked-out, and your record is good, the chances of a deal are quite high. And even if nothing materializes, you will have at least identified yourself as a go-getter, in a nonthreatening way.

The one likely real problem is slightly different. It arises from the requirement that corporate officers exercise "due dilligence" in assuring the best possible deal for their stockholders. The one thing they most dread is the appearance of a "sweetheart" arrangement, by which you, as a corporate insider, are getting a lower price than the open market would set. In the case of the Burroughs Wellcome deal, for example, the company felt obliged to show the division to some fifty potential buyers and keep Mr. Bowman waiting a full year.

Corporate caution is certainly understandable—the appearance of any internal hanky-panky could have easily drawn the unwelcome scrutiny of the stockholders and even, under certain circumstances, the SEC.

Still, no one anxious to get into business is going to enjoy waiting a year or more for the chance. The best alternative is probably to arrange for an outside firm—either a brokerage house or a business appraiser—to set a price. Offer the business on the open market at that price for the standard ninety days, reserving your right to come in with a higher bid if someone else offers. If no one else does offer, you can generally have it for anything near the estimated market value. If you come in at, say, 15 or 20% under, no one will be able to protest effectively—you bought during a down market.

Of course, every situation is unique. If, for example, it can be shown that the company had already offered the division to the public at a rock-bottom price before you entered the picture, or even better, if they had talked with liquidators or auctioneers about selling off the assets, then you should be quite safe with any offer you can make without blushing.

Outsider Sale. Where you lack inside knowledge of a desirable division, your problem is twofold—locating a target, and persuading the parent company to sell to you.

You can still find a gem of a business, but this gem will require some digging. Most of the standard methods for locating distressed firms simply won't work here. The merchant credit associations, for example, won't help, because the parent company will be picking up all the bills, preventing a drop in the firm's credit rating. You will have to duplicate some of the legwork a regular brokerage undertakes to find *its* prospects. In the process, you may discover why brokers collects such large fees.

Brokers have several ways of going about this, any of which might serve for you, depending upon your particular needs. If you just want to find *any* troubled division you can turn around, and don't object to a geographic switch, you can study either business periodicals or companies' annual reports, looking for divisions losing money. Usually, the report will give a brief explanation of the problems being experienced, which, of course, may or may not be accurate. If the accountant's statement in an annual report is reasonably detailed, the division will at least be defined well enough to give you an idea of the size of the operation and the amount of the loss.

When you are determined to stay where you are, another, more efficient approach is to follow the local financial or legal newspapers. You are looking for small items like, "Losses at Ajax Division Depress Acme Co. Third Quarter Earnings", "Local Unit of X Corp. Loses Major Account", or, "Y Enterprises May Close Operations Here." Nearly every issue of any given financial paper will carry one or more such stories. All of them represent potential leads. Many you will follow up to no end, but one or more may prove productive.

Then there's the grapevine. Cultivate people in fields which interest you. If a rumor is about, or if you specifically ask people whether any businesses in their field might be in trouble, follow up on what you are told. And *never* assume a big company will refuse to deal with a private party.

Sometimes, certainly, a corporation will manage to suppress or disguise news of its losses. That does not mean they would be uninterested in selling if approached. Very often the local Chamber of Commerce, the Newspaper, or some comparable organization will publish annual surveys of local business. Generally these will list at least the location, the number of employees, the main lines of business, and the ownership. If there's only one type of business that interests you, this is the place to begin. Especially if there's even a hint of a rumor that a tempting firm might be in trouble, and if a check at the guidebook tells you it belongs to, let's say, the Ajax Division of Textron or Esmark, then you may be on your way to a bargain.

The last step in targeting a company is to conduct a preliminary study, to find out as much as possible about a company's clients, products, and reputation. Of all these, reputation will be most useful. What are its customers' most common complaints? Where management has money to make improvements and problems remain, it means management hasn't been paying attention. With a little care and a few discreet inquiries (and without breaking any laws) you can often discover problems (and so, solutions) which management has not yet thought of. Assuming you turn up no insurmountable problems (such as a pending product liability or class action suit), you are ready for stage two.

Dealing with the Parent Firm.

As with any approach to a seller, your first decision is whether or not to hire a broker to act for you. Clearly this is a case where a known name will be likely to assist you, but only if you pick a firm with a national reputation. A broker to handle the negotiating will minimize the chances of your making a slip and revealing useful information to the parent firm. As always, a reputable brokerage firm will charge you a commission only if a sale is consummated; otherwise, you pay nothing.

Assuming you decide to act on your own, there are several ways in which your approach must differ from that discussed in Chapters 8–12. First, you have to take the additional step of familiarizing yourself with the parent company. You do this partly so you will be able to add some compliments to the implied insult of offering to buy their loser operation, and partly because corporate executives expect you to talk their language, to appear knowledgeable about their world, even if you're only buying a set of their fried fish restaurants. The social world of corporate executives is relatively closed; and you will have to give at least some signs that you're a part of it.

Along the same lines, you have to disregard some of the things we've said earlier about matters such as dress. Here it *does* matter how you dress, and the danger is in appearing to represent too low, rather than too high, a social stratum. The problem of putting off the self-made owner/operator by appearing too affluent doesn't exist here. What you want are traditional business clothes. Obviously, there are other books which can give you more detailed advice than this one, but in general, we're speaking of formal suits for women, and three piece dark solids, pin-stripes or chalk-stripes, or grey flannels for men.

Then there is the advantage inherent in learning the corporate structure and the names of key executives. For the highest officials, of course, you can use the shareholder's annual statement. For local executives, there are a number of guides, among the most useful of which is an annual called *Contacts Influential,* which lists businesses by their addresses and then offers the names of all key personnel. This source is used largely by salesmen, but it will work very well for you.

The idea, in short, is to make yourself—an outsider—sound as much as possible like an insider. Once you have established open communication with whatever corporate officers you need to consult, negotiations will proceed essentially as described in the following chapters—with, of course, the crucial proviso that you must never discuss your future plans. Remember to stick with the *whole* program for examining plants and records. Don't let yourself be deterred by nervousness from steps as important as examining the minutes of the director's meetings. A big company is just as likely as a small one to stick you with a concealed pension plan for key employees.

None of this is meant to intimidate you. In practice, a big company can be as easy to deal with as a small one. In some ways, it can be easier—executives there (once they have accepted you) are actually less likely to stall or make silly attempts to assert their importance. They tend to be efficient and decisive, and you will almost certainly know very quickly whether or not you have a deal, and upon what terms.

And always bear in mind you are helping them as much as they are helping you. If you're gaining a money-maker, they're ditching a loser. There's no contradiction there. Never assume that anything you can do, a big company can do better. In the matter of small business, the precise opposite is more generally true.

7

THE DANGERS OF AN
EXISTING CORPORATION

SITUATION:
*Purchasing an existing corporation means acquiring virtually all
its financial and legal obligations, many of which remain hidden
until the purchase is complete*
OBJECTIVE:
Making the purchase while leaving the risks behind

Beginning in the next chapter, we'll discuss the general tactics for
safely purchasing the existing business of your choice. Right now,
though, we need to discuss a specific problem which arises only
in one case: when you are buying an existing corporation. It's
potentially a particularly grim situation because it hits people who
have found just the business they want, and who could have
safely acquired it if only they'd been shrewd about one fine point.
In fact, I once heard the situation compared with a basketball
player on a fast break, who has a clear line to the basket but fails
to note the slick spot on the floor and winds up flying into the
cheap seats.

As explained in CHOOSING A BUSINESS STRUCTURE, there are many
reasons for wanting to own an incorporated business: prestige,
flexibility, and, above all, tax advantages. Indeed, leaving all other
considerations aside, and granting that tax laws today are in continual flux, the old rule that you want to incorporate any business
which consistently makes over $50,000 a year probably remains
as true as ever.

A corporate structure will let you design your own pension and severance packages, work lease-backs of aircraft and boats, and disperse income by such means as placing family members on the board of directors and then paying them generous honoraria for attending quarterly meetings at fancy restaurants and resorts. All of these advantages can be legally obtained, and any accountant can fill you in on their precise workings.

To those benefits for their owners, we must add the *apparent* benefits corporations offer to buyers. When you buy a corporation, you buy a complete legal and financial entity—a functioning system with all its assets and liabilities. That offers some real temptations. For one thing, it means you'll be getting not only hard assets like trucks and plants, but also all the accounts receivable and the money in the bank. Somehow, that always strikes beginning businesspeople as a plus, as if they're getting something soldier for their dollars—even though they're buying those bank deposits on a dollar-for-dollar basis. More meaningfully, an existing corporation often provides a useful infrastructure; things like managerial chain-of-command, pension plans, and leases are already in place and ready to go. Lastly (and this is a small point, but it does influence some people), an existing corporation will save you the time and cost of filing to create a corporation of your own.

I can understand those temptations with a deal pending. The ball's in hand, the basket's in sight; why not go for the score? You're going to want to incorporate sooner or later anyway; why not buy the whole package all at once?

Well, for thirty years or so, we've been urging people *not* to buy that tempting package. A corporation is a wonderful thing, and certainly you will want to exploit its legal and financial advantages as soon as possible—with a corporation *you've* created. But the very advantages which can make a corporation desirable to own or control can make it extremely dangerous to acquire. And that's the issue here.

What Buying a Corporation Means: The Lesser Dangers.

We have said that a corporation is a complete financial and legal entity. Of those two attributes, the financial aspects create the lesser (though still significant) hazards. In the first place, buying a complete package is going to stick you with *every* deal the company has made. You'll be acquiring not only the bad leases and the leaky buildings, but all the highly idiosyncratic deals the former head of the firm may have cut for himself. Suddenly the flexibility of the corporation seems more like a straitjacket. If the former owner was an aircraft buff, for example, he might have arranged to buy a helicopter and then lease it to the corporation on a long-term basis. That was fine for him, but you're now left lease-holding, say, a Sikorsky S-76—even if you get airsick standing on a ladder. And these sorts of deals are *remarkably* common in successful small corporations.

Worse still are the more mundane financial commitments. Remember that some of the worst of these can be buried in the minutes of the board of directors' meetings. Some will be as open and as easily located as unfunded pension plans. Corporations often commit themselves to large pension obligations towards their workers, but arrange to defer actually putting up the necessary money until the pensions are likely to come into use, years down the road. You, in buying the corporation, become the sole owner of those obligations, which in many cases greatly reduce the actual worth of the company you *think* you are acquiring. Again, companies have been known to protect themselves against take-over bids by setting up huge severance-pay packages for key executives. These can be removed if the entire board agrees, but they still represent yet one more potential danger in acquiring an existing corporation. Remember that some of these financial obligations will be immediately apparent on examination, but others will require careful search to discover.

THE MAJOR DANGERS: OK, catching up on the full extent of your financial commitment in acquiring a corporation can be tedious, but normally (if your incentive is strong enough) it can be done. But the real dangers more often are legal, and they can best be illustrated by an example.

A friend of ours was a business attorney with many years of experience, first on the legal staff of a nationally-based corporation, and then in private practice. He was often in the market for

THE DANGERS OF AN EXISTING CORPORATION 95

sideline investments, and one day he took an interest in a corporation we were offering for sale—a chain of three small magazines of the dollar-a-copy type.

The business was attractive; it had stable, well-controlled markets—one periodical was aimed at the local senior citizens, and had been in business for twenty years or more. It was profitable, neat, and required only a few hours of attention per week. Naturally, since it was fiscally successful, it was an incorporated concern. And that was the source of the problem.

Our suggestion was that our friend break up the corporation, or rather, buy from it only the corporate assets he wanted—namely, the magazines themselves. There would have been no problem in creating his own new corporation, and having the *corporation* purchase the desirable assets. The old owner would have been left with all the company's liquid assets, cash in bank, accounts receivables, etc. Most important of all, the old owner would have kept all the old corporation's legal problems.

Unfortunately, our friend was in a hurry to make the acquisition, and also, perhaps, rather unwilling to go to the trouble and expense of creating a new corporation. He told us pretty firmly that he was a big boy, who knew what to look for in buying an existing corporation, probably better than we did. Given his background (he was a very fine attorney), and his insistence, there was no way to dissuade him, and so we put together a corporate sale.

Then came the slick spot. Our friend had certainly read every available corporate document, and had been right in thinking he had found nothing damnable. The corporation was simple and straightforward. There was, however, one minor item he had overlooked because the early stages of a Federal labor practices investigation are not exactly matters of public record. The previous corporate owners, unfortunately, had been accused of attempting to bribe a union official to block unionization of the company.

Now, obviously, no one is going to be forced to jail for someone else's actions, and there is no way a corporation proper can be imprisoned, but the corporation (meaning our friend, the new owner) can be fined, or restricted in its operations, or forced (usually through a consent order) to make all sorts of concessions, along the lines of immediate union elections or negotiations.

The point of this is obvious. All of our friend's troubles (and they were severe enough to prompt him to sue—unsucessfully—to rescind the sale and to recover damages for fraud) were caused by his insistence upon buying the going corporation rather than the assets.

How do you avoid the problem? Nothing could be simpler: you simply execute a bulk purchase of the assets you want. In theory, this can include *everything* and *anything* owned by the corporation, from hard assets to goodwill to accounts receivable. Normally, of course, you'll want to keep your outlays as small as possible, and so you'll concentrate on buying the hard things you need to run the business: the key fixtures and equipment; tradenames; real estate (if appropriate); and perhaps goodwill at a fair value. You're not obliged to take on the company's raw land, condo in Aspen, or leased turbo-prop—unless you want or need them. Best of all, you leave any potential legal problems sitting safely on the ground while you fly off with the best of the business.

And never worry that you're showing yourself to be overly cautious or bush-league by avoiding the realm of corporate lawyers and securities dealers. Some of the shrewdest big companies around operate this way. When Campbell Soup (which in the past has snagged such plums as Swanson's, Pepperidge Farms and Godiva Chocolates) struck a deal to acquire Mrs. Paul's Kitchens early in 1982, Campbell's president announced, "We didn't buy any obligations. . . . We bought only the tangible assets." *Business Week* magazine, reviewing the sale, applauded:

> Campbell is not acquiring Mrs. Paul's pension liabilities or or receivables. But more important, it is avoiding the problems besetting [Arthur] Treacher's [a Mrs. Paul's subsidiary being sued on antitrust and breach-of-contract grounds]. (*Business Week*, 12 APRIL 1982)

Does this sound familiar? Well, what works to keep Campbell's out of the soup will work for you. Even big companies that don't approach acquisitions carefully often find they've swallowed a poisoned plum: recall the experience of Exxon in the late '70s, simply because it had bought a company (Reliance) which had bought a company (Federal Pacific Electric) which was accused of building dangerously defective circuit breakers. The liability, and the litigation, and the grief all were passed along the corporate chain, with Exxon the ultimate victim.

And what can shock a big company can pretty well fry a small one. So take the trouble, no matter how good the existing corporation looks, to structure a deal which will protect you. Either buy the assets you want personally, or else set up a new corporation to buy those assets. As a rule, closely-held corporations (as opposed to those whose shares are publicly traded) can be established very rapidly. For maximum effectiveness, you can even establish the corporate shell some time before you find a business to acquire. Your articles of incorporation will simply state that the corporation exists to purchase some or all of the assets of firm(s) active in the _____ field, for the purpose of operating them as ongoing businesses. The corporation gets *its* money, of course, by selling you and your partners, if any, shares of its stock. You can usually file papers for incorporation by yourself, but the few hundred dollars needed for the assistance of a competent attorney are generally well spent.

None of this is to say, of course, that you'll *never* want to make an offer on an existing corporation. Sometimes one can be priced so attractively as a complete package that you'll be able to spin off enough of the assets to cover the purchase price and still maintain a going business. Under that circumstance—assuming you've investigated carefully all the corporate idiosyncrasies and outstanding liabilities—the slight risk of buying into hidden litigation is almost certainly worth taking.

But wherever you find a corporation under a legal cloud, this idea of a bulk purchase of assets is your surest umbrella. Whether you buy the assets in your own name, or through the use of a specially created corporation, refusing to buy someone else's old legal troubles is an eminently sensible precaution, and one any fairminded seller will accept. It does more than simply let you make your deal. It lets you go ahead and buy the roses, and leave the thorns, if any, for the fellow who grew them.

8
VISITING THE PLANT

SITUATION:
Once you have found one or more businesses which look good on paper, the next step is an on-site inspection

OBJECTIVE:
Even though there may be restraints on what you are allowed to see, you want to determine the physical quality of any business under consideration

Preparing to Visit.

However you find the business(es) which interest you—whether through reading the ads, asking an accountant, or working with a broker—the next few steps are fairly straightforward. You will likely be asked for a copy of your Personal Financial Statement (or at least a bank reference), to establish that you can afford to buy the business. You'll normally be given at least preliminary financial figures. The owner may not yet show you the books, but he should at least quote you the company's annual volume and net profit for the last two or three years. The next stage may then be either a look at the full books, or a tour of the plant. If a plant tour is suggested, don't be disappointed—if you stay alert, much can be learned from what may seem like an exercise in tourism.

Before your visit, take time to make three kinds of preparations: 1) read Chapter 16: REAL ESTATE, 2) get a small notepad that you can carry in a breast pocket or purse, and 3) if you have not already done so, familiarize yourself with the best types of equipment for whatever kind of operation you are about to visit.

Seeing the Plant.

Never mind what certain hot-shot promoters say about only buying from the books. Sure, numbers are important, but remember that, first, they are easier to doctor than are physical facts; second, even straight, they don't tell the whole story; and, third, as an owner-operator, you are going to be spending a large part of your life on the grounds. You had better like them!

When you are invited to the plant, observe not only ordinary etiquette, but any special conditions set by the owner. The most important of these normally will be that you do nothing even to hint the business is up for sale. If you violate this, and word of a possible sale reaches employees or competitors, you will harm the owner, and probably blow your own chance. So play by the rules.

Even while observing these rules, you must *keep your eyes and ears open.* Clichéd advice, perhaps, but worth repeating simply because a seller with something to conceal will be striving to turn the visit into an empty formality. Don't become so involved in politely touring that you forget to think critically about what you are being shown—and *not* being shown. Because of the need for discretion, notes, or even questions, may not be allowed, but try not to squander the opportunity by thinking ahead solely to the books. Instead, prepare the following mental checklist, and mentally complete it as well as you can while you are taking the grand tour:

1. *Plant Upkeep.* What shape is the equipment in? How much of it is in working order? Is routine maintenance being done? If the plant is a retail shop, how fresh are the window displays? Are items for sale plentiful and of the latest model? (Note: Especially in the retailing of larger items such as appliances, autos, boats, etc, the *"flooring"* or sample display merchandise is either provided or financed by the manufacturer. Scant or dated merchandise here often means the retailer has been slow in paying his suppliers. That is bad trouble, and may mean he is about to have his franchise pulled. Before you visit any retail operation, know what the best brands and latest products are.) Note the presence or absence of any especially reputable or hard-to-acquire lines of goods.

Plant upkeep is a reflection of the amount of capital being put back *into* the business. If the equipment is obsolete, or in poor working order, most likely the business is being milked. Either that, or it has been unprofitable for a very long time.

If you already know enough about the field to rank the quality of individual pieces of equipment you see, so much the better. But at the least, try to get a sense of the degree of newness and repair. Two quick checks for capital spending: one, is there a computer on the grounds? Two, is there an owned phone system, instead of the standard Bell gear?

2. *Plant Neatness/Plant Cleanliness.* This is a different type of question. Now you want to know whether the workplaces are being kept tidy in a plant, or whether the sales areas are clean and appealing in a retail sales operation.

Here you are looking for clues to owner involvement and worker morale. People let things go when they think *they're* going to be let go. Or when they're thinking about quitting. These clues go along with the tone of the person who answers the phone when you call, the kinds of smiles you get when you walk in, and so on. It may not be true that you can always sense a labor action brewing, but at least you can take a subjective impression, one worth recording.

Be careful not to confuse 1 and 2; a neat and cheerful operation will always seem more prosperous than a messy or sullen one, but do keep real and psychological assets separate in your accounting.

3. *Efficiency.* How are things moving along? Are people working, or standing around? Is there a great deal of waste motion, or do actions seem purposeful and precise? Do an impressionistic time-and-motion study, get a general sense. You're not looking for a sweatshop, obviously, just a sense of people going at their work with interest and efficiency.

Try to notice any bottlenecks. Are finished goods stacking up near the loading dock? (Remember, you don't get paid until your product reaches the buyer.) Is the work load evenly distributed, or are some people breaking their necks while others wait for a task? In a retail operation, how long does the customer wait around for help after coming in the door? After picking something out? Do salespeople know their merchandise, or are there lots of costly consultations with catalogues or other salespeople? Are there lines at salescounters?

4. *Safety.* Are there obvious hazards? Are normal safety precautions for the line of work being taken? Aside from the obvious moral issue of asking people (or yourself, for that matter) to work in unsafe conditions, government enforcement of safety codes is growing more rigorous all the time. As of February, 1980, moreover, the Supreme Court ruled that workers may not be penalized for refusing to perform obviously hazardous duties. That decision made safety explicitly what it had always been implicitly, a labor-and-productivity, as well as a moral, question.

Remember, too, that poor safety standards (except where the owner is simply callous or incompetent) often indicate insufficient plant capacity. Whenever people are trying to drive too small an operation too fast, the first thing they sacrifice (after employee feelings) is safety.

5. *Floor Traffic or Customer Activity.* Especially for retail sales, check the floor traffic against the time of day. Later, when you meet privately with the seller, be sure to ask what are the busy seasons and times of day. Also, while out on the floor, try to get an approximate idea of the ratio of lookers to buyers, as well as the average sale volume per buyer. If nobody is coming in, the problem may be simply advertising; if people are coming in but not buying, the most likely problem is the pricing structure. The items may be too far up-market for the neighborhood (in which case you get a lot of window shoppers—very polite people who never buy); or the prices for affordable items are being undercut elsewhere in the neighborhood, in which case you get a lot of comparison shoppers, who look at the price stickers, frown, and walk out. Lastly, if you see a lot of people spending time in a store but not buying, and store security looks bad, you might want to ask the owner how heavy his shop-lifting losses are running—and please don't assume shop-lifting is a problem of poorer neighborhoods alone.

These five points are the essential physical preliminaries. You want to satisfy yourself on the early visits that the place of business either meets your general standards or can be brought quickly up to snuff. More specific analysis—for example, matching up the equipment present with that itemized on the Fixtures and Equipment list—should be put off until you are much closer to a deal. For the time being, you are only concerned with the five main points, and you should be able to take care of them inconspicuously on your first or second walk-through tour.

That is not to say you should approach your checklist casually. Even though the structure of the situation may not allow you to take notes openly, keep as many specifics as possible in mind and *as soon as you are able,* go somewhere (even to a coffee shop, though preferably not in the immediate area) and write up your notes. Remember the limitations of the human memory: within hours or less, you'll have begun to forget details. Even worse, when you visit a whole set of different businesses in a short period, is the danger of details' blurring hopelessly together. Try to record something about each of the five categories, plus anything relevant about the real estate (again, see REAL ESTATE for some tips).

Along with helping you to find a business with the physical potential you want, these notes will do two other things. First, they'll give you an idea (which you'll keep to yourself) of ways the value of the business could be speedily increased. We once showed a woman with decades of restaurant experience a handsome but unsuccessful establishment in a commercial district. On her first walk-through, she noticed two things: 1) a row of cypress trees made the restaurant invisible from the street, and 2) the lunch trade was zero because the menu offered no meals quick enough to serve local office or shop workers. She decided that, by trimming the cypresses and loading meat slicers on carts to provide speed-service at lunch, she could quickly boost sales at least *30%* —and she went ahead with her offer.

Second, your notes may well have a cash value, as negotiating chips when the time comes. If you can convince the seller that you'll have to spend X dollars to make repairs, repaint, or advertise to build the volume up, he'll very likely make a price adjustment to cover the work. For that to happen, you need *specific* points. A lot of half-recalled generalities will get you exactly nowhere.

You will probably want to visit the plant at least twice, once during working hours to get a sense of plant *operations,* and once during nonworking hours to study more closely the details of the *physical plant.* Even on this second visit, you're not out to count paper clips, but rather examine areas you could not conveniently approach earlier—and perhaps to have a quiet word or two with the owner, on his or her home turf. This time make certain you are shown everything that interests you—if any areas are still off limits, you'd better start looking at another business.

But if the situation is either entirely to your taste, or easily corrected, then the next step will normally be a careful examination—with the help of your accountant—of the complete business financial records. There you will be able to discover, among other things, how much of the lovely gear you've seen actually belongs to the company you're thinking of buying. For that next step, please see the following section.

9

LOOKING AT THE BOOKS

SITUATION:

When you have found a going business which seems appealing, the next step is to examine the financial records

OBJECTIVE:

Avoiding deceptions, and coming to a fair general understanding of the company's financial situation before turning matters over to your accountant

Looking at the Books: What You Want to Know.

Once you have met the owner, and seen the physical plant, your next likely step is to examine the books. If you are trained as an accountant, you'll be able to study them easily, but even if you have no background in the field, you should try to reach at least a basic understanding before consigning them to your experts. Remember that you will be the one to make the final decision—and that you'll get more intelligent answers if you know what questions to ask. Also important, accountants and business lawyers are by nature conservative—their main goal is to keep you away from risk. That means nine times out of ten, they'll either tell you to pass, or raise so many trivial objections that you'll lose the deal from delays.

In short, you want to give your experts every chance to find fault, but you must also be able to tell a major fault from a small one. You need to protect yourself from both the excess caution of your experts and the undue eagerness of (sometimes unscrupulous) brokers and sellers.

WHEN YOU ARE ENTITLED TO SEE THE BOOKS. Most serious sellers will make their financial records available to any buyer who has shown the financial ability to make the purchase, and has taken the trouble to see the plant and make relevant inquiries. There are exceptions: a few businesses are sold without any representations of income, and a few sellers refuse to open their books until an offer, backed by a substantial deposit, has been made.

You're probably better off avoiding the closed-book transaction. With a deal requiring a deposit before the books are opened, the only way to proceed it is to make your offer contingent upon the seller's being able to prove his claims once the escrow is opened. Get both his representations of income and expense, and his promise to prove them, *in writing* before you make an offer.

What Records You Want to See.

OK—in a normal transaction, there should be no problem about your seeing the books—except, perhaps, if you already own or work for a competing firm. What records do you request?

Basically, you want to see at least:

1. Any leases
2. Any outstanding notes or other financial obligations, including contracts
3. The profit and loss, or income, statements, starting with the current statement and going back five years, if possible.
4. The balance sheets, with, if possible, itemized lists of fixtures and equipment.
5. The spread sheets, if any have been prepared.

WHEN THERE ARE RECORDS YOU HAVEN'T ASKED FOR. Before you ever see any of those, you may come to a time of hard choices, because this is when many sellers will offer you a chance to see "the real books."

Nobody knows for sure how large the underground economy is, or how large a part small business plays in it. The most dramatic estimates are that unreported earnings by small businesses may equal nearly 10% of the gross national product—a figure which theoretically could total almost $200 *billion*. If the business you're looking at is involved in that, you will probably be offered a look at the "second set" of books, the one showing the "real," tax free profits.

What should you do? Well, of course, no business broker will accept those figures; you'll have to consider them by yourself. Even though we don't touch them, though, we would be naive not to realize they play a part in many of the transactions we assemble. It may be that you will have to pay for them whether you intend to run an illegal operation or not. But do bear this in mind—it's likely that anyone who'll lie to Uncle Sam will lie to you, and if he does, how are you going to get even? Will you take him to court for something which 1) appears nowhere in writing and 2) is *prima facie* evidence that you conspired to defraud the US government? I think not.

That's not to say you should ignore the information entirely; if nothing else, it indicates the kind of volume the business could do legally. Your best bet might be to simply say what many experienced buyers do: "well, you've already had your profit on those sales—tax free—and you can't expect me to take them on faith. If they exist, fine. But I'm only willing to pay for what can be proven by court-worthy documents." You may not get away with it—you may in fact be willing to acquire those off-the-record opportunities—but it's a reasonable starting point for negotiations.

Now let's go on to the more reputable forms of information.

LEASES. To avoid repetition, I've collected most of what I have to say about leases, and other elements of real estate, in Chapter 16. For details, please see that chapter. In general, when considering leases, watch for the following:

1. *The rent.* How much, and with what potential escalator clauses. Is it tied to the Consumer Price Index? Is it written on a net-net-net or "triple net" basis? (Either term means the landlord collects the specified figure, and the tenant pays *all* other costs and expenses.)

2. *The term.* How many months or years remain? Is there an option for renewal? If so, how long, and under what conditions?

Consider that five years (including current lease plus option) is probably a reasonable minimum for a desirable retail location. Otherwise, you're going to have to move just as things are getting rolling. For an undesirable lease in a manufacturing area, on the other hand, two years or so might prove more than enough.

Desirable leases have cash value. You might pay $100,000 or more for a long retail lease at good terms in a hot location—even if the business itself is worthless. A lease so purchased can then be *depreciated on your taxes.* Remind your CPA.

3. *The options.* Is there an option to buy the property (rare these days)? Is there, alternatively, a right to consultation, or a first refusal clause?

4. *The landlord.* Can you find out (from another source) anything about the landlord's reputation? Does he fight with tenants, or cooperate? How does he feel about leasehold modifications? Has he been known to discriminate against groups of people, or to attempt other illegal land covenants?

5. *The transferability.* Can the lease accomodate new tenants? What compensation will the landlord want for agreeing to the change? Is a new lease possible, with extensions?

For some of these questions (especially number 5), you may have to take the seller's word temporarily, simply because he may not want you to talk with the landlord until a deal is finalized. That's a reasonable and common stipulation. Just make sure that any offer you make is contingent upon landlord acceptance—it's another way of protecting your deposit.

ENCUMBRANCES: NOTES AND CONTRACTS. By notes, I mean any money the seller has borrowed from outside to help pay for the purchase or operation of the business. As a rule, the largest single note (if any) should be that still owed to the previous owner.

When you buy through a business broker, the price quoted will be listed as "including" or "plus" encumbrances, if any. Unfortunately, when you deal directly with sellers, these encumbrances often slip their minds, so that you must be prepared for something like this:

"Well, I paid $100,000. If I can get that back, I'll be happy."

"Sounds fair. By the way, are there any outstanding notes?"

"Oh, yeah. I still owe the old owner $58,000. You'll have to pick that up."

Suddenly that $100,000 price is up about 60%. *Find out early about encumbrances to be assumed.* The best thing you can hear is "Owner will clear," which means you start out clean. The worst is when you slowly discover the business owes more money than it is worth. It is a sad, but not uncommon, situation, when a person is trying to sell a business without knowing it's insolvent. Remember, though, that if a majority of corporate debt is to stockholders, they may be willing largely to discount it in order to sell off a troubled firm.

Other obligations are usually less trouble. Service contracts, for example, are usually a *good* sign, because they show the company has spent money on maintenance. A contract for advertising—say, the yellow pages—is probably productive. Most other contracts—for water softeners and so on—represent only small sums. Still, they *are* a part of your total payment committment—keep track of them.

PROFIT AND LOSS STATEMENTS. A good, simple "cash-basis" P and L will detail for you how (and how much) money was taken in and paid out over a given period of time. Note, though, that many P and L's are prepared instead on what is called an "accrual" basis, which means sales and expenses are recorded when they are contracted for, not when the money actually changes hands. While this makes it easier for the owner to tell how cautiously he is running his business, it may give *you* a slightly false understanding. If, for example, he has recently begun lowering his credit standards for customers, he may show a big increase in sales—all at a later cost to you in bad debts. Accrual is a perfectly reasonable system as long as you 1) make sure you understand the terms of the entries, and 2) insist upon receiving the most current figures available.

A second potential problem is the (now common) switch between First In, First Out (FIFO) and Last In, First Out (LIFO) methods of inventory accounting. The older FIFO method assumed that you found the gross profit on any given item by tracking it from purchase to sale. If you bought something for $100 and sold it for $300, you made $200. Fair enough—except that during the inflationary '70s, that often led to ridiculous (and tax-costly) pseudoprofits. The profits weren't real because when you went to replace that $100 item you had bought six months before, it now cost you, say, $180. LIFO, which calculates your profits by using your *replacement* cost as your real cost, is an attempt to eliminate these pseudo or "inventory" profits. Again, one system is as honest as the other, but the changeover can confuse your understanding of the bottom line if you are careless.

Those two accounting rules aside, a small business P and L is generally quite easily understood. Ultimately, your accountant will do the close analysis. For now, just seek obvious problems, like that on a P and L recently shown to me, which listed total annual wages of $22,000—for a firm with eleven full-time workers.

I *think* that was an honest mistake. Sometimes, though, the confusion around a profit and loss statement is not so innocent. There are at least three items I would urge you to watch out for: reconstructions, projections, and "nonrecurring losses."

Of the three, "nonrecurring losses" are a perfectly legitimate accounting category for those particular expenses—defective merchandise, for example—which are out of the course of normal business and not expected to occur again. Unfortunately, some small businessmen will take only a partial write-down on such items, and then leave you, as a new owner, to eat the lion's share of the (entirely foreseeable) loss. Thus, an owner who lists a recent $1500 expense to resole 100 pairs of defective tennis shoes, may actually have sold 1000 pairs. Buy his business today, and you may find yourself having to satisfy the other 900 customers who haven't yet experienced tread separation on the court. "Nonrecurring" losses should be a danger signal. Follow up on them carefully.

Far worse, in some ways, are projections and reconstructions. *Projections* are a process, used by a fair number of business brokers, of simply extending curves of growth as if you were buying a yeast culture instead of a business. Most projections are about as useful as that of Thomas Malthus, who wrote that, because populations grow geometrically, and food supplies arithmetically, the world would starve itself to death before the end of the century—the Nineteenth Century. The number of variables in business is far too great to be handled by any simple Cartesian algebra. When salesmen start talking projections, go get a sandwich.

Reconstructions present more of a problem. A reconstructed P and L is one which attempts to show you how much *you* would have made as owner of the firm during some past period. *Some* reconstructions make sense. If you are going to buy a business which last year had an absentee owner and a manager, and do all the work yourself, you will indeed keep both the profits and the money which had been going to the manager.

The danger comes when some fast-talking salesman sells you on "reconstructions" which are either illegal or impossible. In the worst case of this I've ever seen, a broker convinced a woman that she and her young son would *net* $2000 a month from a health food store which had never done over $1800 in *total sales.* To do it, he used both phoney projections—claiming the business would grow much faster than it possibly could—and impossible reconstructions. He convinced her that her son could do the work of two men, that illegal aliens would handle the rest of labor dirt cheap, and even that the landlord would lower the rent because it was unfair.

There is, in short, no end to the inventiveness of some salespeople when it comes to "reconstructing" P and L statements. Hear them out—occasionally they hit on a genuinely useful idea—but stick mostly to the reconstructed profit that your own (or your family members') labor will add. Even then, remember that you are giving up whatever value that labor might have outside the firm. (For more on P and L's please see APPENDIX 1.)

Updated Figures. The need for current figures cannot be overemphasized. Remember that a small business has nothing like the stabilizing bulk of a large one: the profit and loss picture can change almost literally overnight. Be suspicious whenever the most current figures are over thirty days old. It's often a precipitous drop in sales or profits which is prompting the sale. Brokers and sellers play out this scene time and again:

POTENTIAL SELLER: As you can see, we made about $140,000 last year. Of course, I haven't got the books back from the accountant yet for this quarter, but . . . on the basis of the trends. . . . well . . .
  BROKER *(Having heard it before):* About how much would you say you lost?
  SELLER: Maybe $25,000, plus no salary since December.
  BROKER: What happened?
  SELLER: A national chain opened up two blocks from here, and they're beating our brains out.

Up-to-date figures are a must! If my father goes to price a business on Tuesday, he requests not only the latest financial statements, but the owner's estimate of unpaid bills *as of Tuesday morning.* Working that way, he's avoided many an unpleasant surprise.

A good accountant should get a small firm's books back in forty-eight hours if asked. It takes longer during tax-time, of course, but anything over a month is out of the question—suggest they change accountants. (Note: in a pinch, if you're buying a small business with retail sales, just ask to see their state or city sales tax receipts, which provide at least the latest sales volume figures.)

THE BALANCE SHEET. The balance sheet should tell you what the company owes and what it owns. Again, remember that obligations to the old owner (usually the biggest single obligation) may not show, if they are carried as private obligations of the present owner of the firm. On the other hand, even if you are thinking of buying a business on the basis of "book value," remember that you are only dealing with a mythical number, one which may not at all accurately reflect what the owner will want—and often, deserve—for particular items.

Here's an extreme example. The Tax Act of 1981 says that vehicles used in research and development may be depreciated off the books in three years. Suppose, then, that the owner of a company you are considering bought, through the company, a $30,000 automobile two years ago, and now carries it on the books at somewhere around $10,000. That's fine for tax purposes, but suppose too the car is a turbodiesel Mercedes Benz. At two years, its true resale value is probably somewhere around 90% of original retail—or about $25,000–27,000. Should you expect to be able to buy it for $10,000 just because that's the book value? Don't hold your breath. (Actually, since there is a recapture factor when a depreciated item is sold, you very likely won't be offered a chance to buy the thing at all).

Odds are that anyone claiming a turbo-Mercedes as an R and D tool will need to do some fast talking with the IRS, but the point remains. The figures carried on the balance sheets as assets are really only abstractions. Some assets (like real estate) often appreciate after purchase; others (furniture, for example) depreciate even faster than the rates assumed by our tax laws. The price you finally pay for assets will likely prove to be a compromise between their book value, and what it would actually cost to replace them.

SPREAD SHEETS. The last of the useful financial guides you can ask for are spread sheets. Prepared by brokers, accountants, and corporate acquisition teams, among others, spread sheets are a way of turning the "snapshots" provided by P and L's and balance sheets into something nearer to motion pictures. They let you see at a glance the changes in financial situation—from net sales to total net worth—over a period of up to five years. They are made simply by transfering relevant data from each year's financial statement onto single sheets of graph-like paper. In miniature:

	1984	1983	1982	1981	1980
Net Sales	$3,653,195	$2,741,308	$2,237,877	$1,519,427	$902,888
Net Profits	268,945	144,519	88,072	29,515	8,542
Total Inventory	415,000	250,000	195,000	125,000	65,800

And so on. They are, however, time-consuming, and so most brokers prepare them only for larger businesses. If the deal you are considering does not qualify for them, you might make up simple ones yourself—they *do* give a very useful picture of how the financial situation is changing.

Calculated Factors: Ratios. If you do go to the trouble of making up your own spread sheets, you may as well take the last step towards professionalism, and include one or more of the calculated factors known as "ratios." These ratios will not only give you more usable information about the company's financial situation—its liquidity, ability to turn over inventory, and so on—but will allow you, thanks to the existence of annual national surveys, to compare its performance with that of comparably-sized companies nationwide.

Published surveys of ratios are available from several sources. *Dun's Review,* for example, provides one each fall. Probably the most widely used survey, however, is published by Robert Morris Associates, which is the national association of bank loan and credit officers (Robert Morris Associates, Philadelphia National Bank Bldg, Philadelphia, PA 19107). The Robert Morris volume is not only thorough, but contains, in its Introduction, probably the most lucid explanation of what ratios do that I've ever read.

If you are planning to calculate ratios, or to compare given ratios with industries' standards, you would be wise to invest in a copy of the Robert Morris *Annual Statement Studies.* Here, meanwhile, are some of the ratios to be found in that handbook, along with explanations of my own design. (I've also included, at the end of this section, a plant-updating ratio of my own.)

1. *Liquidity Ratios.* These measure the ability of a company to meet its current liabilities promptly. (Current liabilities are those due within one year.) The most widely used of these is the "acid test":

$$\frac{\text{Cash and Equivalents} + \text{Accounts and Trade Notes Receivable}}{\text{Total Current Liabilities}}$$

A company with an "acid test" ratio of less than one would probably need to liquidate inventory or other, similar, assets in order to meet its liabilities.

Another of the primary liquidity ratios is Cost of Sales/Inventory:

$$\frac{\text{Cost of Sales}}{\text{Inventory}}$$

If you take the cost of all the goods sold by the company in a year, and divide it by the average inventory (also at cost) during that period, you will know the number of times the company turned over its inventory; that is, how efficiently it was merchandising its goods. (Remember, though, that a very high number *may* only mean an undernourished inventory.)

2. *Leverage and Coverage Ratios.* These are the ratios likely to be least exciting to you, and *most* exciting to anyone thinking of loaning you the money to buy the business. *Leverage* shows how much borrowing has been done to create or maintain the business: in general use, it's the ratio of a business's debt burden to its net worth. *Coverage* inverts this, measuring the likelihood that creditors will be able to get their money back in case of trouble. The two simplest of these leverage and coverage ratios are 1) Fixed Assets to Worth:

$$\frac{\text{Net Fixed Assets}}{\text{Tangible Net Worth}}$$

"Net Fixed Assets" are hard assets (buildings, machine tools, etc) after accumulated depreciation. "Tangible Net Worth" includes both those hard asset and *liquid assets* (cash in the bank, etc) but excludes abstract assets like good will. The smaller the resulting ratio number, the smaller the percentage of the company invested in hard assets like machinery, which would be difficult for creditors (or you) to liquidate. In general, then, the lower the Fixed Assets/Worth ratio, the better.

And 2) Debt to Net Worth:

$$\frac{\text{Total Liabilities}}{\text{Tangible Net Worth}}$$

"Tangible Net Worth" is defined as above; "liabilities" are any monies the company owes. Obviously, the lower the ratio number the better, although the danger point varies greatly from industry to industry. Real estate, for example, is generally hugely leveraged —that is, it carries a high ratio of liabilities to net worth.

3. *Operating Ratios.* These show how productively the company's assets are being used, and are often taken as indicating the quality of management. The most generalized of these is the Percent Profit Before Taxes/Total Assets Ratio:

$$\frac{\text{Profit Before Taxes}}{\text{Total Assets}} \times 100$$

You, as buyer, can calculate a *potential* percentage of return on your investment by dividing Profit Before Taxes by the asking price for the business:

$$\frac{\text{Profit Before Taxes}}{\text{Asking Price}} \times 100$$

Obviously, this is highly speculative, but if the percentage return on your investment is, say, lower than prevailing bank interest, you are probably looking at an overpriced business.

4. *Expense to Sales Ratios.* The Robert Morris handbook allows you to compare the business you are considering, to industry norms for expense percentage ratios for Officers' Compensation, Lease And Rental Expenses, and so on. These are extremely handy for helping you discover which expenses (if any) are inflated.

Those are some of the standard financial ratios used by credit and loan people to decide upon the worthiness of a business. Some will be of more use to you than others, but you should be aware of their existence.

In addition, there is one ratio I would strongly urge you to consider, even though it is not usually found in ratio surveys. In fact in my opinion the fact that this ratio has been widely ignored by American business is a main reason why so many of our basic industries have become uncompetitive by world standards. I mean the capital reinvestment ratio.

Plant Updating. What you want to know is whether the business has made a regular and significant effort to keep its plant modern. Many American businesses have fared badly in this regard—while the Japanese have turned over their *entire* industrial plant every ten years on average since the war, some of our industries haven't managed one complete cycle in this *century.*

Take the Japanese ten-year cycle as your ideal. To achieve it, the business you are considering should be *annually* spending an amount equal to at least 10% of the total value of its fixtures and equipment on *new* fixtures and equipment—exclusive of maintenance. Particular industries may at times require much greater reinvestment, but 10% is a fair average *minimum.*

Calculating that ratio will not always be easy, but it can be done. Thanks to the Economic Recovery Act of 1981 (ERTA-81), anywhere from the first $5,000–10,000 worth of new equipment bought each year beginning in 1982 can be expensed directly through on the profit and loss statement. For earlier years (assuming the firm's accountant will not provide you with a breakdown of expenses), you can check the year-to-year change in the (nondepreciated) figure for fixtures and equipment.

For each available year, subtract the vanity expenditures from the amount spent on fixtures and equipment. That new Cadillac may please the president, but it hardly boosts productivity.

From the resulting figure for Productive Equipment Expenditures, you calculate the ratio for any given year:

$$\frac{\text{Annual Productive Equipment Expenditures}}{\text{Total Installed Cost of Fixtures \& Equipment}} \times 100$$

Even if you can't get precise figures, at least eyeball for that 10% ideal. A company with a plant worth $175,000, for example, should be spending around $17,500 per year on new capital improvements. Anything less requires close study: either the business does not generate enough cash to justify its size, or the owners are milking it and running it down, or (least likely), the firm is undercapitalized.

The business is being milked if the owner's profit or (for a closely-held corporation) the officers' salaries stay high while the company is not meeting the 10% reinvestment figure. In that case, watch out—you are probably being handed a business which is being run into the ground. Very shortly you will face either a decay in your competitive position (when better-equipped companies start undercutting you) or else the heavy costs of deferred improvements.

A more hopeful possibility is that the company is undercapitalized and is burning up its profit paying off high-interest, short-term debts. You might have a real opportunity here if your pockets are sufficiently deep. Suppose, for example, you find a business showing no profit, but making the interest payments on $300,000 in short-term 20% obligations. If you could get hold of it by assuming the debts and immediately paying them off, you'd have a business paying *you* that $60,000 a year, and offering a sound basis for further growth. Sometimes known as "blowing off" debt, this process can work very well if you've picked a sound business, *and* you go in as a working owner, not a pure investor.

If the money the company takes in is ending up neither on the bottom line of the P and L, nor under the Assets listing of the balance sheet, nor even in the retirement of outstanding debt, then probably the venture is unsuccessful. You're better off thanking the owner for his time and moving ahead to look elsewhere. Above all, don't get discouraged and begin tampering with the numbers to make them come out the way you'd rather have them look.

Those are some of the ways in which an analysis of financial data can help you decide—without being an accountant—whether a particular business makes sense for you. If financial analysis is not your strong point, you had better be careful to find an accountant who is both trustworthy and willing to take the time to explain matters to you in detail. Even then, it's worthwhile familiarizing yourself with the material so that you can, first of all, ask the right questions, and, second, be alert for some of the *unfair* manipulations of unscrupulous sellers and agents.

10
FOUR FINAL QUERIES

SITUATION:
After you have seen the books, but before you prepare your offer, is your last chance to ask tough questions
OBJECTIVE:
Uncovering hidden problems

Seeing the books is the last major step in your investigation of a business, but you should never overlook any chance to pick up stray information about the firm in question. Aside from watching the local business and financial pages, and asking friends in the field for stray gossip, here are four useful questions you should ask before preparing an offer or approaching potential backers. The questions really can be asked anytime earlier, but they seem to go down easier—and to draw more complete answers—after buyer and seller are better acquainted.

WHY ARE YOU SELLING? The odd thing about this most obvious of questions is that if you ask it at the right time, you will often get a useful answer. The most frequent answers are "illness" or simply "personal reasons," but a seller who has gotten to like you may respond with something as frank as "nobody who isn't a Spanish-speaking deep-sea diver will ever make it in this business." It's usually trusting people who get sold businesses they are not qua-lified to run, and they're usually too decent to try to stick someone else in turn. Wanting to know why a person is selling is human nature, and everyone—including acquisition people from major corporations—asks it sooner or later. So go ahead and ask, but if the answer is, "personal reasons," leave it at that.

WHAT DOESN'T GO? That is, "what items on the balance sheet or anywhere in the physical plant that I've seen is not included in the sale? "Personal effects" is usually the first category mentioned— and is perfectly reasonable, as long as you get the term clearly defined. Fancy company cars are another standby, but obviously two or three $20,000 Cadillacs being taken out of the company changes the value of what you are buying. Again, fair enough, as long as you know it in advance.

Two warnings: First, watch out for the guy who keeps bumping the "does not go" list up another notch every time you turn around. He is likely out to leave you with nothing, and will keep altering one point or another until a business deal turns into a shell game.

Second, try to get a final itemized list before the negotiations begin in earnest, but for Heaven's sake, allow a little slack. If the seller remembers at the last minute that the wall clock used to belong to his grandfather, let him have it.

I say this because some years ago we put together a deal on a contractor's school—then worth about $250,000—which was highly beneficial for all parties. Just as the final papers were to be signed, the buyer and seller exploded into an argument, which turned into a virtual fistfight—in a downtown bank—over a desk and a chair. Shortly before our $25,000 fee flew out the window, we persuaded the seller to sell *us* the precious desk and chair—for a princely $300—which we then gave as a present to the buyer.

My point is not our cleverness in saving the deal, but rather that the "Does Not Go" list often becomes a focal point for fears and suspicions as the negotiations get tough. To remain sane, narrow the list as precisely as you can early on, and then flex a little at the end.

ARE YOU FACING ANY LABOR ACTION? If the owners of a corporation have received a strike notification, they are generally required to so inform anyone considering buying the firm. Don't wait to be informed; ask early on. Find out anything else you can about labor relations. Have there been strikes or organizing efforts in the past? Are the workers there generally happy with conditions (count your impressions from the walk-throughs), or is there a big turnover among employees? Remember that if you take over a strikebound firm, you may never get the doors open.

ARE YOU FACING ANY LITIGATION? Obviously, this is most important if you are buying an intact corporation (as mentioned in Chapter 7), or where the litigation is of a sort—such as product liability—which might carry over even to a noncorporate buyer of manufacturing assets. Minor litigation can perhaps be overlooked, but watch out for the real crunchers. Along with asking, it's wise to keep an eye on the legal notices and the court calender, just in case.

Again, none of these questions will automatically produce revelations. Still, you are obliged to ask them—or any other, comparable, questions inspired by your suspicions—partly on the chance of getting useful information, and partly because if something *is* being hidden, your legal position will be much stronger if you can establish *willful* misrepresentation of material facts. Whether the question draws an honest answer from an honest seller, or a blazing lie from a crooked one, you're better off for having asked.

11

PRICING AND NEGOTIATING

SITUATION:
*Both pricing and a business and negotiating for its purchase
constitute arts rather than sciences*
OBJECTIVE:
*Buying the business as safely and cheaply as possible, while still
making a friend of the old owner*

Buying Bebop, Inc.

OK—after some days, weeks, or months of searching, you've
found just the business you want. The plant looks good, the books
stack up, and the seller and broker both seem honest. They've
quoted you a price. Now you have two questions: first, is the price
fair, and second, fair or not, is there any way I can improve on it?
That is, how are prices determined, and how are they negotiated
down?

To answer those, first understand that—no matter what brokers
or consultants might claim—business prices are neither scientifi-
cally determined nor (in a great many cases) rigidly maintained.
Our policy for getting sellers to set fair and firm asking prices is
probably tougher than nine out of ten other brokers, but I'd still
guess that one-third of all our businesses ultimately went for less
than the initial asking prices. Some brokers, moreover, will delib-
erately set unrealistic prices, figuring that if you talk them down,
fine and if you fall into the trap, so much the better.

The reason all this can happen is that each business is unique.

Even the best-intentioned people in the world could not standardize prices, because the number of variables is infinite. All that can reasonably be done is to set a *range* of fair prices, and then let buyer and seller horse-trade until they have a deal.

To see what that means in practical terms, consider the following hypothetical case:

The company you've decided to buy, we'll say, is called BeBop Electronics, Inc. It's a fairly large, single-outlet retail electronics firm, which sells a large range of hi-fi gadgets, but gains its name from the fact that it is the area's exclusive distributor of hot-selling components from the BeBopsu Company of Yokohama—with six years remaining on its eleven-year exclusive marketing agreement.

The key figures on BeBop Electronics are:

1. The book value of the company is $150,000, which includes carrying the value of the exclusive marketing arrangement at a heavily-depreciated $20,000.
2. The inventory has been built up substantially over the last year, and now stands at $200,000.
3. Two years remain on the lease, with no option to renew specified. The location is good, but facilities border on being too small.
4. After a steady officer's salary for the owner of $30,000, pre-tax net profit developed as follows:

1981	1982	1983	1984	1985 (Projected full year)
$60,000	$80,000	$100,000	$120,000	$140,000

5. The asking price is $500,000 plus inventory, or $700,000. Good deal or bad? (Take a minute to decide before reading on!)

The Art of Pricing.

Whether you answered "good" or "bad" you are probably about equally right (or wrong), because the probable truth is that the price is stiff but fair. Here's why:

The price breaks down as inventory at cost, plus $150,000 for tangible assets (fixtures, equipment, automobiles, etc.) at book value—plus $350,000 which represents the intangible value of the business. This intangible is usually called, "good will," and the usual justification of it is that anyone starting from scratch would have to spend an amount equal to it to build the business up to this stage of profitability. That's logical enough, but what constitutes fair good will? If you pay $350,000 to make $140,000 a year, are you doing well or poorly?

Well, the usual rule for calculating goodwill—and of all the dozens of pricing formulae, it's probably the one that makes most sense, says that good will should never exceed *two-and-a-half times* the current income (if stable), before taxes but after deduction of owner's salary.

In this case then, the BeBop Company passes the test, if only barely. Two-and-a-half times $140,000 is $350,000—the asking amount for good will. The business is priced right on the upper limit of acceptability.

But a fair deal is not necessarily a good one. Might there be a lower fair value?

In fact, yes. The *whole* rule for fair pricing holds that the fair price must fall between a *minimum* of the book values of the company (which, normally, the seller could get simply by liquidating) and that *maximum* value of book plus two-and-a-half times current adjusted income.

So the fair value of BeBop actually falls somewhere between $150,000 and $500,000, exclusive of inventory. In between, friend, is contested ground and it's in your interest to gain as much of it as you can.

Steven spielberg, inc: determining fair good will. Of course, some people—and some major corporations—simply refuse to pay good will at all. They also spend a very long time waiting for something to buy. The rest of us are willing to pay good will, but want to make sure we're getting fair value, and not simply automatically paying top dollar.

Good will is worth top dollar if it is *stable, defensible,* and *transferable.*

In small businesses, which reflect the personality of the owner,

transferability is often decisive. Let's put it this way: anyone with
sufficient management acumen and training could run IBM. The
company is huge, employing hundreds of thousands, and scarcely
depends upon the personality of any one person.

But imagine a hypothetical company called Steven Spielberg,
Inc, which owns the rights to make Steven Spielberg films. Based
on earnings from *Close Encounters, Raiders of the Lost Ark, Jaws, Poltergeist,
ET,* and other films, the good will of the company would be im-
mense—hundreds of millions of dollars at least. But unless Spielberg were staying with the company (or you're a buyer with
comparable genius), the transferability would be nil. That's why
smaller, highly personalized businesses—including accounting
practices, even barber shops—generally have little good will involved. (Barbershops are usually too small to be handled by
brokers, but accounting firms are sometimes sold on a "retained
accounts" basis, where the good will value of the sale is based on
the number of old accounts still with the firm six months or a year
after the sale closes. This is fine for the buyer, of course, but
extremely risky for the seller.)

Now, in the case of BeBop, transferability doesn't seem to be a
problem. If you can handle retail sales, you're probably OK. What
about stability?

Stability simply means that the earnings have held up for a
number of years, or better yet, shown steady progress. Beware of
the guy who's made $30,000 a year for the last decade, except that
last year he made $125,000 off a rare hot product—and now wants
$300,000 in goodwill for the place. Similarly, make sure the busi-
ness has been around long enough to justify all that goodwill; a
business in operation for eighteen months is probably out of line
asking top-dollar goodwill.

BeBop, Inc, seems to be alright on this count. Income has moved
up steadily from year to year. On the other hand, year-to-year
percentage growth has been slowing. From '81 to '82, it grew 30%,
but the next year was only up 25%, the next 20%, and so on—
the boom is losing steam. Is the market peaking? Is the current
store too small or poorly located for further growth? These are
clues to possible bargaining chips.

They also raise the last question mark about goodwill, that of *defensibility.* How vulnerable is BeBop to competitive pressures? That eleven-year exclusive contract looks good—it means no price-cutter is going to open down the street. But suppose BeBopsu has been using old-style transistors, and now ShaNaNap Industries of Cupertino, California is bringing out an integrated circuit model that's twice as hot? Your market share is suddenly up in the air; does BeBopsu have its own replacement ready to go on-line, or are you going to get stuck with a turkey farm? Remember, good will is predicated on the assumption that you can foretell the future by judging the past—but it's up to you to decide how well the two correlate.

It's easy to name factors which might make the good will hard to defend. Are labor troubles brewing? Are there major challenges nearing from the loss of a patent, a lease, or even a key employee? Bebop looks vulnerable here, because the products are aging, the building's small, and the lease is running out.

Your ability to exploit these circumstances will vary according to the situation of the owner. Is he tired of the business? Is he ill, or reaching retirement age—or is the business in fact in the hands of a caretaker? Such factors, though unmentionable in the framing of your offer, will influence your ability to negotiate a low price. On the other hand, you may be up against an owner who is merely testing the waters—willing to sell if he can get top dollar, but unwilling otherwise. We used to deal regularly with two superannuated gentlemen who owned an air-conditioning and heating company. Once each Spring they would call us up and announce they wanted to sell, and we would dutifully dispatch a couple of people to help them determine the company's worth. Usually they would look the figures over and decide that they had changed their minds. Occasionally, if the price quoted were sufficiently high, they would give the authorization to sell, and then, when a week or two had produced no sale, cancel out the listing. If, during that brief interval between their signing and cancelling, some buyer had walked in with a check for their full price, *perhaps* they would have sold, but basically, they were only collecting a free appraisal.

The best person to tell you how vulnerable a seller may be, is the broker. Unfortunately, the broker's primary legal responsibility is to the seller, not to you; he is expected to get the seller the highest possible price for his business. There are ways around that, which we'll discuss in a minute. But first a word about a method of pricing businesses meant to give the *art* of business buying an undeserved veneer of science.

WATCH OUT FOR FORMULAS. It's only human nature to want to do business as systematically as possible. One attempt at bringing order to the chaotic work of pricing businesses has been the use of formulae based upon the monthly gross *sales* (not profits) of particular *kinds* of businesses. There are separate formulas for each type of business in order to account for the variations in both desirability and profit margin among business types. These formulas—which are by no means standard from year to year, or from region to region—range from the plausible (the goodwill of an advertising agency should equal 35–50% of average annual billings) to the bizarre (the goodwill of a mortuary should equal $1000 per average annual planting). The worst formulas are simply arbitrary concoctions meant to justify clear overpricing; the best are informal guidelines worked out by brokers to approximate average business selling prices in their region. But even the best formulas should be used with caution—especially when they call for a price much above the "two-and-a-half-years' net" rule for goodwill. Here's an example of the dangers:

Bottled liquor in California used to come under what were called "fair trade" laws, which meant that the state set the minimum prices, and so guaranteed the profit margin, on every bottle sold. A separate law restricted the number of off-sale alcohol licenses available, and those two laws taken together virtually guaranteed that a California liquor store would be a money-maker. As a result, not only was an off-sale license worth $80,000 or more on the open market, but the "formula" for a liquor store said it was worth anywhere from five to seven times its monthly gross. That meant a small store doing $30,000 a month was worth up to $210,000 goodwill, plus $80,000 for the license, plus inventory of, say, another $60,000—fixtures and equipment were generally accounted negligible. That's $350,000 for a not-very-large operation. At the peak of the boom, the stores were being snapped up as fast as they were offered, and brokers were practically shooting each other in the streets for listings. The store owners were as arrogant as lords; every time they boosted monthly sales another $1000 (a case or two of good wine), the value of their stores went up $7000. And buyers were told that seven-times monthly sales formula was inviolable.

Then fair trade was abolished. Liquor profit margins fell, and the glamour of owning a store fell even more. With fewer people attracted to the business, the licenses were less valuable; they sell today for around $40,000, which is nearly a 75% drop in inflation-adjusted value. And the sacred formula of the mid-'70s? Today a liquor store will probably bring *two* times monthly sales —if it's a nice looking store. So that $30,000-a-month store will bring something like $60,000 in goodwill + $40,000 for the license + $60,000 for the inventory = $160,000. That's less than *half* what it was worth during the boom years. Formulae, in short, are merely ways of giving quasimathematical expression to current going rates. They can be a useful rule of thumb, but never let any broker or accountant persuade you they are sacred.

Making an Offer.

OK, business prices—whether set by formula or not—are meant to be negotiated. How do you go about it?

The first concrete advice is that you are generally unwise to engage the seller in a lot of price-talk before making your offer. Asking a lot of questions like, "Well, do you think you might take thirty-five down?" tends to either 1) harden a seller's position, or 2) create false expectations. If he says he'll take $35,000, but you were only fishing for information, what then? Perhaps your subsequent analysis will determine that the down payment should only be $19,000, but the seller thinks you're already verbally committed to the higher figure. It's only trouble.

A wiser approach is to gather all the data, go home, work out what you consider a fair price (or better, the price you *want* to pay and the maximum you *will* pay), then submit a formal written offer.

This offer (at the *want* price) can be submitted on either a broker's form (of which a sample can be found in the Appendix), or a form of your own design. In either case it should not much exceed one typewritten page, and should be reviewed in advance by your attorney. It should include:

1. The name and full address of the business

2. The price, including approximate inventory at current wholesale, with exact amount to be determined by inventory at time of your taking possession, and the price to be adjusted accordingly.

3. Form of payment. How much you are providing, what encumbrances you are assuming, and what new encumbrances you are creating. Include specific amounts, monthly payments, and interest rates.

4. Seller to provide:

A. Bill of Sale free and clear of all but specified encumbrances.
B. Transfer or granting of lease. Offer to be subject to your approval of that lease.
C. Warrant that the property meets all relevant codes and regulations.
D. Complete list of fixtures and equipment (to be mutually approved by buyer and seller). Seller promises that all equipment will be in good working order at the time of possession.

5. Your right to examine and approve all business records, with offer contingent upon your approval. Deposit to be automatically refunded in case of previous misrepresentation. (This is a key escape clause. Some firms—ours, for example—have never kept a deposit check which a buyer wished returned. Others consider all deposits nonrefundable, and will use the fact to pressure you into completing an ill-advised purchase.)

6. The Disposition of Deposit: All parties agree that the Broker is to keep the deposit check uncashed, until it is placed in escrow or returned to the buyer. (A second protection of your deposit.)

7. Termination Date. The offer should only stand for three business days. Create whatever psychological pressure you can for a sale—and limit as far as possible your own exposure.

8. Arbitration. (Optional) You may want to specify that disputes arising from the offer will be submitted to the American Arbitration Association (or some similar organization) for settlement. (Please see: AVOIDING LITIGATION, Chapter 15)

The bottom of the form will normally have spaces for the broker's acknowledgement of the deposit, the acceptance by the seller(s), and (occasionally), the sellers' countersproposal, if any.

The deposit backing the offer should be modest—a reputable broker will normally want a check for about 1% of the total consideration, rounded up to the nearest $500. That is, $500 for a business worth up to $50,000; $1000 for one worth between $50,000; and $100,000, and so on. Run from any broker who says 10% is the standard deposit—he's just looking to pocket an unearned commission, or force you into completing an unwise purchase.

NEGOTIATING A DEAL. Submitting an offer, then, is quite simple. The real art comes in, first, finding the lowest acceptable price, and second, winning the offer's acceptance.

Let's return to our example. The asking price for BeBop Corp. is $500,000 (which includes $150,000 book value plus $350,000 goodwill) plus $200,000 in inventory. You have no particular passion for consumer electronics, yet you like it well enough. In fact, you basically like everything about BeBop, but with some reservations. First, top-dollar goodwill seems excessive when the company's growth is slowing. Second, it will need to move to a bigger location shortly. Third, you doubt that you can move that $100,000's worth of type-A, old-style bopifiers. With some slack on these points, you are willing to buy, but otherwise, you'll walk.

Instead of simply tendering full price for BeBop, you now go to the broker, explain your specific objections, and ask to write up an offer on your terms. You might offer $290,000 for the business (full book value—$150,000, plus one year's income—$140,000, for goodwill), and stipulate that the owner must agree to liquidate the stock of type-A BeBopsu equipment. Your total offer, then, is $290,000 plus $100,000 in approximate remaining inventory.

Will the owner accept? In truth, much depends upon factors beyond your control, such as how eager the seller is, and how many other offers he's received. The only way to guarantee acceptance is to offer the full price and terms, but that's as expensive as it is certain. The bargain price you want will normally take some dealing.

You can, however, usually get a hint of your chances well before your hear the seller's response. Nominally, a broker is not supposed to prejudge an offer; in fact, the laws of most states require him to submit *every* offer received. In practice, an unwritten code allows brokers to tell flakey buyers, "Mr. Jones, here's the telephone. I don't believe I can present that offer in person with enough enthusiasm to carry it." From an honest and competent broker, that is the signal your offer is unreasonably low.

Such a response is unlikely in this case; your offer for BeBop, though tough, is within the fair range. More likely, the broker will urge you to prepare a written offer of the sort discussed earlier. In that case, he really is trying to help you, because he knows that a vague verbal proposal tends to crash, where the same offer in written form, with a check behind it, is very likely to fly.

Not only will the broker help you write up your ideas, often he will provide some usable suggestions of his own. If you had not thought of it yourself, for example, he surely would have proposed the seller's liquidating that unwanted inventory. If, by this time, you've come to trust the broker, then pay attention to these hints—he's doing what he legally can to take your side.

Once the offer is written, you have only a short time to wait for an answer. You've written in a three-day termination, but a well-organized broker may have the seller's reply in a matter of hours. If it's "yes," you've got a deal—and you've avoided the troubles of negotiating. If it's a categorical "no", because the price is firm, you'll likely look elsewhere. But if it's a counteroffer, then you'll begin negotiating in earnest.

That in turn may mean sitting down face-to-face with the seller and wheeling and dealing—a prospect some people find exhilarating, and others face with dread. The people who most dislike negotiating seem to view it as a kind of aggression, and to fear either inflicting, or suffering, injury. If you must, you can hire a broker to take your part, paying a flat fee if he gets you the business at your price. Better still is learning to do it yourself.

Dozens of books have been written on the art of negotiating—one which many people find helpful is *You Can Negotiate Anything* by Herb Cohen—but perhaps these few rules will help most in business:

1. *Do Your Homework: Know Your Strengths.* You've already done this in studying the books, seeing the plant, and calculating your offer. A grasp of the facts should protect you from appeals to your vanity, your sympathy, or some false sense of social responsibility —and remember that a broker trying to talk you up in price will appeal to them all.

By the same token, emphasize your own strengths, the things you are giving to the seller. Stress not only a fair price, but your expertise, reputation, even eagerness—anything suggesting that the business (which you are likely buying over time) will be safe in your hands.

2. *Know When to Quit.* Sometimes a negotiation is over before it starts. If BeBop starts at $700,000, you offer $390,000, and the seller counters with $695,000, you're probably too far apart. Some gaps are simply too wide to bridge.

3. *Find Points of Accord First.* Spend as much time stressing where parties agree as where you are apart. Avoid creating the feeling that there is only going to be one winner.

Personality clashes hurt many negotiations. Adept negotiators try to match styles with the other party. If the other party if all business, the negotiator is all business; if they're just country boys, the negotiator is just a country boy, and so on. At least make allowances for differences between you and the seller.

4. *Trade Concessions, and Get a Big One for a Small One.* Make those small gestures which set an (often frightened) seller at ease. I once saw a buyer offer to advance $65 to a seller who had forgotten to bring her checkbook, and so turn her hostility into warm and cooperative friendship. Since she had inherited the business from her husband, our client was the first person who had not rushed to cheat her. He made a friend and got his deal.

More rigorously, trade a future concession for a present one. For example, if you can get a seller to let you in for less money down, you don't mind paying a bigger price overall—because that money is due way down the road. Get yourself into business now—you can either pay, or renegotiate, the balance years hence.

5. *Deal Firmly.* You've done the homework, you know the facts —make sure your personal style reflects it. Review the information before every meeting, and use a "cheat-sheet" if you need it. Speak confidently.

As confident as you want to seem, please remember one cardinal rule: don't knock the business. Even if negotiations become heated, and even if certain weaknesses in the firm are obvious, avoid criticizing the old management.

Not long ago, a pair of examples showed me the rewards of a pleasant personality. I saw an experienced buyer get precisely his deal on the purchase of a small trucking company. He began by praising the seller's performance to the heavens and presenting his own low offer as an unfortunate economic necessity. The seller was delighted to be dealing with him, and the deal went smoothly.

A few days later, I watched another buyer lose a deal, despite offering the seller's full price and terms. As the negotiating meeting began, she confronted the seller with a tirade about how she demanded respect, was nobody's fool, and so on. Before she finished speaking, the deal was dead: *this* seller felt threatened and humiliated.

I can certainly understand that some people become aggressive trying to protect themselves, that their aggression is covering fear or lack of self-confidence. Remember, though, that we're all a bit frightened in big negotiations. The way to protect yourself is, first, to prepare carefully, and second, to deal firmly but with dignity and kindness.

If you recognize no other reasons, you want to keep talks civilized because sellers often change their minds a few days after talks break off, and because you don't want anyone bum-repping you all over town. Outside of New York, Chicago, and Los Angeles, the business community (especially for any given industry) is generally surprisingly small, and if word spreads that you tried to stick it to old Joe, you are going to run out of prospective sellers very quickly. Alternatively, if, two or three days after negotiations break off, old Joe decides your offer really was acceptable after all, you don't want to have said anything which would make it hard for him to call you up and say you have a deal.

Except where one of the parties is a major corporation, small business negotiations rarely extend over more than about two weeks. If no progress has been made by then, simply let everyone involved know that you've offered the most you think current circumstances justify—that you'd be grateful if they'd inform you if the situation changes, but for the time being you're going to have to look elsewhere. This may prompt movement by the seller, and at least hints politely to the broker that if he can work his client down, you'll be interested. *Don't* say anything like, "Well, if you ever decide you'll take $490,000, let me know, and we've got a deal." Business situations alter rapidly—that's why your first offer stood only seventy-two hours. The guy could go out, lose $200,000 the next week, and announce he's accepting the offer you made in front of witnesses. Why commit yourself unnecessarily?

In a great many cases, though, your sensibly devised offer—perhaps renegotiated to some extent—will be accepted. If you lose it, well, you simply recall your deposit check, tear up the offer, and start looking again. You've lost some time, but nothing worse.

If, on the other hand, the offer is accepted, you still have at least one tough bit of negotiation ahead, that of the actual sale or escrow contract. Even so, cheer up; you're more than halfway home.

12
ESCROWING AND TAKING OVER

SITUATION:
To complete the purchase of a going business safely, escrowing the sale is your best insurance
OBJECTIVE:
To find a reputable escrow company, and to write an escrowed agreement which is both safe and efficient. To take charge of the new firm without complications

Escrow: Doing Things Right.

You've found the business you want. The plant and the books look good, the owner's honest, and the price is fair. You strike a deal. Now how do you safely and quickly carry it out?

First, recognize that buying a business is more like exchanging hostages than it is like, say, buying a toaster. The problem lies in dealing safely, so that you hold onto your money, and the seller, his business, until all the myriad details from transfers of leases to approval of bank loans have been completed.

The best solution is an *escrow,* which simply is a place where a legal document is held until certain of its provisions have been executed. Since a business escrow is more complicated than the better-known real estate escrow, it's worth our time to discuss briefly 1) how to find a suitable escrow, 2) how much to pay for escrow services, and 3) how to recognize safe escrow instructions. This is not meant to replace a lawyer's, or a broker's advice, but merely to get you thinking along the right lines; as with any contract, you want to work for your own security.

FINDING AN ESCROW COMPANY. Technically, anyone willing to hold papers and money for you and your seller could qualify as an escrow. In fact, you are wise to pay a fee for expertise and fiscal strength. You want an escrow which 1) knows what it is doing and 2) will be there in the morning.

Most of this country's escrow firms work mainly with real estate, and so handle business sales only poorly. Of the few which escrow businesses frequently, fewer still are truly expert. Your business broker will certainly know the names of these. If you aren't using a broker, you can still get advice; simply call up a major brokerage, explain that you are handling a transaction privately, and ask which escrow company they use. Normally, they'll be glad to make a recommendation.

Financial strength is another matter. In most states, escrow companies are fairly well regulated, not only frequently audited, but subject to minimum financial-strength requirements and backed by some form of state-sponsored insurance.

Unfortunately, the regulation isn't perfect. When State auditors discovered that one of California's best-respected escrow companies was short nearly $600,000 of clients' funds, the regulators did step in—by freezing all the company's assets and pending transactions. Today—more than a year after the discovery—the funds and the deals remain frozen while the state tries to decide whom to prosecute. People with deals pending will, it now seems, finally be reimbursed, but for many, the wait has already been disastrous.

There's no absolute way to avoid such a mess (which, again, is a rare occurence), but you should 1) act on the advice of someone well connected to the business grapevine, and 2) if possible, choose an escrow company affiliated with a big, solid general financial services firm—either a bank or a conglomerate of the TransAmerica ilk.

WHAT GOES INTO THE AGREEMENT. I don't mean to scare you with that story—with any good-sized escrow company the chances of trouble are vanishingly slight. A more legitimate concern is that you receive an escrow *agreement* which protects your interests. Your broker, lawyer, and escrow officer should all cooperate to see it's done right. A good broker will assemble the basic agreement by choosing instructions from an escrow "kit" containing twenty or forty pages of standard clauses and documents, and then working with the lawyers to add any needed special instructions. Make certain the result is a complete legal document, one stating name and place of business, price and terms, and so on. Beyond that, look particularly for the following:

1. *The Noncompete Agreement.* You deserve a promise that, the day after escrow closes, the seller won't simply open up a new place a block away and swipe all your customers. Such a guarantee is called a "noncompete agreement." As long as it specifies realistic limits of distance and time ("seller not to compete within ten miles for a period of three years" is typical), it is a standard and perfectly legal request.

One potential problems comes from tax considerations. Here's how:

An agreement only has force if there are penalties (called "liquidated damages") for breaking it. Let's suppose you and the seller agree that breach of the agreement will cost him $50,000 in such damages.

Fine—except, unfortunately, the IRS will assume that, of the price received for the business, $50,000 was paid for that noncompete. You don't mind a bit. Because you can capitalize that $50,000 figure and then depreciate it like any other asset, you get quite a tax break.

It's the seller who'll howl, because money he gets for a noncompete is taxed as ordinary income. For him, it's far better to receive the same amount of money as payment for his *"good will,"* which is taxed as capital gains. You don't like that, because you can't depreciate good will—it's a dead loss to you until the time comes for you in turn to sell the company.

So there's the difficulty. The total amount to divide between good will and noncompetition is fixed—you won't pay more than the fair intangible value of the company (the $140,000 you agreed to for BeBop, Inc., for example). But the way the money is divided up makes great differences in tax considerations. You're entitled to a noncompete with some teeth in it; after that, you're trying for as much larger a figure as you can grab—but be willing to compromise somewhat.

2. *Owner Must Keep Premises Open Normal Business Hours until Possession.* A nice simple clause, but you want it, because otherwise, the day you deposit the money in escrow, the seller can just lock the company's doors and go on vacation—and by the time you take possession, the firm's good will won't be worth a fig.

3. *Seller Warranties Premises:* The seller warrants to you that the premises of the business will meet all governmental codes on the date of possession—again, simple enough. You don't want to show up at your new restaurant, and find the health inspector and the fire marshall arguing over who gets to condemn it first.

4. *Seller Warranties Fixtures and Equipment.* Seller warrants to you that on date of possession, all fixtures and equipment shall be in working order.

5. *Seller Guarantees Inventory.* Seller guarantees to maintain inventory at normal levels during escrow period. He agrees to deliver to you an inventory value of at least X dollars, or to adjust your price accordingly. Most sellers will strive to hit the target, but do specify the way inventory is to be priced—current Blue Book, current wholesale, or whatever.

6. *Seller Warranties No Warranties or Guarantees.* The seller guarantees there are no existing warranties or guarantees on any products or services he or she has previously sold. You want no undisclosed liabilities.

7. *No Rental, Advertising, or Promotional Contracts.* Seller should guarantee that no such contracts exist, except those specifically listed in the escrow papers.

8. *No Employee Benefits.* Seller agrees to take care of any due or promised employee benefits, such as bonuses, vacations, etc. Where you buy a corporation, you will automatically acquire such items as pension fund obligations, but otherwise you should be exempt. Watch this one—you'd be surprise how many owners have told key employees, "Boys, the day I sell out you each get a month off with pay."

9. *Presence of Existing Security Agreements, etc.* You authorize the escrow officer to inquire of any relevant governmental agencies whether there currently exist any effective security agreements, debts or encumbrances, naming the Seller, and affecting any of the fixtures, equipment, or inventory being sold. The seller agrees to clear any such encumbrances—except for those you specifically agree to assume.

10. *Real Estate Option.* If the seller of the business also owns the building it occupies, and has vaguely offered you an option to buy it too at some future date, this is the time to get it in writing.

11. *Instruction of Buyer.* The seller agrees to instruct you without charge for N number of days in the conduct and operation of the business, *instruction to begin no later than close of escrow.* (Leave the last part out, and he'll look you up when he gets back from Tahiti— in about ten years.)

12. *Possession by Agreed Date.* Assuming that you deliver all of the required funds to escrow, that you qualify for required loans and permits, and that you have not deceived the seller on any material point, the seller agrees to give you possession of the premises on or before a specified date.

All right—those are twelve points of protection you want for yourself. What should you allow to the seller?

1. *Approval of Books and Records.* You agree that you have read, understood, and approved all the documents of the business (as many or as few as may be). This protects the seller against your coming back two weeks later and saying you thought the company made more or owed less. You can still sue for actual fraud, but otherwise, the seller is clear.

2. *Approval of Lease.* You agree that you have read, understood, and approved the lease(s). As above, reasonable protection for the seller.

3. *Cash for Stock.* Because stock can be stolen or simply sold off, the seller is entitled to receive cash up front for all stock present on his shelves the day you take possession.

Those are three general safeguards any seller deserves. In addition, he is entitled to one or more forms of *failure to complete* protection. If you are unable to complete the deal because you cannot get needed licenses or an expected loan, or simply because you suffer a change of heart, then the seller (and broker, if any) are entitled to some compensation for their time, trouble, and expense. In general, expect the figure named to be no more than about 10% of the total price of the business. You will also probably be required to pay all escrow fees and charges—as is only fair. The seller will expect this to be protected by an *Irrevocable Assignment of Funds,* an escrow deposit you'll get back only if the *seller* defaults.

How long should it take; how long is the document? Because most brokerages have standardized kits and can phone in escrow instructions by number, a basic escrow can normally be opened within twenty-four hours of your offer's having been accepted. We usually then like to have both parties read and sign the escrow instructions together at the escrow company's offices. Your lawyer can be present if you wish, but normally you will already have had the chance to query him about any doubtful clauses. By bringing a lawyer with you, you are inviting a display of lawyerliness— unnecessary objections meant to show a lawyer is earning his keep —but if his presence reassures you, bring him.

If no serious objections are raised, your presence should only be required for an hour or two. A very basic escrow agreement can can be as short as five pages, plus ancillary documents. More complex deals need proportionally longer instructions, but an escrow requiring a full day of your time would be uncommon. If anything unexpected or vague appears in the instructions, don't let yourself be buffaloed into signing; you're entitled to contact your attorney, even if it means delaying the escrow a day. If it ends up costing you an extra hundred or so in legal and escrow fees, it's still cheap insurance. Do be efficient, though, and collect all your questions before calling for help—it's only fair to other parties involved.

Assuming no hitches arise, the escrow will last only long enough to execute all its instructions: to deposit funds, transfer leases, acquire permits, and so on. Most escrows should close within two weeks, although those involving tightly regulated permits (liquor, gambling, etc.) can take several months. Anything longer is rare.

WHAT DOES IT COST? Escrowing is not expensive. For an unincorporated business without a liquor license and worth $100,000 or less, most escrows will charge around $600–700, plus perhaps $100 for miscellaneous fees. Prices go up from there, but they are unlikely to exceed, let's say, $1500—to be split evenly between buyer and seller.

TAKING CHARGE. Taking charge is usually far less trouble than most people expect. You've already learned much about the business by studying the plant and the books. The owner will normally spend another ten days or two weeks teaching you his basic business routines—how orders are routed, where he buys supplies, and so on. You've paid for trade secrets, clients, and a ready work force. Your permits, licenses, and insurance are already in place.

A FEW PRECAUTIONS. In spite of that, you need to be ready for certain potential transition-time problems:

1. *Physical Hazards.* It's amazing the number of owners who manage to injure themselves in the first few days of business possession. Sure, you're enthusiastic, but take a week or so to learn your way—and especially go slow with any repairs or remodelling if you aren't experienced. We had a client, a professional of some sort, who bought a large restaurant. The second day he owned it, he decided to make some sort of minor repair—change a lightbulb, I think—so he used a stepladder to climb up to the top of one of the cooking range hoods. Unfortunately, no one had told him that even scrupulously clean restaurants often collect thin layers of condensed oil and grease in unlikely places. He lost his footing,

went flying, and ruined his back. He went to the rest home for six months, and the business went back on the market. So go slow, and learn your way around.

2. *Employees.* The last thing you want is to have key employees quit on hearing of the sale. The best approach, it seems, is to have the old owner call the workers together and make the official announcement—but not until the escrow is about to close. It's also nice if you can say a few words. Stress your belief in continuity, and your willingness to hear about their ideas and problems. Be as upbeat as possible. Don't commit yourself to any firm job policy; instead talk generally about the firm's bright prospects. You won't in any case want to make many personnel changes until you've had time to study the exact performances of individual workers. The main thing just now is fielding a complete team.

3. *Clients and Accounts.* You'll probably find most people with whom the company has dealt to be extremely supportive of your efforts—especially if you get out and contact them, stressing your willingness to meet or exceed the performance of the old owners. Your suppliers, who need you as a customer, should be particularly helpful. Often they'll aid you over the rough spots with all sorts of advice about storage, transportation, and even promotion of goods. You may well discover they have fine ideas for you that the old owner was too stubborn or too old-fashioned to adopt.

Even while cultivating the company's long-standing relationships, you must beware of slow-paying clients. Some of your less-desirable accounts will likely use the confusion of the transition period to dodge their payments.

The old owner almost certainly had a tagging system, either colored tabs on account cards or (better) a computer kick-out on delinquent accounts. As soon as you get one of these warnings, act promptly but cautiously. Remember that honest mistakes happen, and that sometimes your firm, and not the client, will be at fault.

As a bill goes ten to fourteen days past due, most companies send a friendly second notice automatically, sometimes politely disguised as a "replacement bill." After that, phone calls are more economical than customized dunning letters. Simply get your delinquent account on the phone, explain the problem in one sentence (eg, "We haven't received your payment for March or April")—and then dummy up. Remember the old salesman's axiom that in a dispute, the first one to speak loses. The other fellow may offer excuses for a while, but finally, embarrassed, he'll ask whether you're still on the line. At that point, you can say, "Yes, but I've been waiting to hear when we could expect our payment. When will that be?" The excuses have been exhausted, and you should get a committment of some kind.

Be flexible. Sometimes by extending payments or offering a count for settlement, you can save a valuable customer. At least, you'll save the problems of collection agencies (which will keep half of most small-to-medium collections), or lawyers, who will cost you time as well as money.

Remember that anytime you have to seek outside help collecting accounts, you're the loser. Your best long-term defense is to tighten your credit policies. Deal as far as possible with cash- or bank-card customers (taking checks only with guarantees), and extend credit only after careful investigation. If your bad debts ever go as high as 5% of total sales in any given quarter, it is time for *much* tougher credit standards.

You'll probably take more credit risks in your early days than at any other time, simply because you feel you need the business. When our company was starting in the late '40s, it seemed that half the deals we handled ended up with the lawyers or collection agencies. By the late '50s, that was becoming so rare that we were able to resell with guarantees notes we had accepted. Between 1968 and 1983, so far as I can discover, we had only one default on money owed us. As our own business had grown, we had simply become strong enough to reject financially risky clients. The same thing will happen to you, sooner or later, so be patient. Don't rush to extend credit just for the sake of sales—you'll suffer in the long run.

In general, taking control of your new business should be an exciting and pleasurable, if hectic, time. Remember that the old owner, your broker, your suppliers, and your employees are there to provide no-cost expert advice. If problems arise, don't hesitate to ask. Take a few days to get squared away before chasing debtors or making wholesale reforms. When the time comes to engineer improvements, move on to the following chapters.

One Final Tip.

Sometimes your first weeks or months in business will reveal gaps in your skills. Don't panic. Not only will the following chapters help, but there are growing numbers of high-quality support services for small business owners. One of the best is a program recently begun by the Control Data Small Business Centers. The sixty centers each offer some 100 well-focused courses to help you run your business better. The courses—average price, around $160 —range from writing effective business letters to running market research. Control Data underwrites the courses—as well as services from word processing to office space—to try to foster future customers. They're hoping you'll remember them five years from now, when you're fat and sassy and out buying commercial credit and high-ticket computers. Sounds fair to me. It's a true bargain, and a sign that the big guys believe in your future—it at least deserves a look. Over 7000 small firms have joined up already, and it's easy to see why. Check it out.

13

INSURING THE BUSINESS

SITUATION:
Insuring a business is really a complex process involving risk analysis, risk reduction, and several kinds of insuring
OBJECTIVE:
Obtaining cost-effective protection for all vulnerable business operations

From its modest beginnings as a Fourteenth-century Italian proposition to protect against maritime loses, insurance has grown today into a dizzying enterprise, offering a staggering range of policies, from the mundane to the most exotic. To name only a few:

Astronaut Life
Business Liquidation
Business Purchase
Computer Damage
Errors and Omissions
Fire
Health

Kidnapping
Malpractice
Personal Liability
Radioactive Contamination
Space Accident
Theft and Burglary

And on, and on. Certain kinds of insurance can make the difference between happiness and misery, even (through risk-reduction) between life and death. Others are unnecessary, overpriced, and even (if they fail or cheat you in the face of disaster), positively lethal. Given that some of the world's largest, best-financed sales organizations exist to sell whatever is best for the insurance firms, instead of what is best for you, how can you possibly play the insurance game and win?

Well, most medium-sized businesses, and many fast-growing small businesses, usually discover that the problem requires the presence on the payroll of one or more full- or part-time insurance managers.

Even before reaching that stage, you can do well with insurance if you recognize this crucial principle—before you think about insurance, think about risk. Once you understand the ways you are at risk, you can protect yourself intelligently. That protection may include risk reduction, retention, or insurance, and the insurance may come in several forms, but until you decide for yourself exactly what your hazards are, you are going to be the natural target of every fast-talking insurance salesman in the world.

Risk is a complex and, in many ways, a dreary topic, but unless you want to wind up on the six o'clock news talking tearfully about how you never thought a tornado would hit Kansas, you'd better learn something about it. You start by relying upon:

1. Your lawyer
2. Your accountant
3. Your personal convictions and goals
4. Your own thought experiments and walk-throughs

Your Lawyer.

From your lawyer, find out about your risks and obligations from 1) statuatory law and 2) general civil liability.

STATUATORY LIABILITY. Technically, statuatory liability means laws extending your liability beyond ordinary bounds. Examples are "tavern owner" or "dramshop" laws, which hold merchants liable if they sell alcohol to persons subsequently involved in accidents.

Similarly, you may find that your state laws require you to post bonds or contribute to insurance funds according to your line of work. In California, for example, corporate securities dealers are required to post $100,000 bonds to guarantee transactions. You will also likely be required to provide *Workmen's Compensation,* by either contributing to a state insurance pool, or buying private coverage. Workmen's Compensation is a part of most general business insurance packages, but be sure yours covers even part-time workers, and those hired for a single, one-time task.

CIVIL LIABILITY. Also ask about the ways your business might be sued. Possibilities include: *Contract Actions* (breaching, voiding, etc., any verbal or written contract); *Equitable Actions* (defrauding, misrepresenting, or making mistakes costly to others), and *Tort Actions*. *Torts* are either *intentional* (like trespass, assault, or false arrest), or *unintentional* (involving negligence or omission). Remember that about *90%* of all cases for personal injury and/or personal property damage involve *Unintentional torts,* and that, in most cases, the business is responsible for the actions of employees. (Also, realize that I've mentioned only a few of the possible forms of liability. For the details, a fine textbook to consult is *Risk Management and Insurance* by C. Arthur Williams and Richard M. Heins. It's published by McGraw-Hill, and is both readable and highly informative.)

Lastly, ask your lawyer to name a general dollar figure for the amount of coverage you need. He or she should have a good idea of what recent settlements have brought.

Your Accountant: Finding Out Your Financial Exposure.

From your accountant you need to know the value of everything the company owns. You need to work with your accountant, because technically, every item will have several values: original cost, cost less depreciation, use value, replacement cost, and so on. You also need a realistic evaluation of your financial strength, to see 1) how much insurance you can afford, 2) whether you can afford to self-insure any operation, and 3) whether you are running on such narrow margins that interruption-of-business insurance is essential. Your accountant will also be able to explain the insurance requirements—if any—of any outstanding loans, and also help locate potential white-collar crime weakpoints.

Personal Reflection: Your Own Needs.

Through quiet reflection, decide what you expect the business to do for you, your family, and your employees.

One possibility might be *key man* or owner's life insurance. "Key man" is life insurance to compensate the company for the death or incapacitation of some key employee. It is sometimes coupled with a policy naming family members as beneficiaries—which has often been considered a fairly desirable perk because of its tax advantages for the insured.

But the main form of small business life insurance has been that for the owner, to protect his or her family from the devastation of federal estate taxes. Before the tax reforms of 1981, even families receiving estates as small as $400,000 often had to liquidate businesses when the owner died. When the new code takes full effect in 1987, estates up to $1.2 million will be effectively tax-free— a much fairer figure. Still, you might consider company-backed *owner's life*.

If no family member is interested in succeeding you, but there are employees who might want to carry on, you might consider *Business Purchase Insurance*. In this plan, your employees (usually) agree to buy the business upon your death or incapacitation at some set price, and then you insure your life with a policy dedicated to that purchase. Along with helping your employees to guarantee their futures, you insure that your family will not be stuck holding (and trying to run) a business in which it has no interest.

One other possibility—of many—is employee medical/dental beyond the required workmen's compensation. Many owners consider it their duty to protect their workers this way; some will find it a competitive necessity. Recent years have brought an increasing number of small-business medical/dental plans, some specifically designed for companies with, say, fewer than ten employees. Remember that employees with access to affordable care will likely treat problems while they are still minor—and so not only protect themselves, but prove more reliable, productive workers.

By the time you have decided on those personal goals—life,

business purchase, health policies and so on—you will have invested several hours in insurance planning: perhaps an hour with your attorney, a like time with your accountant, and some period of personal reflection. The next step requires doing something that rarely comes naturally to an entrepreneur. You must steel yourself to *think negatively*. Whether the business is actually in existence, or still on the drawing board, you must try to anticipate every every possible disaster. In a certain way, frankly, this is rather fun, but you must be methodical.

Thought Experiment.

A "thought experiment" is simply the asking of a set of hypothetical questions to help you understand a *possible* sequence of events. You want to determine, by both observation and those hypothetical questions, every place you might be vulnerable to the legal or financial risks you've discussed with your accountant or lawyer. Ask yourself how your customers, employees, products, and financial infrastructure can cause, or suffer, harm. Sometimes, happily, you'll find cures so simple that you'll be able to reduce risks the same day you find them.

CUSTOMERS ON THE PROPERTY. Put yourself step-by-step through a process something like this: "OK. A customer comes onto my property. What's the first thing he encounters? The parking lot? OK—what hazards? Is the paving OK? Are the slots marked? How about traffic flow? Now he's up to my front door—how can he get hurt? Door opens in his face? OK—we put up a sticker: "Caution: door opens outward." OK—he's up to the counter. Any dangers? What about this paper cutter? Alright, post a notice for employees: 'paper cutter to be under the counter at all times.' What else?"

And so on. Think of your average customer as an over-eager five-year-old, and you'll accord him or her the kind of protection juries expect of you. If this seems like a poor use of your time, remember that in 1979, according to Insurance Company of North America, the average judgement for a *knee* injury was almost $40,000.

Above all, keep work and sales areas separate. If you have to meet with customers at a coffee shop to keep them out of your machine shop, do it. The inconvenience beats having someone back into a bandsaw. Lastly, remember to review risk every time you make changes.

YOUR PRODUCTS. First, product liability. "Is the manufacturer making me sign a 'hold-harmless' clause on any of the orders I place? If so, will it stand up in court, and with what limitations? What about products I make. What quality slips would make them dangerous—faulty wiring, low grade chain-guards? Now, suppose the customer gets the product home. How could he *possibly* misuse it so as to injure himself? Five different ways." OK—list those in red in the instruction manual, and throw in a general warning about product misuse.

People out to collect on product liability often skip the small fry and go after the ones who can pay big. That's why Proctor & Gamble, instead of neighborhood drugstores, got sued over Rely, the tampon allegedly implicated in some toxic shock syndrome cases. On the other hand, don't expect any slack for a good overall record. Look at what happens to US airlines whenever there's a crash.

Second is product loss or damage. "Is the roof tight, and the building secure from theft? Suppose the power goes out—what about temperature changes? Suppose it rains for twenty days—are we on high ground, or in a flood channel? What if there's a warehouse fire—who fights it, and who calls for help? And where are the fire extinguishers? How are products packaged, and bulk-packaged? Any way they can get damaged in shipment to me, or by the customer before they reach home?"

And so on. Do the thought experiment of following products from manufacture through arrival in the customer's home. Find out which risks are yours, which can be reduced, and which must be insured.

YOUR EMPLOYEES. First, their safety. "Are there any slick floors? Sharp edges? Unprotected equipment, frayed wiring? Do any of my people seem to have problems with alcohol or drugs? Is their protective gear and clothing the best available?

This is one area where you may have more help than you want. In spite of repeated promises of legislative reform—and the recent elimination of some 2,000 excess regulations—the rules of OSHA, the Occupational Safety and Health Administration, still allow a government inspection of your premises whenever there is a complaint from one of your employees or a union representative. *You* cannot request practice reviews from OSHA—that's one of the biggest complaints against the system—but you can get help from either the National Safety Council (if there's a local chapter) or the federal National Institute of Occupational Safety and Health.

Next, consider harm employees might *cause.* "Do they know the products, or will they get me sued for misrepresentation? Do they know that contract sales can be cancelled within three days? Do they ever leave the grounds on company business—OK, better check my auto insurance. Nonowned auto coverage is cheap, but some insurance salesmen neglect to mention it because the commission is correspondingly small. Do my people ever call door to door? Better warn them about trespass. Are they ever likely to face irate customers, or picketers? Better warn them against making threats or, worse, settling affairs with their fists."

And so on. Employees can hurt you either intentionally (see below) or, more likely, unintentionally. That unintentional harm, from knocking a competitor in a slanderous way to leaving a company car unlocked, can only be checked by a *continuing program* of employee education. Make the safe conduct of business a recurring topic.

YOUR FINANCIAL INFRASTRUCTURE. "How does money move through the company, and where does it collect? Who has access to it, and what controls have I installed? Where are key records kept, and how are they protected—in UL-approved fireproof safes and files, in the computer system, or in boxes in the back room?"

Beyond taking the steps mentioned in SECURITY, you want to consider fidelity bonding your key employees to protect against their misbehavior, along with, perhaps, fraud insurance.

Do whatever you can to protect your records. Fireproof files are expensive and extremely heavy, but a wise precaution. You can insure computers not only for their cost, but for the value of information stored—but it still pays to keep duplicate discs off-site. Remember that a loss of records will also make it harder to collect on other claims, including lost inventory. It's not a bad idea to keep photo- or video-tape records of the premises to back up any claim you may have to file. Lastly, you may want to insure the general survival of your financial entity by an *interruption-of-business* policy.

Planning Action: Insuring, Retaining, and Reducing.

Once you have a clear idea of your goals and problems, you can begin designing your *risk* and *insurance strategy*. This means deciding what risks to retain, what to reduce, and what to insure.

RETAINING. The first way to deal with risk is simply to *retain* it. You assume that some risks can neither be neither be eliminated nor cost-effectively insured, so you simply face them. Some of these will be the "one-in-a-million" risks—like meteorite damage. Others will be forced by economic necessity. In its early days as an armaments company, DuPont built a small plant which somehow placed a gunpowder drying room next to an operation requiring open charcoal braziers. With the country needing arms, the company retained the risk—that is, pushed ahead. Shortly after going into operation, the plant blew up. Since DuPont went on to become the world's largest chemical company, the risk was presumably correctly calculated, but keep in mind how much you gamble when you retain risk.

CO- AND SELF-INSURING. Basically, you only want to retain risk where there is no affordable alternative, or where the risk is slight enough or spreadable enough (if you have nine stores, the likelihood of their all being robbed the same week is extremely slight) that you can certainly afford the loss.

Two alternatives to risk retention are *coinsurance* and *self-insurance*. *Coinsurance* means you share the risk with your insurer. Most business property insurance policies automatically involve coinsurance: that is, even after the value of your lost property has been determined, the insurance company will pay you only a percentage of that value, usually 80 or 90%. Where there are formal coinsurance clauses, it is essential that you use them as key elements of your comparison shopping. Obviously, a 90% coverage is worth far more than an otherwise comparable 80% policy.

Beyond formal coinsurance, you are informally coinsuring any time you carry less than full value coverage. Sometimes this is sensible. If, for example, you are using an ornate 1920's building for a warehouse, but would be just as happy with a cheaper modern structure, you might want to insure for the lower *use* value of the building, rather than its replacement cost.

Self-insurance is the process of retaining some part of your company's earnings or net worth to cover losses or liabilities. Where this is to replace some type of legally mandated insurance, it will be subject to governmental supervision, but even then it *can* be done. Some forms of self-insurance—*bad debt reserves,* for example —can be used to shelter income from taxes.

Various other economic arguments have been made in favor of self-insurance, including the avoidance of insurance-company mark-ups. Personally, I'm reluctant to see it. The real danger is *general liability self-insurance,* because then a pending lawsuit can so obscure a business's net worth as to make it unsaleable. Some years ago, we were asked to try to sell a fast-growing, multi-state car-rental firm. Unfortunately, during the preceding years of high profits, someone had decided to retain cash by self-insuring all the cars. That worked fine, until a single accident produced some $3,000,000.00 in lawsuits. Since that roughly approximated the net worth of the whole company, there was no possibility of completing a sale until the litigation was settled—some two or two-and-a-half years later.

RISK REDUCTION. Whatever kind of insurance you adopt, you have a vested interest in risk reduction. In fact, I've known many a small businessperson to develop a passion for risk reduction. The reason,

I think, is simple. Insurance is a financial necessity; risk reduction (especially where human lives are involved) is a moral imperative. There's satisfaction in knowing you've made your workplace safer for those around you. Once you begin, you'll see what I mean.

You can get helpful pamphlets on risk reduction from most major insurance companies or from the SBA. More personal help will come from people in your own field: try trade associations, SCORE, or even one of your competitors. Consultants—usually safety engineers or professional claims adjustors—can constitute money well spent. The simplest steps you took while walking through. Other tips follow below.

· Arrange machinery to provide maximum clear space commensurate with efficiency.

· Check daily to see that paths are kept clear, emergency exits are unlocked, and that rubbish—especially flammable rubbish—has been carted off the grounds.

· Make sure safety equipment (medical kits, fire extinguishers, etc.) is in working order, and don't hesitate to spend money for new and better models. See that emergency numbers are posted by every phone.

· Hold frequent safety meetings, and, if you have quality control circles, make workplace safety the subject of both solicited ideas and direct instruction.

· Consider a small bonus for one or more employees to enroll in a certified first-aid course.

· Keep production schedules reasonable. When you overwork people, either by demanding too many hours, or by pushing them to work too fast, accident rates skyrocket.

· Don't let obviously unwell or overmedicated people work around machinery—the risk is too great. (For that matter, such people are likely to make financial errors too.) Better to send them home, or give them harmless work, for the day.

· Risks which cannot be reduced, should at least be clearly labelled. Put warning and "keep out" signs everywhere they are appropriate—bilingual signs, if necessary. Write cautions into your instruction manuals—and affix them to your products, if appropriate. As a matter of self-interest, write "hold harmless" and "limited liability" clauses into your contracts and warranties wherever you can.

Combine these suggestions with those in SECURITY, plus the results of your own walk-through and thought experiments, and you will be well on your way to a workable risk-reduction program. Remember, too, the practical benefits of risk reduction. A safer company has a better chance of making a "contributory negligence" defense against liability, because the victim is likely at least partly responsible for his own troubles. Some risk-reduction efforts will produce direct insurance savings. The presence of a night watchman, for example, should earn you a discount on both your theft- and fire premiums. If your broker doesn't mention these options, get another broker.

Buying Insurance.

That brings us to the last part of the program. Even businesses with strong, ongoing risk reduction programs will always need a fair amount of insurance. How do you buy it without getting stung?

1. Complete your risk-analysis before you start shopping; know your special needs. If you are just starting out, take a look at the general business insurance with the best "comprehensive liability" section: for simple start-up companies, a well-chosen basic plan may do the job—at least initially.

2. Deal with an experienced *broker,* not a salesman. Use specialists (in health, liability, etc.) even if that means using 2 or more brokers.

Ideally, you want a broker with previous experience with businesses like yours. He should have clear knowledge of the typical risks, and a proven record of helpfulness when claims have been filed. Get recommendations from trade associations, competitors, independent adjustors.

3. The broker should have a range of policies to show you, and speak knowledgeably about their differences. He should be the one to compare their relative exclusions, breadths of coverage, etc.

He should be willing to look as far as necessary to find the coverage you need. It's not unknown for a small business to need twenty or more separate policies under some conditions.

It's good if your broker at least considers policies from some of the newer insurance companies specializing in small business policies. Some of the best of these were founded in the late '60s and '70s by small business owners (or groups of owners) who could not get the coverage they needed from the majors. Today, they are providing other entrepreneurs with some of the finest insurance available.

4. Shop comparatively, among as many qualified brokers as possible. Expect from each one an on-site inspection, and a written report of recommendations, before making your decision.

You are looking not only for the best price, but for the most detailed analysis, the report which uncovers risks you had missed in your own search. Give least credit to the report which simply recommends a standard "broad-coverage" policy from a major company. As already noted, if you've got a simple start-up operation, one of these might serve, but it's still likely to have gaps, and it won't tolerate much growth. The broker who proposes it won't have done much work.

The insurance industry unfortunately lacks rigorous licensing or training requirements: while some salespeople are superb, many are simply hot-shots hired to move a lot of paper. One recommendation is qualification as a Chartered Property and Casualty Underwriter—although many of the finest independent brokers and agents will lack the needed coursework. With any broker or agent, beware the usual salesman's tricks of excess joviality or personalization (it's none of his concern how your kids are doing in school), or the old reverse psychology of trying to talk you out of a policy *he's* just proposed.

Resist the policy which offers too many obscure coverages—these usually mean either gravy for the insurance company, or a cover-up for gaps in more important coverage. This is why you do your own initial risk analysis—so you'll know what's worth buying. Check and double-check any exclusions.

Watch the start-up dates of policies. They should be written with binders, to come into effect the minute you come into ownership of the business. At least once, I've seen a showplace restaurant burn down the day the escrow closed. Remember that accidents are more likely when you first assume a new operation than at any other time.

Check the cancellation clauses carefully. Any legitimate insurer will guarantee you at least thirty days' notice before cancellation —enough time for your broker to seek a replacement. If you ever *are* cancelled, find out why. Sometimes, your broker misreported something to the insurer. Sometimes a minor change in your operation will get coverage restored. Sometimes, the insurer is simply leaving the field—in which case, ask the reason. If too many insurers begin dropping the coverage you need, that's a sign that the risk, or litigation, picture is deteriorating. It may be time for you to consider getting out, too.

Whatever broker or brokers you choose, be sure to get *certificates of insurance,* which make the *broker's* insurance liable for any losses *you* suffer from his accidental errors or omissions.

The broker's insurance won't cover you if you forget to mail in a premium check, so track *insurance renewal dates.* The best brokerages will send you renewal notices in plenty of time, but mistakes happen. Keep an *Insurance Calender,* and don't ever let needed coverage lapse.

Your broker should have a policy of frequent (say, semi-annual) reviews of coverage, including on-site visits. Automatic inflation adjustments are fine for a house, but make little sense for a changing, growing small business. Moreover, getting people onto your property will help if you ever later need to verify a claim for losses.

The amount of coverage you need depends upon your particular business, of course, but remember it's cheaper to raise the coverage limit than to lower the deductible. Low (or zero) deductible arrangements cost the most. Since you are paying quite a high percentage for insurance protection, most experts tell you to insure only for the losses you can't afford to sustain; a $1000 deductible makes more sense than one for $100. When you set your limits for liability, whether for $500,000, $1,000,000, or more, be sure you do it on a *per-claim* rather than *per-occurrence* basis. One incident can produce half-a-dozen or more separate claims.

Filing a Claim.

The real test of your insurance comes with the first claim you file. Some experts suggest that you should suffer minor losses quietly rather than risk having your rates raised or your policy cancelled. The counterpoint is that a minor claim will help you judge the quality of your insurers. If they try to squirm out of a small claim, what will they do when you have *real* trouble? It might be worth your time and money to see just how reliable they are.

When you file a claim for losses—especially where something as changeable as inventory is involved—you will need to provide documentation of your losses. In nearly every case, the insurer (quite willing to settle before you know your full losses), will immediately dispatch a company claims adjustor. You want to work *with* him, but not let him dictate the final claim. After all, you know far more about what was lost than he does. Resist that quick settlement; instead, start in immediately getting contractors' and repairmen's *estimates* of what work is going to be needed. If you're going to need time to file your claim—if a manufacturer in Georgia can't quote a replacement cost for another six weeks—that's fine. Just make sure the adjustor understands your problems, so he in turn can explain matters to his office. Otherwise, he'll get a lot of flack, and you'll be suspected of "cooking the data"—filing an inflated claim. Allow time for all your losses to become apparent.

If you can't get the kind of cooperation you expect from the company's adjustor, you can hire a public claims adjustor, who will charge you a negotiable percentage of the claim—or, occasionally, a flat hourly rate. Albert Lowry, in a strong chapter on "Insuring Your Business" (please see this book's BIBLIOGRAPHY), makes the interesting suggestion that you cultivate insurance adjustors in advance, inviting them periodically to examine changes in your operation. I've never known any small businesspeople to do this, but—if you have the time and the contacts—doing so would make a great deal of sense.

Finally, remember that an uninsured casualty loss can be taken off your taxes—if you have the records, and bring them to your accountant's attention when tax-time rolls around.

All of this should suggest why most medium-sized businesses, and many smaller ones, have one or more part- or full-time insurance managers on their payroll. Well before reaching that stage, though, you should already have begun a careful program of risk- and insurance management. At the very least, keep in mind:

1. Insurance is a complex legal and financial product, meant to blend retention, reduction, and insurance of risk, and to be analyzed with the help of your attorney and CPA.
2. All programs are ongoing, changing as business changes.
3. Insurance should be bought from a brokerage competent to handle your kind of business—and not from the first smooth talker who walks through the door.

14
SECURITY AND SAFETY

SITUATION:
Operating a business requires protecting it from criminals and competitors alike
OBJECTIVE:
Achieving safety and security at reasonable cost, and without *destroying the pleasure of being in business*

Checkpoint Charlie: How *Not* to Do Business.

Some years ago, I had the chance to examine a business—a liquor store—set up according to what some experts thought was going to be "the plan for the '70s." This particular store was in a custom-designed building of cinder-blocks, built on a small artificial rise. The land surrounding it was cleared as a field-of-fire, metal sheeting reinforced the door, and anti-intrusion grills covered the two small windows. The building itself was mustard yellow, but had been painted over with block-lettered black signs saying "No loitering within fifty feet." "Warning: Employees of this store are armed." It looked like the East German army was trying to run a Speedy 7-11.

The store owner, of course, only wanted to protect himself from the kinds of armed robberies which are far too common these days, yet his efforts had nearly ruined his business. He couldn't keep employees, his customers were almost all scared away by the intimations of violence, and he himself was turning anxious and depressed by working in an armed camp. He brought us in to sell the business off, but without success. Potential buyers would take one look at this mini-Stalag and turn and head the other way.

The point of this is obvious but important. When you design for the safety and security of your business, you've got to counterbalance your plans with the need to make a place of business attractive to your clients or customers, and pleasing to yourself and your employees.

That is not to say you can ignore the dangers of crime. At the very start, you must realize that no part of the country is automatically safe. Not long ago, I was living in the sort of quiet, upper-class neighborhood where nothing ever happens—except that a few days before I moved away, two men walked into the tiny local jewelry store, demanded some loot, and then forced the owner into the back room, and let him have it with a sawed-off shotgun.

Blue-Collar or Street Crime:

OK—everyone has his share of horror stories. Even if these armed crimes don't represent the greatest *financial* threat to business, they are still the ones that worry us most. The ruthlessness of American small criminals—their willingness to take lives over seemingly trivial amounts of money, is a source of national shame. Still, short of turning your place into a fortress, and handing out M-16's to all your employees, what can you reasonably do?

Actually, quite a lot. Before you shop for antitank guns, consider the following:

1. In the first place, if the insurance companies are right, those sealed-up fortresses of stores might be going at things backwards. The safest stores, it seems, are well-lit and offer clear lines-of-sight from the street all the way to the back of the store. Don't turn your business into a hand-built dark alley. Criminals don't want to be on TV, and they don't want to be visible from the street. Most new convenience stores, for example, put their cashiers right up front. Anyone robbing them will be out in public.

Lines-of-sight are crucial. Don't get in the habit of stacking stock up in the front of the store (an old retailer's trick to make it look like business is booming, or a hot sale's going on.) Neither should you leave promotional posters (or those cultural announcements some businesses post as a courtesy) stuck up blocking windows after dark.

2. Create as much motion as possible in a store. That means not letting your salespeople look like they're asleep at the switch. Just like muggers, armed robbers will generally go after anyone who looks feeble or off-guard.

It's a good idea if you're planning to be open after dark to run some inexpensive promotions to keep up floor traffic—a lot of small stores, for example, give away free coffee and make a point of inviting the local police to drop in for a cup anytime.

3. Carry *absolutely* as little cash as possible. Make your bank deposits daily; if possible, see that your salespeople deposit excess cash immediately in an on-premise safe for which they do not have the key. (Deposits are made through a one-way slot.) Make sure that your low-cash policy is *clearly* posted on the premises.

4. Many fine business writers have commended the program of the Southland Corporation (parent of the 6750 Speedy 7-11 Stores) for its innovative studies of the psychology and sociology of armed crime. I asked Jerry Lowery, Sr., the man who launched the 7-11 program in 1973, for some parts of the Southland plan which could be adopted by the average small businessperson. Here are the highlights:

A. After removing the window obstructions, train your clerks to watch the street for anyone parked outside too long; have them phone the police if it seems the store's being "cased."

B. Except when completing a transaction, clerks should stay *away* from the cash register. Registers belong up near the front of the store, but 7-11s studies showed an armed robber can use that to his advantage: if the clerk's right at the register, a gunman can step into the store, demand the cash, and be gone in under twenty seconds. If, instead, the clerk is dusting a shelf fifteen feet away, the gunman will need a minute or more to pull him to the register and then clean out the drawer: the extra time makes a patrol car arrest far more likely.

C. For even more protection than the standard locked drop-safe provides, consider the (more expensive) electronic safes which dispense rolls of change (but not bills) at preset intervals. If your clerk needs a role of quarters, he can get one—but then can't get another for, say, two hours. You get flexibility and safety. Southland was so impressed with these, it bought the company, Tidel, that makes them.

D. Teach clerks to recognize and deal with the "culture of violence." Nearly all the crime victims Southland interviewed said they had known they were about to be robbed. If you (or a clerk) has a bad feeling about someone, the proper thing to do is to *immediately* strike up a conversation. Even better, Jerry Lowery says, is to hail the person by name—any name. You can always apologize, by saying, "Sorry, but you're the spitting image of my friend Joe Blow." The potential crook will probably pass you by, because he knows you've got his picture clearly in mind. And you've been friendly, not confrontational.

E. A big one: Southland studies have shown that, because inexperienced young people commit most armed robbery, the *victim* actually has a period of roughly ten seconds after the money has been handed over *during which he or she can take charge of the situation.* During those ten seconds of uncertainty, you must suggest nonviolent ways to end the confrontation: "What should I do now? Should I lie down on the floor, or do you want me to go into the back room?" Don't give orders, make suggestions—but show the fellow with the gun there's a resolution which doesn't involve your getting shot. Southland's research suggests this is crucial: otherwise, a young man wanting to prove his toughness to his peers is too likely to pull the trigger.

F. Jerry Lowery is so opposed to the general use of handguns that, even though he's a firearms expert himself, he won't carry one simply because it sets a dangerous example. The chances of your using a gun effectively are very small; the chance of your getting pistolwhipped by a robber who frisks you and finds you armed, are excellent. (The discussion of firearms on the following pages is included for the sake of full information. But do consider the advice of Jerry Lowery, and of most other experts.) Southland limits each store to a maximum of $30 in accessible cash; why risk anyone's life for that?

Over the past six years, Southland has reduced armed robbery in its stores by an astounding 64%—and today, fewer than 2% of all Southland robberies result in injuries of any sort. Achieved during an era of skyrocketing crime, and put across without either high-tech gadgetry (except for the electronic safes) or confrontational violence, the program deserves the highest possible praise. Southland's security people sponsor frequent seminars, lectures, and demonstrations: if you have the chance, check one out.

5. To discourage thieves (who go after property, not people), you need to keep all goods under close control. That means keeping people out of your storage areas, and excess goods away from high-traffic areas. Above all, watch receiving and unloading areas. Discourage not only loiterers but passersby. Try to schedule deliveries for early in the day, and make sure everything you receive is safely inside under lock and key before the business day ends: don't leave loaded trucks or goods stacked on loading docks as easy targets. If deliveries are frequent, or more than one or two trucks will be there are a time, consider a locked and guarded yard: insurance company studies have shown this to be the very best security going. Your clerks won't be able to watch everything at once; sometimes, they'll be distracted by one group and ripped off by another. Modern industrial parks are often built with this kind of security in mind, but if you are working from an old plant—

especially in an older, downtown area with narrow streets, lots of alleys, and a great deal of traffic—you can have your delivery slots designed with foam exclusion bumpers which keep anyone from getting on the blind side of your trucks (that is, putting the truck itself between your people and their escape path.) If you're located in one of those old, tough neighborhoods, where hijackings and dock rip-offs are common—and if you can't get help from the community, your best security measure might simply be to move.

6. Invest in reasonable *passive* security measures. Good locks are essential. Security screens on warehouse windows should be of high quality. Security paints (which stain, often with fluorescent dyes, the clothing of anyone who comes over your fences) work fairly well, and are more pleasing to regular customers than barbed wire. Anti-intrusion chain link will at least keep out pranksters and casual vandals.

7. Develop good relations, and a general anticrime plan, with other businessmen in the neighborhood. When that jewelry store owner in my old neighborhood was shot, a fellow from the real estate office next door ran over to ask what was wrong. One of the gunmen told him there was no problem, and he went back to his own office. When the police finally showed up, he wasn't even able to give a usable description. His *instincts* were right, but he lacked proper training.

The more people participating in your cooperative self-defense program, the better. You need to get to know the police in your neighborhood, and to engage their help in designing your plan. If possible, involve other people in your community in the program as well. Your regular customers should know what to do in case of problems, and you can also work out a set of signals for letting people know you are in trouble.

Further Measures.

Those are the basic, inexpensive steps every business should take. After those, we come to two more difficult questions. The first is spending on more expensive systems, and the second, the really tough one, is the matter of *active* defensive measures.

You should shop for more sophisticated anticrime equipment with great care: a lot of it is less useful, or more complicated, than many people realize. Remember that the market is fragmented, and only a few, larger, companies have the money to develop first-rate gear. Automatic cameras are time-tested and effective; some small businesses get away with simply buying the shells of the cameras and mounting them on scanning platforms, which may deter at least the small-time crook. Most of those tape-on-glass alarms, on the other hand, or the systems which simply run circuits across door locks, are easily bridged; they won't deter even semiskilled thieves.

More useful (and more expensive) are systems using ultrasonics, pressure detectors, and infrared photo-electrics. Remember that *any* system needs to both detect intruders and notify authorities. If your unit is not tied to a central dispatch station, its effectiveness (beyond scaring intruders off) will depend upon a passing patrol car or a good citizen. Tying your unit into a central station *is* more costly (aside from installation, you'll pay a monthly dispatcher's fee, with total cost around $100 to $150 a month), but makes a great deal of sense. If you do choose to use one, make sure the dispatcher (like all of your own hardware) meets Underwriters' Laboratories standards. Be sure, too, to pick up the service contract on *any* alarm system you buy. At around $35 a month (and up), it is obviously essential insurance.

You will find alarm systems available from $50 or so for (not very useful) kits, up to several thousand dollars. Choose yours *according to the value of what you are protecting,* and without any regard to the "safety" of your neighborhood.

ACTIVE DEFENSIVE MEASURES. Active defensive measures are those which will, one way or another, *do* something to intruders. The most obvious three are guards, guard dogs, and weapons.

Guards are often hired right at the minimum wage, although if you go through an agency, the fees are naturally higher. The problem, of course, is in finding trustworthy people to do the job.

Each of the big three in the business—Burns, Pinkerton, and Wackenhut—claims to screen its people carefully, but in general the only *legally* required qualification for a security guard is that he not have been convicted of a felony. That's hardly iron-clad security, so use care before letting anyone have the run of your establishment alone at night.

Guard dogs seem to have vogues of popularity. Dogs are hardy and active, and are often used to guard, for example, expensive-car dealerships. They *do* frighten off vandals and sightseers, and they'll never steal from you, but remember some of the problems. A serious intruder will shoot or poison them. Too, dogs are difficult to train and relatively expensive, even if you are paying monthly fees to a guard dog service. If you do want animals, you want *guard,* not attack dogs. It is enough if they scare off or corner an intruder, without mauling him. If you're training your own, consider one of the guard breeds (Briards, for example) which instinctively knock intruders down instead of biting them. Otherwise, the likelihood of hurting a policeman, a fireman, or one of your own customers is too great.

Weapons. Probably the most natural first response of any victim of crime is to want to get a weapon—especially a gun—and to lie in waiting for the next SOB who tries the same thing. It may be a natural response, but bear in mind that arming yourself or your employees raises a whole set of moral, legal, and practical questions.

The moral questions I will not presume to touch. The legal questions are more complex than you may realize, and you would be wise to discuss the legal situation in your state with a lawyer. English Common Law once recognized a principle of "wall or ditch," which allowed you to use violent means to defend yourself once you had retreated until you could retreat no farther. Nothing like that remains in use today. Between the liberality of a state like Texas, and the rigor of a city like New York, even your right to own a handgun varies from region to region. In California, for example, you need a license to conceal a weapon—and concealment can mean as little as placing it in a glove compartment. Beyond criminal liability if you start blazing away, there is the possibility (nearly incredible, but quite real) that the fellow you plug will turn around and sue you.

At a minimum, then, before you consider firearms for a business, you *must:*

1. Carefully inquire into your legal rights and responsibilities. Acquire any necessary licenses, for anyone who will be in a position to use those weapons.

2. Choose weapons with intelligence, and with an idea of their ultimate function. It's a dreadful idea that you might have to shoot another human being; it's an even worse prospect to think you might have to defend yourself with something that won't do the job.

3. *Get proper training for anyone who might be called upon to shoot.* You need training in gun safety, gun maintenance, and marksmanship, and if you let anyone lacking those skills—or anyone you suspect of emotional instability—get their hands on firearms, you are a menace.

4. Consider the moral issues involved. Having used firearms is something you'll live with your entire life. Equally to the point, you don't want to draw on someone and then discover you haven't the will to shoot. If they're armed, you're probably dead. As far as possible, decide under what conditions you'll use a gun.

5. Consider the *practical* difficulties. Remember that you'll need a great deal of luck to actually get the drop on anyone. It's far more likely that passive measures—the kind that keep gunmen out of your store, or improve the chances of a quick police response—will work. If a handgun makes you so overconfident that you neglect passive measures, it represents a clear net loss of security.

Just one last tip: never think you can solve your crime problems with a little dose of pure machismo. Many years ago, we were asked to sell a liquor store for a man who had been held up at gunpoint twice in the preceding two months. Not only had he been armed from the day he opened, but he was at that time a star player for the San Diego professional football team. We had to advise him to sell off the stock and the license, and just board the business up. If the people in his neighborhood weren't afraid of a pro cornerback who kept a .45 under the counter, who were we going to find as a buyer? Conan the Barbarian?

Shoplifters.

Shoplifting is, in practical terms, far more likely to ruin a business than is outright armed robbery. If, in a normal neighborhood, you are robbed more than once during a year, it would be odd. But shoplifters will hit you day in and day out. It's like being nibbled to death by ducks. Remember that on average you will need to sell about six of any given item to make up your losses on any *one* that's stolen. If you're in a low-margin business, the replacement ratio is that much higher.

Shoplifting can probably never be stopped entirely, but you should early on pursue at least the following:

1. Announce, post, and follow through upon, a program of prosecuting shoplifters. Remember that shoplifters are often from middle- and even upper-class families, and that you may face all sorts of blandishments not to prosecute. Stick to your program. Don't worry about ruining some young person's life. The courts almost never jail first offenders, and in the long run, a young person will suffer more from a false belief that crimes go entirely unpunished.

2. Stay alert to the traditional danger signals. Beware of people who wander too long without buying, lingering before costly items, but drifting away from your employees. Be doubly alert if these people are wearing loose-fitting clothes, keeping their arms too carefully against their sides, or acting unduly nervous. See that purchases made, and then carried, within the store are bagged and stapled shut *with receipts attached.* Always have a manager visible near the checkouts—say at a "customer service" stand.

Concentrate your surveillance intelligently. According to the

Christian Science Monitor (see below), almost 50% of all shoplifting takes place in the space of just thirty days, between Thanksgiving and Christmas each year. During this period, an average of *50,000* people a day will be caught shoplifting. By doubling your security just one month a year, you could conceivably cut shoplifting losses in half.

3. Keep expensive items under glass or otherwise controlled (as by use of locking hangers for clothes, or in wall cases in back of counters, watched by clerks). Control the number of items any customer may examine at one time. If they want to examine five different pocket computers, fine—but only one or two at a time.

4. Make sure that at least some of your people keep in continual motion, to make it that much harder for your operation to be cased. The impression of an alert staff is worth at least as much as those gimmicky solutions like having nonexistent security officers paged by the public address system.

5. If your volume is sufficiently large to justify it, hire undercover people or employ electromagnetic tagging systems. Remember, though, that the tags also require someone to make the arrests, either you, or a professional security person. If you do have to make the arrest, remember to make it outside the store, and to act in as polite and nonthreatening a manner as possible. You want to avoid noise or violence, and to diminish the danger of getting yourself charged with anything like false arrest.

In 1981, a fine *Christian Science Monitor* article, " 'Tis the Season to Deck the Shelves—and Guard against Shoplifters," profiled a group called Shoplifters Anonymous International. According to SAI, almost 75% of all shoplifters (especially during the holiday season) are "soft core" criminals, essentially honest people overwhelmed by a desire to provide gifts for friends and family. Partly by warning these people of their legal risks, and partly by teaching them how to observe an old-fashioned, home-made Christmas, SAI was able to reform the great majority of shoplifters sent to it. Only one person out of every 100 referred to SAI was ever rearrested. I'm usually a hardliner on crime, but these Christmastime shoplifters are surely a special case. You might well urge your local court to develop an SAI-type program. It seems more humane (as well as more economical) than simply jailing people who may have been wrong but were hardly wicked. Remember, though, that even reform begins with the arrest.

As with most crime prevention programs, what you want to do is to make it known that you are not a target of opportunity. You don't want to pursue the problem past the point of diminishing returns, but the first four points above are all highly cost efficient for even the smallest firm.

White-Collar Crime.

According to Laventhol & Horwath, the giant accounting firm, white collar crime is expected to cost American business $250 *billion* annually by 1990. Even the 1980 figure—50 billion—absolutely dwarfs the comparable costs for violent crime (L & H *Perspective,* No. 1, 1982). White collar crime is, in general, crime committed by manipulation of financial data. It can be in conjunction with theft, like the clerk who runs through phony credit slips or billing orders so his friend can walk off with a new bicycle, or it can be simple manipulation of funds and accounts. Preventing it outright will probably require the help of an outside accounting firm, which can 1) identify trouble areas, and 2) (if necessary) recommend detective- or industrial security firms to help you crack down on specific offenders. Even before reaching that stage, you should be alert for any of these danger signals:

1. Inordinate inventory "shrinkage" or losses to "damaged merchandise."

2. Undue consistency in your company's suppliers. If your list of suppliers doesn't show at least the traditional 20% annual turnover rate—a bit higher for high-tech fields, a bit lower for mature ones—then your buyer may have established "kickback" or other collusive arrangements. The same holds true for any pattern of accepting merchandise from obviously second-rate firms, or for which you've had an inordinate number of complaints.

Anyone in a position to do buying for you will receive a fair number of "Christmas presents." You can't stop these outright, but you can suggest a maximum dollar value—and make sure they aren't arriving in May, June, and July as well. If necessary, you can provide a compensatory Christmas bonus of your own. You want employees to know who they are working for.

3. Any employee who consistently refuses to take vacations or sickleave. You may simply have a workaholic on your hands, or you may have someone with something to hide—something a replacement worker would be likely to detect.

4. Any department or aspect of your business which does a large amount of cash business. What many small businessmen do to Uncle Sam, your employees may be doing to you. (Occasionally I've been told that a key employee—perhaps a popular bartender at a successful restaurant—is stealing, say, a steady 5% of the gross, but that he is too valuable to lose. If that's how you feel, fine. But make sure you know what's going on.) The simplest way to spot these small-time crooks, by the way, is to watch for the fellow who doesn't close the cash register after every transaction. If he's dealing straight from the cash drawer, the odds are he's helping himself to some of the owner's profits.

5. Any distant warehouse or depot over which you have limited supervision. Periodic inspections are essential, or you can find the place has been sold out from under you.

6. Any one person with sole access to the company computer system. (Please see Chapter 19). More and more major accounting firms are developing computer audit software: at the very least, make sure you have someone there you absolutely trust.

7. Any employee with apparent personal problems, especially a problem with gambling. A part of your company health program should be set up to deal with emotional problems; at least you can steer anyone with a problem to a community counseling program —and meanwhile, see that he or she is closely supervised, and given only moderate work.

In general, your best protection requires a two-part program. First, you need a widespread effort to see that your employees are happy with their work and feel that they matter to the company. Second, you need a set of cross-checks so that no one person has complete control over any major part of the business, purchasing, selling, or accounting. Folk wisdom says that the unhappy employee is the most likely white collar criminal. Sometimes that's true. But it's also often true that you're being cheated by someone with the strongest reasons for gratitude, someone motivated simply by greed. That's why you need both the incentives to loyalty, and the cross-checking systems.

A Special Reminder. If you ever have to terminate anyone with access to the computer center, be certain you 1) get their keys immediately, 2) deny them any further access to the center, except to pick up personal belongings and then only under escort, and 3) have all the center locks changed that day (in case a duplicate key was made). As covered in Chapter 19, computer sabotage is one of the few things which can absolutely destroy a company overnight.

Part II: Security.

Along with these precautions against white-collar and street crimes, you will also need to guard yourself against the loss of valuable information to competitors. You don't want a raving mania for security, just a plan to reduce the obvious risks.

Nearly any business has at least *some* information worth protecting, even if only the details of a forthcoming sale or promotion, or the proposed site of a new outlet, or the name of a low-cost supplier of some important item. For many small businesses, that means only exercising secrecy on a few occasions and for short periods of time. But for other, higher technology or more competitive firms, security has to become a way of life.

PERSONNEL. Of all the ways sensitive information leaves your firm, the easiest is for one of your own people to simply walk out the door with it. A close second—and probably even more galling —is for one of them simply to give the information away through ignorance or carelessness.

Rarely can you stop people from leaving with what they can carry in their heads. Except for a few specific items—patented processes, research for which they have already abandoned their claim, and so on—people have traditionally been allowed by the courts to leave a firm with whatever they have learned. Consider the case of Activision, the video-game software company started by a group of former Atari employees. Activision reached some $50 million in annualized sales virtually overnight, and its first products were all Atari-compatible game cartridges. Atari went into court to get them to desist, but ultimately won only a modest compromise. Activision remained very successfully in business.

Even if your legal rights to prevent people from leaving with information (hardware is, of course, another matter), are limited, you can still take some steps to control your losses:

1. Provide information on a "need to know" basis. People will be less likely to pass along information if they have to work to get their hands on it. If they work too obviously, perhaps you'll catch them.

2. Impress upon your people the harm that can be done by idle talk. Many leaks are caused by people who never knew there was a reason *not* to talk.

Make sure, too, that your salespeople know how not to give away the store. Often, if you're selling high-priced services, a good half of your "buyer inquiries" will just be fishing expeditions by people looking for free information so they can set up an in-house operation.

3. Include a "trade secrets" clause in your employment contracts. Even allowing for the difficulty of prosecuting, a written promise to protect certain *specified* elements of your operation will give at least a beginning ground for legal action.

4. Control documents. Important information should exist in only a finite number of copies, and away from photocopying equipment. (See below). If you terminate someone, collect their copies of all important documents *at once.* Even people out for revenge will have trouble relying on unassisted memories. Don't make it easy for them.

5. Perhaps best of all, consider bringing key idea people into a profit-sharing, or even a partnership, role. This is the surest way of keeping their abilities permanently with the company—and of eliminating the dangers of defection.

Most people will suffer very little unreasonable overseeing. Just establish a livable policy, and try not to vary it much. Remember, too, that having the competition catch up with your old tricks is sometimes the best incentive to inventing better new ones. I've even known people who have developed an improved way of doing business to quietly "leak" their old method to the competition. It can't hurt to try.

Industrial Espionage.

A whole industry exists to help you keep documents and other hard items out of the hands of competitors. Some of the equipment meant to foil industrial spying is quite modest, and some of it—like hand-geometry identification systems or the antiphotocopying paper which fluoresces under bright light—is suited only to the most competitive of high-technology fields. More basic precautions include paper shredders and the use of high-security, multistrike typewriter ribbons like IBM Tech III: the film ribbons of IBM (and comparable) correcting typewriters can be read back by anyone with sufficient patience. Beyond that, you begin reaching towards antibugging equipment (I was recently shown a bug-detecting belt buckle, for example), computerized card-entry systems, and so on.

PROCEDURES. However limited your initial budget for security hardware, you ought to consider the following *procedures:*

1. Control *outflow* of documents and samples. Keep itemized lists of important documents mailed out to clients. Keep these giveaways at a minimum—it's wiser to have a conference room set aside where they can come in to see them. A cover letter should stress the confidentiality of anything important you send out.

Remember that often salespeople from the competition will be more than willing to borrow anything you've left with potential clients—just to work up a comparison, of course.

2. Do as much printing as possible in-house. Printing shops are a common place for leaks. If you do go out-of-house, be sure you recover not only all copies, but all the plates, dittos, negatives, etc., used in the printing.

3. Resist giving any information on trade secrets to the government. Under the current Freedom of Information Act, anything you give the government (unless it involves national security) can be had by your competition just for the trouble of filing an inquiry.

(As I write, the Freedom of Information Act is under review, but be sure to inquire about it if you ever must deal with government inspectors. If it hasn't been amended by the time you read this, write your Congressman and tell him it should be.)

In addition, avoid tipping your hand on announcements which must eventually become public. Aim to make announcements soon enough that you get optimum publicity, but late enough that your competitors cannot react effectively. The worst procedure is to announce a new product before it is ready for release, fail to bring it out on time, damage your reputation, and give your competition an idea to follow up on.

The first thing you can do is to defer as long as legally possible any required publishings or filings. Obviously, you must do whatever the law requires in such matters as building permits. But you can still execute a little discreet disguising. If your company is Buzzard Al's Pizzerias, for example, there is no reason to buy up land or take construction bids under that name. Try calling your real estate wing something like "Hawkesworth Real Properties, Ltd."—and let your competitors at least hustle a little to discover where you're opening your next spot.

The next thing to do, where appropriate, is to get the cooperation of your suppliers. If you sign a big contract of a sort which will tip your competitors off to your plans, you can still require the suppliers to keep the deal silent for, say, ninety days. They'll want to publicize their own success, of course, but they can wait a reasonable time before doing so.

Remember—every day you can keep the competition from following your new idea is a day you have the market to yourself. With hard work, a short lead can turn into permanent market dominance.

High-Tech Security.

Security in high-technology fields is often complicated by the tiny size of valuable products. From the early days of genetic research comes a famous story of a research team trying to acquire a sample of a kind of virus, called a bacteriophage, which attacked only bacterial cells. When the director of the competing lab refused them, they simply sent a second request addressed to him at his lab. He immediately sat down and penned an angry second denial at his lab bench. The research team then calmly took this second note and ground it up in a Waring blender—and extracted their bacteriophage sample. Like everyone else in his lab, the director had been well coated with the little phages (harmless to humans), and had in turn thoroughly contaminated his own stationary.

As that story suggests, when you enter high-tech fields, you are almost certainly committing yourself to the use of both professional industrial-security firms and a great deal of patent-law litigation. Indeed, I once heard an electronics firm executive, whose company was spending more money defending its products in court than developing them, claim that his company was really run like a law firm with a sideline in communications technology. Perhaps the story also suggests why high-tech, research oriented firms (like Cetus and Genentech) have such huge capital requirements for such small manufacturing bases. If you want to get involved in high-tech products—and if you lack *very* deep pockets —you are almost certainly better off beginning by refining and repackaging someone else's fundamental research. This was the original strategy of Apple, and of many other "begun in a garage" high-tech firms.

If you do decide to try a high-tech business, remember there is a philosophical conflict between the business need for security and the American scientific tradition of free exchange and publication of research data. It's hardly an impossible problem—Bell Labs has managed to average about one patent a day over its fifty-seven years of existence, while still winning seven Nobel Prizes for research—but you *will* need to work out an intelligent compromise, especially with any academic scientists you place under contract. Otherwise, you may find your top-secret new product plastered on some graduate student's poster at a national conference.

Foreign Travel/Terrorism.

By and large—except for a brief period in the early '70s, and scattered incidents since—Americans have been spared the horrors of terrorism found in many places abroad. Still, since experts persist in warning that we will not remain exempt forever, and since American businessmen abroad have been targets in the past, here are a few of the basic precautions you might consider:

1. Avoid devices which draw attention to you, or which in any way make you easy to identify in public. This means no outlandish automobiles, and even (if you take the program seriously) no vanity license plates.

2. Avoid any publicity about your personal life. Keep out of the social pages, and *especially* keep your travel plans out of the press. See that your office provides only vague information on your whereabouts to unidentified callers.

3. Avoid establishing a fixed daily routine. Vary your routes to and from work (one of the smartest real estate investors I know has been doing this daily for thirty-five years, and claims to have spotted some of his shrewdest investment opportunities during his daily digressive commutes), and avoid settling on one particular restaurant for your usual lunches or dinners.

4. Avoid publicizing any connection or interest you might have with any foreign country or ethnic group. Whatever you do (within the law) is of course your business, but there are potential risks in drawing too much publicity to your association with any entity which has been an object of terrorist attack.

5. Consider at least minimal electronic home security. Here you need a system which automatically alerts a central dispatcher. Nearly all the lag time in police response stems from citizen unwillingness to use 911 numbers—a gap eliminated by dispatcher-tied units.

6. If you intend to travel to a country with known antibusiness terrorism, you can dress down to the occasion. Assuming your credentials precede you, you won't need to impress anyone on arrival. A few American businessmen abroad have even taken to wearing blue jeans and staying in *pensiones* to keep from drawing attention to themselves.

Responsibility and Social Action.

This book has emphasized aggressive action, because aggressive action is fundamental to business success. Remember, though, that the problem of crime cannot be solved solely by digging in or hunkering down. We have far more police in this country than we did twenty-five years ago—far many more locked doors and security guards and surveillance systems—but our safety has only deteriorated as our efforts to protect ourselves have redoubled.

Every business person has an obligation to battle not only individual crimes, but the greater root *causes* of crime. How you choose to become involved is up to you, but here are a few ideas for starters:

1. *Political Action.* Let your legislators know how you feel about such issues as the sentencing and paroling of those accused or convicted of violent crimes. Consider following the performance of your local courts on plea-bargaining, suspending sentences, and so on.

2. *Economic Action.* A major contributor to crime is unemployment —especially among the young and the minorities. If each small business in the US found just *one* job for a young person, we'd go a long way toward solving our problem. It may mean taking some risk on a person who'll need a fair amount of training—and you may have to stretch your budget—but if the end result is a reduced risk of violent crime, improved community relations, and a good employee found, I'd say your efforts were rewarded.

3. *Personal Action.* This is supposed to be the era of decreased governmental involvement and increased individual commitment. Get involved! Whether it's Cub Scouts, Boy Scouts, Girl Scouts, Junior Achievement, or whatever, lend a hand—and remember that the lower down the social ladder the people are you help out, the more your actions matter, if only because the poor kids never get a shot at summer camps, tennis lessons, or dances at the country club.

In short, while personal security is certainly important, never forget how much your own safety depends upon the safety of the community as a whole. Do what you can to improve the moral strength and the social character of your community, and you will be repaid many times over.

15

SURVIVING LITIGATION

SITUATION:
Unresolvable Conflict/civil action
OBJECTIVE:
Winning outside of court

Being sued, probably the worst thing that happens to a business-person, is becoming more common every day. America has become a litigation-prone society. In 1970, a real estate broker had one chance in ten of being sued during the year; by 1980, that likeli-hood had increased to *six* chances in ten. With a whole class of American lawyers priding themselves on their ability to put the screws to people to force them into settlements, *your* chances of facing a suit have similarly skyrocketed. You'd better be prepared.

In a moment, we'll try a live ammo exercise and see what you can do to protect yourself against being sued, or to minimize the damage if you are. Before that, let's do the arithmetic to establish why "If you don't like it, sue me!" are probably the stupidest words a businessperson will ever utter.

Lawsuits cost you in money, time, and stress. If you're on the receiving end of the suit, all costs are multiplied several times over. First, there's the cost of an attorney. If you were suing someone else in a matter with a large potential settlement, you would likely be able to hire an attorney on a contingency basis, letting him collect (usually a percentage of the judgement) only if you win the suit. As a defendent, you will almost certainly pay on an hourly basis. Neither should you trust a cut-rate legal clinic. You need a crack business attorney, who will generally charge you from $100 to $150 per hour. Court time is usually priced higher—a $100 per hour attorney will often get $1000 per courtroom day. You will also be billed for all clerical and research services at around two and a half to three times cost. That means every time the attorney needs a 10¢ photocopy, it will cost you 30¢, and every time a $10-per-hour clerk spends an hour in the library, you're going to be tabbed $30. Just as a rough ballpark figure—and it's hard to generalize—you can figure a three day trial using a $100-per-hour lawyer from a competent law firm is going to cost you $8000– 10,000—*if* you win. If you lose, of course, you can throw in the amount of judgement, plus court costs. Strictly as a matter of economics, you're wise to stay out of court.

Then there's the time. To get into court on a civil action in a major city today can take anywhere from two to five *years;* your right to a speedy trial holds only in certain criminal matters. During that time the legal process will likely be doing little for you, except costing you money and making you nervous. (Even if you're the one suing, you won't gain much, because, whatever preliminary injunctions you may win, the court will almost certainly turn around and lift the restraints upon posting of bond— most judges, quite rightly, are reluctant to let a spur-of-the- moment decision made in advance of a trial have the force of law during those two to five years before the case is heard).

Stress, of course, is highly personal. Some people can face even a stack of lawsuits with nary a tremble; others will wake up sweating in the middle of the night, thinking that some crazy judge just might award their opponent the $100,000 he wants for that cracked waterglass that ruined his dinner party.

In any case, if you're getting the idea that being sued is a curse, you're getting the right idea. Lawsuits are so great a threat to business that in 1981 a minor miracle of cooperation occurred, when erstwhile bitter adversaries, Ralph Nader and American big business, cosponsored a conference on managing corporate legal expenses. For big businesses, legal fees can run into the millions; for small businesses, they can easily prove ruinous.

Now that you have a notion of the risks, let's try that example:

You own a medium-sized insurance company in Los Angeles. An acquaintance of yours has a brother-in-law in New York who wants to come to California and get into insurance. As a favor, you call him long-distance and explain what's needed to become an insurance salesman. You talk to him for maybe twenty minutes, and tell him that if he ever meets the requirements and moves west, you'd be glad to give him a job interview.

A year goes by. The brother-in-law shows up in Los Angeles, and demands the interview. You set it up, and he behaves there in an arrogant and unaccomodating manner, telling your sales manager he already has a guaranteed job. Your sales manager is turned off, and recommends against hiring.

Now the brother-in-law comes storming into the office, insulting you, demanding the job, and, finally, promising to sue. He storms out of the office, and a week later you get a letter from his attorney. You have caused his client grievous psychic damage, and he is suing you for $50,000.

What do you do?

Basically, you've already made a number of mistakes. In the first place, avoid making casual or long-range commitments. Even if you're only intending to be kind or helpful, there is a certain class of human being who is going to try to nail you for every decent gesture you make. The proper response to a request for free, long-distance services must be entirely noncommittal, even as it is extremely helpful. You might, for example, have sent along the address of the California Insurance Commission. And any response *should be in writing*. Who knows what took place in a phone conversation? Worse still, if phone records show *you* made any of the calls, the court will likely assume that you lured the plaintiff out West. *Put it in writing; avoid open-ended commitments.*

Even after the fellow appeared for the interview and blew it, you still made a mistake. Always be as concilliatory as possible. Suggest a second interview. Offer to review the results of the first personally, and to send him your findings. Take him out to lunch and talk it over. Try to work out a deal. *Negotiate*—after all, there's at least an even chance that something not his fault *did* go wrong in the interview, and he *wasn't* fairly treated.

Even after negotiations seem to be going nowhere—even if the fellow really is an unredeemable jerk—you can still stop short of a courtroom trial by suggesting arbitration.

Arbitration is the use of a (binding or nonbinding) hearing concerned, not with assessing guilt or innocence, but with helping all parties reach a fair settlement of a dispute. Informal arbitration works like this: you and your opponent each nominate an arbitrator, and those two agree on a third arbitrator. Finally, all three hear your case and vote on their decision.

Formal arbitration, moreover, is increasingly available, either from the standards committees of such groups as Realty Boards, or from professional firms like the American Arbitration Association. In either case, the arbitrators assigned will strive for a deal both sides can live with, rather than assess huge penalties. In our case, for example, they might say to you, "Ms. Jones, either give Mr. Smith the job you clearly offered, or pay his expenses back to New York, plus his hotel bills here." Or, they might say, "Mr. Smith, Ms. Jones didn't offer you a job; she offered you an interview. Since you came to that interview completely unprepared, we don't see that she owes you anything. If you come to her six months from now with all your licenses in hand, she might be nice enough to give you a second interview. But that's entirely up to her." No traumatic blows, no sudden windfalls, just a fair compromise—usually, with no legal fees. You pay only the arbitration fee. The AAA, which is available in most major cities, charges a minimum of $150, and cases involving up to $10,000 will be heard for $300. Arbitrators often know their field better than judges, and are perhaps less antibusiness. Use them if you can.

Fair arbitration resolves a tremendous number of disputes. Even if the ruling goes against you, you will be spared time, money and stress, and most often, even if neither party leaves arbitration deliriously happy, neither do they leave feeling they've been robbed. They can put their disputes behind them, and get on with their lives.

Arbitration and negotiation are not only morally proper; they are in some ways a kind of preliminary groundwork for a legal defense, should that become necessary. After all, the unfortunate fact is that, in some courtrooms, you as the businessperson are going to labor under a burden of implied guilt simply *as* a businessperson. At the very least, the opposing attorney will try to portray you as the fast-talking, big-city racketeer who set out to take advantage of his poor, innocent client. If your record since the first dispute shows that you've remained cold and unapproachable (even arrogant), you're going to have two strikes against you. If, on the other hand, you can document that you offered, first to make amends through negotiation, and then, to accept an arbitration board's ruling—well, the psychological battle will rank at least as a draw, which these days, means a victory for the businessperson. After that, the facts of your case will get a fair hearing.

In sum, negotiation and arbitration together offer three advantages:

1. They are speedy and economical
2. They work without assigning guilt and innocence. No one's an absolute loser, and you may even make a friend.
3. They establish your good intentions should the matter eventually come to trial.

Still, let's go on, and assume that efforts at negotiation and/or arbitration fail, and that there is going to be a lawsuit. What happens next?

Keeping a file. The first thing to do is to begin keeping a file on the disputed case. Save not only any relevant documents (invoices, letters, sales receipts), but also the most thorough notes you can manage about what precisely took place over the course of the dispute *including* dates, places, and summaries of conversations. It's hard enough to get matters straight now; wait until the trial takes place, two, three, or four years down the road. At the same time, make sure that anyone else in your firm—secretaries, clerks, or whoever—makes whatever other notes he or she thinks important, and see that those are added to the file as well. At some point before the trial, the attorney for both sides will take the depositions (or statements, with questions and answers) of all the prime witnesses, but the notes are absolutely invaluable refreshers.

Moreover, remember that employees like secretaries have a tendency to move on after a few years, and the expense of bringing in witnesses from out of state (assuming they can be found) is downright staggering. A file is not the same as a sworn statement, but it is a useful tool nonetheless.

It's not a bad idea to jot down a few notes after every dispute you have—just for safety's sake. If the dispute goes on more than a couple of days, or a couple of conversations, you'd better think about a file.

Contacting the Insurance Company. As soon as any dispute arises which might result in some form of a claim, determine whether you have any insurance coverage relevant to it. (See INSURANCE). Depending upon your line of work, you might have malpractice, auto, personal or product liability, or any other useful form of coverage. If so, you insurance company will handle all or part of the defense, and it is essential that they be notified *at once.* Don't wait for the papers to be served.

Getting an Attorney. If the amount of the lawsuit overruns your insurance coverage (increasingly likely these days), or if, as in the test case we're using, you have no appropriate coverage, then you need a lawyer or lawyers of your own.

Superficially, there should be no trouble in finding one. Law is a boom business in this country. In 1970, we had about one lawyer for every 600 Americans; by 1980, there was a lawyer for every 410 of us. As of August, 1981, there were 535,000 of them admitted to practice in the U.S. (American Bar Foundation *Research Reporter,* Summer, 1981). The problem is finding a *good* lawyer. Price is little or no help. Neither is reputation, since reputation was earned in the past. And neither is size of the law firm, since newer or smaller clients are generally shunted off to the recent law school graduates.

About the only general guidelines I can give you are these:

1. Make sure you get a business attorney—ideally one with a business background outside of his legal training.

2. Get one with recommendations. Ask people you know for a business attorney who can be tough—and one they know personally to have won tough cases.

3. Know from the outset whether your attorney is a trial attorney or not. Many of the best business attorneys confine themselves to negotiations only. That can be fine, as long as you are prepared to make the shift (generally to another attorney in the same firm) if the matter does reach trial.

4. Make sure you can talk with your attorney. It sometimes seems that the attorneys who talk toughest with their clients are the first ones to cut and run when the other side begins putting on the heat. Again, you want a record of performance under fire.

Make sure, too, your attorney is open to suggestions. Start out by saying something like, "I understand that you're the attorney, and I won't try to run the defense or teach you the law, but I intend to take an active interest in what you do, and at times to stress facts or make suggestions. Does that bother you?" If he or she says yes, you'd best keep looking for a lawyer.

5. Above all, remember that choosing an attorney doesn't end your responsibility. You must monitor his or her performance. Once we had a senior partner from a major law firm representing us. He was a fine man with a fine reputation—who unfortunately had a nervous breakdown while handling our affairs. He left settlement checks made out to us sitting in his files. He failed to notify us of court appearances and other important dates. By the time he admitted he couldn't continue his practice, he had left many of our affairs (and those of many other clients) in a sorry mess. And it was our tough luck—in law, as in the boxing ring, the rule is to protect yourself at all times.

(Of course, the ABA has a format for review of its members. Persuading three lawyers to condemn a fourth, however, borders on the impossible).

Those are only cautionary notes. They do not amount to an absolute guideline, but unfortunately, good business attorneys are a scarce commodity. Probably the best general approach is simply to begin looking before you really need one—because these days, the odds are that sooner or later, you'll need one.

Using Your Attorney. One of the minor disadvantages of engaging an attorney, of course, is that from that point on, you'll be expected to do any negotiating through him. That means that the back-and-forth discussions that used to be free will now be costing around $100 an hour—actually more, since your attorney will be relaying to you the results of each conversation with the opposition, either by another phone call or by letter. Beware, too, of the tactic of prolonged and insincere negotiations. The opposition, whose lawyers' fees are contingent upon settlement, may try to break your nerve by holding hours and hours of negotiations which always seem just about to produce a settlement, but somehow never do—until you are faced with thousands of dollars' worth of bills for wasted negotiating time. The only defense is for your attorney to announce that, until better faith is shown, you are calling off the negotiations. Indeed, if your attorney is any good, he or she will be the first to suggest this.

That brings us to a second, touchier topic—attorney's bills. Modern firms send out their bills with amazing, computerized, speed. Since clients are reluctant to pay off a losing lawyer, law firms want as much of their money as possible up front. You likely will be expected to pay a few hundred dollars even before your first meeting, and the bills will appear with sharp regularity from then until the end of the case. If you're wondering what happens if you don't pay, just check your local court calender to see how many people are sued by law firms on any given day. And don't assume that the clown who lost your case will be such a clown when he goes after you for overdue fees. It's amazing how much better a job the average attorney does when it's *his* money at stake.

Some attorneys will let you work out a payment plan in advance. Beyond that, you can stretch payments according to the limit specified in the bill (say thirty days), and then hold off payments as you near trial. If you win the case outright, you'll want to pay in full and continue the relationship. If you lose but your attorney was impressive, again you'll want to pay. But if, in your honest opinion, your attorney failed you, then those last, withheld payments (which can amount to $3000–5000 or more, can be a useful bargaining chip. Remember that it costs an attorney plenty to go after you in court, too. At the same time, if he's a reasonable human being, he'll be feeling some guilt about his performance, and you may be able to shave the bill by perhaps $1500–2000, which may be all you'll ever salvage from a rotten experience.

The Trial: Winning and Losing. When you move into the trial situation, the stakes of the dispute are automatically raised. Now you are dealing with guilt and innocence, punishment and reward. If the judge decides you willfully did Mr. Smith $10,000 worth of damage, he can award Mr. Smith treble damages, or $30,000. Again this is the kind of hazard arbitration avoids.

This is also why you may want to make one last effort to settle "on the courtroom steps." Without giving away the store, you may want to offer whatever you expect to spend on the trial, plus a small sweetener—in this case, say a total of $4000–5000. Known as a cost-of-defense settlement, this is in no way an admission of guilt. If the plaintiff's attorney thinks he has a mediocre case, he may grab it. If not, you have a trial.

Nominally, your lawyer will have been building towards the court appearance from the day he took your case. He will be researching precedents, interviewing witnesses, structuring arguments—and you, meanwhile, will be feeling less and less in control of your own fate. This may explain all the mystical theories put forward about how to appear best in courts: dress humbly, dress like a winner; have your spouse and children in the courtroom, *don't* have your spouse and children in the courtroom; act outraged, act downtrodden; and so on *ad infinitum.* Personally, I'd like to believe facts alone determine the outcome. If you are frank, courteous, and thoughtful, that should be sufficient.

On the other hand, be alert to efforts by the opposing attorney to portray *you* in a damaging light. Note that "damaging" may not mean unflattering. Indeed, these days, one of the most damaging portrayals may be that showing you a great success. Juries, like most Americans, tend to sympathize with the underdog. Fend off any irrelevent references to the size or profitability of your business, the number of your employees, and so on—and make sure your attorney reminds the court that the opposition is writing melodrama, not trying the case.

The Judgement and the Appeal. In the vast majority of cases, you will receive a fair examination upon the law and the facts. If the right is on your side, and if your lawyer has argued your case well, you should prevail. If the judgement is in your favor, the case may well be over. You can sue to recover your legal fees, but that begins another long process, with attendant loss of time and money. You may want to try striking a deal whereby you pay your own fees and your opponent foregoes his appeal.

Of course, your opponent may insist upon appealing, thereby placing you almost back where you started. Although the court will only hear an appeal if substantially new evidence can be brought forward, should an appeal date be granted, you will again have to decide whether to offer a cost-of-defense settlement. This time, of course, your case is stronger by reason both of the victory and the fact that most of the costs of defending are behind you. You may only want to offer half of what you offered before, unless the new evidence introduced seems overwhelmingly strong.

But what, on the other hand, if the judgement goes against you? Basically, there are two categories of negative judgements—the minor, nonpejorative sort, which you may well wish to pay, and the disastrous judgement, which you (or your insurance company) are obliged to fight.

In a minor settlement, the judge may concede you've done nothing specifically wrong, but still award Smith some compensation for a misunderstanding. Instead of $50,000, he may award, perhaps, $4000, double damages—or $8000. Now he's put you in a bind. At $50,000, you'd certainly appeal. If he'd let you off entirely, the decision would have been up to your opposition. But $8000 is awkward. On appeal, you might prevail, or the appellate court might double or triple the award—or even up it to the full $50,000. Basically, your odds are poor. Unless an important principle is involved, you'll be wise to settle. Try for a compromise figure, but pay up if you must.

Suppose the court decides against you for the full amount—$50,000, or $200,000, or even $1,000,000 or more. What can be done then?

Dishing Off and Bailing Out. Unless you are vastly rich, or carry tremendous insurance coverage, you will appeal. But if you seem likely to lose again, then what?

Your first goal is to buy time. An appeal process can run a year or so in the normal course of events. You can stretch matters out by secondary filings of papers, delays for illness, substitutions of attorneys, and so on. Meanwhile, you can hope that new evidence or arguments will arise, or that the person suing you will lose heart, or soften his position.

Still, about this time, many people begin thinking of either dishing off assets or simply cutting and running. I would never encourage you to try circumventing the will of the court. Equally to the point, there are practical as well as moral problems with trying to avoid paying on any judgement against you.

Never assume, for example, that you can hide behind the legal fiction of a bankruptable corporation. Officers of a corporation have substantial personal liability for that corporation (which is why you should never agree to sit on a friend's board just as a courtesy). Courts often transfer corporate liability to the individual officer(s). Known as "piercing the corporate veil," this process can puncture a dozen or more corporate entities at once.

Similarly, hasty postjudgement attempts to give away assets to friends and family almost always fail. The courts nearly always view these as attempts to defraud creditors, and order the money returned.

On the other hand, some businesspeople are crafty enough to begin quite early in their careers giving away assets to family members, partly as gifts, and partly as compensation for work done. Doing this, they not only reduce their taxes, but provide themselves with insurance against future litigation. When you win a case against them, you find their net worth far smaller than you ever imagined. Persons who take this approach to self-protection are, I must admit, very difficult to touch. Often, though, they discover their spouses have absconded with assets given them for safekeeping, and again, this is not an approach which can be taken after the case is decided—if, indeed, it is *ever* morally right.

In theory, of course, you can also leave the state, or even the country, when a big enough decision goes against you. People who leave a state can be tracked quite easily, though, and as for leaving the country, I think it is beneath discussion. Remember, no matter how bad the judgement against you, you can always begin anew. The kinds of judgement which courts sometimes award these days are terrifying, I know, but ultimately you are wisest simply to stand your ground.

Still, the possibility of such disastrous judgements suggests the ultimate danger of lawsuits, a danger you are well advised to avoid. The best policy, then, is one of prevention, which involves the following:

1. Avoid dubious dealings; don't try to take customers for that very last penny. Make the occasional generous gesture; it's not only good for the soul, it's good for business.

2. Stick to a careful risk reduction program (See INSURANCE, please). Make your place of business as safe a place to visit as possible.

3. Practice conflict containment. When something goes wrong, when there's a dispute or a problem, move quickly to correct it amicably. If it means splitting a disputed claim, or apologizing, or paying for a lunch, or whatever, do it—anything within reason.

4. If you can't come to terms informally, then *arbitrate before you litigate.* Arbitration can often be successful for a tenth the cost, and in a tenth the time, of litigation.

5. Get a tough, effective attorney, but one you can talk with. Don't assume big name firms will give you the best service; often they'll shunt you off to the low man on their team. And if you lack confidence in the attorney you choose, make a change as soon as possible. Cut your losses.

6. Even up to the day of the trial, don't exclude the possibility of a negotiated settlement. Never let your feelings get involved. Take the deal that makes the most sense from the standpoint of reputation and economics, and never mind getting even.

There will be times when you'll have to turn to the courts—either to sue or to defend yourself. But civil litigation is slow, costly, and painful, and it is beginning to overburden the American court system as a whole. Before you go to court, try every other fair and reasonable way of settling.

16
REAL ESTATE

SITUATION:
Finding and acquiring business commercial/industrial real estate

OBJECTIVE:
Acquiring usable *real estate at minimum cost and without committing capital which would be better invested in productive assets*

Business Real Estate: Making the Right Choices.

When major corporations need real estate, they can almost always rely upon their own in-house experts, or even wholly-owned real estate subsidiaries. When you first look, you're likely to be a committee of one. How can you compensate?

Part of the answer is that you can use the services of a real estate firm specializing in commercial and industrial properties. But even the best real estate people won't be able to help you unless you can 1) accurately determine your needs, 2) sensibly evaluate properties you are shown, and 3) understand in general the terms of real estate contracts. Those are the subjects of this Situation.

A FIRST NOTE OF CAUTION. Here's a first law of buying business property for your firm:

DON'T CREATE CONFLICTS

That is, don't get yourself in a situation where your goals as a real estate speculator are in conflict with your goals as a business owner/operator. Too often, people thinking they're onto a hot real estate deal move their company into a bad location, sap the firm's profits to keep up the mortgage payments, and then either lose the building because the anticipated buyer doesn't materialize, or get the buyer they want, and find out the business can't survive the move to a new location.

So unless you choose to become strictly a real estate speculator, the only sensible way to proceed is to decide what property your business needs, and then to gun for your best real estate value within those limits. Before even talking with real estate specialists, then, you should first consider the following:

1. Physical Requirements. The types of land and buildings you want
2. Zoning/Land Use Requirements. Any legal restrictions which might affect your choices
3. Personnel/Labor Force Requirements. The needs and availability of your work force
4. Transportation. Partly, as above, the ease with which your workers can reach you. Also the availability of needed shipping, airports, etc.
5. Energy costs and availability
6. Fiscal Restraints. What you can afford to pay

You should begin by searching for a property which optimizes your needs in each of these areas. You can compromise later.

PHYSICAL TYPE. What sort of plant and/or acreage do you need? Do you need space for offices, retail sales, light industrial, agricultural, or heavy manufacturing? What are your image requirements? Does the plant have to be the most modern, or can you use something a bit tarnished, if the price is right? Do you have precise design criteria (requiring virtually a custom-built operation) or will most general-purpose buildings serve? How much do noise and privacy matter? Will you pay for the "association factor," the privilege of being near to prestige businesses, or are you going in low, with the idea of building your own chic?

How big a location do you need, in square feet? (You can get an idea of this by either pacing out other people's existing operations—or simply asking them—or by use of some standard formulae. Any number of business associations, as well as the Small Business Administration, will assist you with guidelines. For retail sales, for example, try *The Retailer's Guide to Shopping Center Leasing*, from the National Retail Merchants' Association.)

When thinking of installed leasehold improvements, remember the resale value of these often hugely expensive items—special lights, walk-in refrigerators, etc.—drops roughly in half the minute they are installed, and depreciates to an effective zero within about five years. After five years, such items might even technically have negative value, if they cost more to rip out than they will bring as salvage. So if you can make do with some slightly dated improvements, be sure to mention that fact to your real estate person. Workable used installed equipment can be decisive in determining your best deal. (If you're thinking of an R and D-oriented business, this can go doubly, because laboratory suppliers are in the habit of sticking it to government-funded researchers. An *extension* of an existing distilled water line can run you $100 per ft. Again, see if you can find such things already installed.)

Lastly, decide whether you might actually need more than one site. Don't get into the bind of paying prestige office rates to store inventory that ought to be in a warehouse somewhere, or you'll be spending, say, $12 per square foot for what should be costing around 80¢ per square foot. If you can efficiently mix property types, *do it.*

ZONING/LAND USE. Zoning codes and land use plans vary greatly from city to city, and so you (or your real estate advisor) will have to determine which parts (if any) of the city allow for the type of business you are planning. Generally, developable land will be zoned (with whatever nomenclature) as residential, business/professional, retail sales/commercial, light industrial, or heavy industrial. There will be subgradations, and some areas may be graded multi-use. Some cities will effectively bar certain forms of development. San Diego, for example, has nearly banished heavy manufacturing, favoring instead such clean industries as electronics assembly: the economic rationale is to protect the local tourist industry.

Find out, too, about any other generalized restrictions. Virtually any construction work done along the coasts of Oregon or California, for example, requires governmental approval, and the California Coastal Commission is notoriously strict. You also ought to know whether your area requires environmental impact statements for construction work, and if so, how long they require for approval. The difficulty of undertaking new construction might rule out your looking at raw land even this early on.

Remember that simply meeting an area's zoning requirements does not mean you can go ahead and undertake the work of your choice. Even if your area is zoned for industrial uses, you will still need special permits—likely to require one heck of a fight—for endeavors which produce toxic fumes or effluents, including furniture stripping, smeltering, acid etching of metals, paper manufacturing, and so on. You can have similar problems with *anything* likely to offend your neighbors, such as the smell from a tuna canning operation. In that case, it only makes sense to scout for areas where you'll be fairly well isolated, or where similarly noxious activities are already underway.

ONE WARNING: be sure to stress that you are not interested in any land under consideration for *eminent domain* condemnation. In the past, eminent domain was usually invoked only for such things as new freeways, but it is increasingly being used to condemn older business districts (the areas favored by many beginning small businesses) as part of urban renewal projects. The process is often one way big businesses use government to stick it to small businesses. In San Diego eminent domain was invoked in the late 70s to force the demolition of all the small businesses in a major part of downtown, to allow a (Canadian-controlled) land developer to build a regional shopping mall. Your tax dollars at work!

Still, the point is clear—even though properties under threat of eminent domain condemnation will rent cheaply, you're better off staying away. And once you are in possession of a property, it's in your interest to get involved in any governmental land-use decisions likely to affect you. *Get in there and lobby for your interests.*

PERSONNEL/LABOR FORCE. You have to choose your sites with an eye to the availability of labor in the region, and to the ease with which workers can reach them. When Harcourt Brace Jovanovich announced its plans to move its operations from New York City to California, Ohio, and Florida, one of the declared reasons was that its many female employees found the New York City subways unsafe, and the company was finding the cost of moving them by taxi probitively expensive.

You want a location not only near to your workers, but attractive to them. If you get dirt-cheap rent under a freeway or next door to a glue factory, your turnover in workers will probably cost more than what you save in discounted rent.

The main thing here is to offer *competitive* physical surroundings, and that means knowing what comparable firms in the region are providing. In a few places where the competition for workers is fierce—as in the semiconductor industry of Silicon Valley—you may be obliged to go whole hog, with hot tubs, jacuzzis, and swimming pools. Of course, the Japanese firms (so often taken as the norm today) also spend heavily on on-site recreational facilities. But remember that 1) plenty of Americans still prefer to go their own way after hours and 2) you can get stuck with some pretty expensive improvements as fads peak. If you put in tennis courts today, are you going to switch them to racketball tomorrow? Underwriting employee memberships in health spas is a much cheaper alternative.

Still, if spending for aesthetics does pay off, this is where it will —in a work force which is productive and stable.

TRANSPORTATION. This is a two part concern. The first follows from the above: can your workers reach the place reliably and cheaply? You want not only closeness (it costs between 45 and 60 ¢ *per mile* to run a car), but *redundancy*. There should be a back-up transport system (buses, light rail, etc.) in case of bad weather or energy shortages. Consider promoting car- or vanpooling. Because you are dealing with a real gain in efficiency, you can provide your workers with a positive gain at little or no cost—and some benefit —to yourself.

The second issue is the ready, cheap and safe movement of your goods. Make sure that your warehouse and/or manufacturing points all have close proximity to the most efficient land, sea, or air shipment means. Each trans-shipment (transfer from one means of shipment to another) multiplies your costs. Short lines of communication between you and your suppliers are essential for a "just-in-time" delivery system (see Chapter 20), and that can mean *big* savings in reduced inventory and interest charges.

The *safe* movement of goods means both a location in a safe neighborhood—one which either provides or makes easy the sorts of security precautions mentioned in Chapter 14—and one which will expose your shipments to the least physical damage. Thus, if you are operating in the Pacific Northwest, you want provisions to keep shipments dry during torrential rains; if you're in an area where the train tracks are in terrible shape, you want to be near an alternate form of shipping (say, UPS or Greyhound). Remember that every improvement in the gentleness of your transportation system will contribute to your bottom line, through fewer losses, cheaper packing costs, and so on. Ford Motor Co., for example, once calculated that the worst stress an American car undergoes during its normal lifetime is the rail trip it makes from factory to dealership.

ENERGY COST AND AVAILABILITY. Are you in an energy-intensive business? If so, remember that, in the event of another energy crisis, the power companies are quite capable of doing what they've done in the past—rationing power. If that happens, only the efficient will stay in production. Tell your real estate advisor you favor the following:

1. *Passive Conservation.* A tight, well insulated property is worth a premium. So, too, are double-glazed or heat-screen coated windows, sun-shading adjustable awnings, well-placed deciduous trees, and the like.

2. *Active Conservation.* Look kindly on plants with efficient energy control systems. Automated controls can save you 30–35% on your total energy bill. In some regions, installed solar hot-water

systems make strict economic sense, and may offer tax benefits as well.

3. *Well-Chosen Energy Sources.* Favor buildings using the region's lowest-cost methods of heating and cooling. For medium-to-large operations, consider a site with cogeneration capacity. Even newly installed, those generators have a *very* quick payback period; second hand, they can be a *terrific* bargain.

Similarly, if you have in mind a business which can burn its own by-products for fuel, give preference to any site with adaptable boilers. Wood products companies, for example, have achieved remarkable economies this way—some reaching complete energy independence.

Fiscal restraints. The last of your parameters, and in many ways the hardest to calculate in advance, is the amount you can afford to pay for rent. Ideally, your rent should be calculated as a percentage of your anticipated sales—with different experts telling you a dollar in rent should generate $5, $10, or even $20 in sales—but in practice, you might do better when setting out by budgeting your rent as a percentage of total overhead. That percentage will vary according to your line of work, of course. For some service businesses, rent may constitute 40–60% of monthly overhead; for a manufacturer, 5% might be closer to the ideal. You need to ask your accountant or a trade association what's average for your line of endeavor. When you first open your doors, meanwhile, your *total* allowable monthly overhead should be determined by what you can afford to lose in the two to six months before the firm turns profitable.

If that won't buy you quite as much style as you had hoped for (and if you are interested in retail sales or services), direct your search toward areas adjacent to the most fashionable ones, and especially areas being renovated by eager young professional couples. They're often prime customers, and you can get low rents in their neighborhoods if you move fast enough.

Alternatively, consider making a virtue of your poverty by building or acquiring the cheapest exposed-conduit warehouse you can find, preferably in a low-rent, out-of-the-way location, and turning it into a mini discount operation. If you really do pass along all your savings, these operations can grow like wildfire. Not long ago I saw one, started by two immigrant brothers speaking very little English, go from zero to $6,000,000 a year in sales (with a reported profit close to $200,000) in less than three years. They just found an old building about 100 yards from the railroad tracks, painted it international orange, and started moving out those goods.

Finding Your Site.

Whether or not you're cut out for high-volume discounting, running through the above factors—physical type, zoning, etc.— should prepare you to search intelligently for property. Now you can go to a real estate specialist and talk effectively: "I need about 5000 square feet of C-Zone property somewhere near the I-60 Corridor and within three miles of the airport," or whatever. Normally, between the efforts of agents, and your own casual searching, you should come up with a number of potential properties. To decide which is best for you, I'd advise making up a set of *comparison sheets,* and then evaluating each potential property according to (at least) the following five points:

1. *Aesthetics.* This is most important in retail sales or prestige professional services, but it matters in manufacturing as well. Include things like landscaping, color schemes (is everything battleship grey, or olive drab?), quality of fixtures, views from windows, even the way other people in the building or area dress (are there a lot of characters wearing blue-jeans jackets with logos like "Angels of Destruction" walking around the neighborhood?). Of course, your willingness to pay for these features will vary according to your situation. Still, note what's there: if your only objection is the paint-scheme, probably you can have a change thrown in as a lease-sweetener.

2. *Access.* Is the place as easy to reach in fact as it seems to be on the map? Is it near major freeways? Are directions to reaching it easily described in an ad or over the telephone? Is the access blocked off by periodic traffic jams, or is any major construction scheduled nearby? What about one-way streets, or no-left-turns? You don't want the kind of access which scares off potential customers.

What about parking? Is it pay or free, and how plentiful? How many slots are reserved for you as tenant? Are the elevators up-to-date? Hi-speed or not? Is there a freight elevator?

Ask, too, about after-hours access. Is the neighborhood still safe? Do the elevators still run? Can you arrange to have the heating, ventilating, and air conditioning system switched on? (Remember that, especially these days, many buildings' HVAC systems are largely shut down after business hours—and working in a sealed, unventilated building, especially on a weekend, can be stupifying.)

Is there access for the handicapped? After all, why exclude a whole class of customers?

3. *Structural Quality.* What's the condition of the roof? Floor load rating? Are the loading platforms easily reached, and of the right height for your trucks? Are the ceilings high enough—at least twelve to fourteen feet for general manufacturing? In a new industrial area, is the sewage system fully operational? (Even if you can trust a future installation date, remember that sewage installation will tear up the roads for weeks, perhaps longer.) Are installed sewage, electrical wiring, etc., all in in good repair? Is there an adequate fire-suppression system? (Overhead sprinklers are best, except that certain sensitive equipment, such as computers, may need more costly CO_2 or inert-gas systems.) *Note:* in some very high-ceilinged buildings, overhead sprinklers fail because the water they scatter turns to droplets and then to steam before reaching the fire.

Try to inspect each likely property yourself. Unless you know a lot about contracting, though, it's probably wise to seek an expert's opinion before signing any long-term lease. Ask your architect (if you plan changes), or borrow a bank's property appraiser (even for a fee), to inspect the place. Any small fee will be well spent for security and peace of mind.

4. *Services.* This matters most when you are renting space in an existing building. Is the building or the area guarded? By hardware, guards, or both? How good are the cleanup crews? What temperature settings are used for the HVAC system? How do other tenants feel about the landlord's record on answering complaints?

Note: if you are starting a service or professional company heavily dependent upon services, consider first renting from one of those firms which combine office space with a whole set of communications and administrative services. These firms usually take a floor or more at prestige addresses in a number of cities, and then sublease space for which they provide area receptionists, conference rooms, word processing, Telex, and other services. Typically, because costs are pooled among a number of sublessees, these services (some carrying a user fee) can be provided much more cheaply. The result can cut your total office overhead by up to *40 or 50%.* Generally meant for start-up or temporary operation, these rental packages usually offer fairly small spaces on fairly short leases (often six to twelve months). So, they are a way to get yourself into business for a *very low* initial outlay—and they make those rapid early expansions as painless as possible.

5. *Availability.* Lastly, when can you move in? Remember, this depends upon both the date of lease availability, and the downtime for any necessary modifications. If a location is going to require extensive modification by *you,* you need to get not only construction bids, but time estimates (from reliable firms). Start-up time can kill you—favor the place which needs the least modification.

Signing Up.

If you've comparison sheets covering the above five areas for each property you've examined, you'll be able to sit down at the end of the process and make your decision without relying upon your memory. How many places should you look at? Well, the glib answer is to keep looking until you find exactly what you want.

Clearly, that's going to be possible only if you have 1) lots of potential places to consider and 2) plenty of time to spend. Some experts say you should compare at least half a dozen locations. Sometimes, though, a crowded market will force you to move more quickly. If you've taken care of all the preliminaries mentioned above, you'll be able to decide almost instantly whether the offering meets your needs. Otherwise, especially if you are already successfully in business, and only looking to branch out or expand, get in the habit of scouting future sites in your spare time. See that one or two high-quality commercial real estate people have your name and number, and a clear idea of the type of property you're seeking. The more you know about general real estate conditions, the better you're likely to do.

Lease or Buy.

As a general rule, the beginning small business is far better off leasing than buying, for three main reasons: 1. *likelihood of miscalculation*, 2. *likelihood of expansion*, and 3. *conservation of capital*. Your first time out, even with professional help, it is very difficult to anticipate your exact needs. Equally to the point, many small businesses grow exceedingly quickly. You'll likely have to make one or more moves in your early years, even if you've guessed exactly right to start with. Finally, remember the large down-payment necessary to buy property will deplete your capital for investment, and strain your credit capacity early on.

Recall that there are generally said to be three ways for a piece of real estate to create value: tax sheltering, cash flow, and proceeds of sale. If you find a location you want, you aren't going to want to sell it, so there go proceeds of sale. Your first months in business are unlikely to prove profitable, so the need for tax sheltering is dubious (although you can carry forward the benefits). Your cashflow situation is similar. Unless (as sometimes happens) you buy a large enough property cheaply enough to be able to rent out your excess space at a big profit, buying a business property will give you a big *negative* cashflow for some time to come. Since, moreover, the real estate boom of the '70s seems clearly ended, the reasons for buying your own business property appears less than compelling.

WHEN TO BUY. That is not, of course, to say you should *never* buy property. Buying makes sense in several situations:

When the Price Is Unbeatably Low. Rarely, a distress sale will make buying nearly as cheap as renting, and virtually guarantee a large profit on resale. To act in this case, though, you need *personal* expertise in real estate. You cannot rely upon the opinion of some salesman out to make a sale. Remember, too, that against "guaranteed" profits on the resale, you must match your losses from being forced to vacate the premises after a sale. (See, however, Sale/ Leaseback, below.)

When Nothing Suitable Is Available. You might want to buy property and build your own building if nothing suitable is available. First, though, consider the possibility of a *build-to-suit* arrangement, where a well-heeled landowner will put up the building of your choice in exchange for your signing a long-term lease. But if "nothing is available" because you insist upon being in, say, some absolutely prime retail location, look out. Any land you want to buy there will, by definition, be selling at absolutely top-demand prices. There won't be any bargains. See whether you cannot lower your demands, or find an alternatively fashionable location.

When You Want to Shelter Earnings. Once your business becomes highly profitable, of course, your tax situation changes, and looking at investing in your own real estate begins to make more sense. I still think you are better off investing in ways of boosting your productivity and market share—in branch locations, new machinery, and so on—but when you've reached the limit of that, real estate begins to make a good deal of sense. It's a useful way for professional corporations, especially, to keep earnings safely within the company. If you've got a profitable legal firm, for example, but have no desire to add partners beyond a limited number, and if you have already bought the best in word-processing and other office equipment, why not go ahead and buy a free-standing building—or even a small office building? You not only get direct tax benefits, you defer excess immediate profits while realizing a likely capital gain on your eventual sale of the property, *and* can enjoy the psychological satisfaction of building or remodelling offices exactly to your taste, like those finely restored Colonial or Victorian buildings made into legal offices.

SALE/LEASEBACK. Owning your own building has one other potential advantage, since it can (once you've built up some equity, or the land has significantly increased in value) serve as a pool of capital when real emergencies or opportunities present themselves. Loans taken out against real property will cost you much less than those secured by any other business assets, especially those against intangibles such as accounts receivable. Even more dramatically, if you think the real estate market has matured, you can sometimes take out your capital gains while still keeping your valued location(s) through a sale and leaseback, whereby the person who is buying your property simultaneously grants you a long-term lease on it. These deals make particular sense where you have exhausted the tax depreciation schedule for the buildings on your property, generally after a period of ten or more years of ownership. One of the most dramatic of these sale/leasebacks was executed by the May Company department stores a few years ago, when they sold and leased back virtually all of their shopping center land, in a transaction which generated some $200,000,000 in new capital. Again, this is something you *build for* when you first start acquiring your own sites. The benefits are much less powerful over the short haul.

RENTING OR LEASING. OK—the odds are that the first time you go shopping for a location (or take over a business already in existence), you are going to be dealing with leased or rented property. What do you watch for, what do you ask for?

Well, the first point is that if you've never leased or rented anything other than, say, a place to live, you're in for a surprise, because it's not uncommon for even a lease for a small amount of retail space in a major shopping center to run to thirty-five or more pages of grade-A legalese of this sort:

> (23.k.4) In the event that any portion of the Demised Premises shall be, during the lease term or any extension thereof, taken through condemnation under the power of eminent domain as in this article defined, this lease shall terminate as to that portion of the Demised Premises so taken on the date when actual physical possession of said portion is taken by the condemnor. . . .

etc., etc. So unless you are yourself a lawyer, it's crucially important that you spend the $100 or so one will charge you to read any lease before you sign it. Along with that, you should also take the time to familiarize yourself with many of the common key terms of leases, in order to provide yourself with minimal protection. You are not obliged to agree automatically to any of these clauses, but they will be a part of the majority of leases you are offered. Here are some of the reasonable terms and expectations of any typical retail lease—probably the most complicated type faced by a small business person:

Attornment. You agree to recognize as your new landlord anyone to whom your old landlord has lost, sold, or assigned the property. When that occurs, the terms of your existing lease should remain in force, and the worst you can suffer should be the inconvenience of a new, perhaps less pleasant, landlord. A secondary problem arises if you've signed the lease on the basis of some verbal guarantees by the old landlord, because those guarantees are probably lost. That should be yet another incentive to get everything in writing.

Merchants Association. Most retail centers will require you to join a nonprofit merchants association, and to abide by its rules. These associations are generally organized by the landlord, and exist partly to encourage proper business ethics, and largely to undertake group advertising and promoting, and, in some cases, lobbying. They are a reasonable idea, but there will be, probably, both membership fees and special assessments. Find out what you're getting committed to.

Right of Access. Landlords of commercial property generally reserve the right to enter the premises whenever they must inspect for damage, make repairs, post legal notices, or show the property during the last six months of the lease period—in short, whenever they like. As long as you keep the premises in good shape and make payments promptly, though, this is rarely a problem. Commercial landlords are usually professionals with better things to do than annoy tenants.

Holding Over. Under certain strict legal terms, a landlord who accepts a single payment from you after a lease period has expired may be held to have issued a *new* lease for a period equal to the expired one. "Holding Over" clauses simply specify that the landlord's acceptance of such payments grants you only *month to month* tenancy of the property.

Assignment and Subletting. Subletting of your property is often one of the safest and cheapest ways of breaking your lease—if the landlord goes along with it. Nearly all leases require the landlord's *written* approval of any subletting or assignment. *You* should require a statement *in the lease* that said approval will not be unreasonably withheld; it's reasonable insurance in case you ever decide to sell.

The landlord will likely consider himself entitled to some compensation for making the lease transfer. One likely compromise is to agree to an immediate recalculation of the cost of living adjustment (COLA), in advance of the normal adjustment period.

Competitive Business. There are two variations on this: in the first —which you should request—the landlord agrees not to allow into the center any specialty business (department stores are excluded) which competes directly with yours. Normally landlords are sympathetic to this, since direct competitors, which hurt each other, also hurt the center's take on percentage of sales. The smaller the center, the more likely it is to agree.

The less desirable form is a "competitive business" clause which states that if you operate another, similar, business within three to five miles of the perimeter of the center, the gross of *that* business will also be subject to the percentage rent clause of your lease with the center. This is completely unreasonable, and though most centers try to get you to sign for it, most will line it out if you squawk. So squawk.

Insurance, Improvements, Maintenance. Maintenance and insurance for the building proper should be the business of the landlord, but note that plate glass windows and front doors are generally your problem, which means you bear the brunt of any vandalism or attempted break-ins. All other responsibilities are also yours, and you will probably moreover be required to have any improvements you desire to make first approved in writing by the landlord. The lease will also probably stipulate that you take out comprehensive public liability insurance worth at least $1,000,000, and name the landlord as coinsured.

All those points are common, and most—especially the coinsuring of the landlord—are fair and reasonable, but you should still negotiate for as many improvements as you can. The larger and more prestigious your operation, and the longer the term of the lease you are willing to sign, the more you should be able to demand as sweetener. When one of our clients took a lease in a small shopping center, he was able to require the landlord to first install, among other things, a new floor, new acoustic ceilings, new lighting, two new toilets, and all the gaslines necessary for a set of fireplace displays—close to $10,000 worth of improvements in all.

Note:

Your chances of generous inducements improve whenever business is slow. If a center is showing several vacancies—or if it's newly opened for leasing—you should (politely) hold out for concessions before signing a lease.

Recapture. Recapture clauses allow a landlord to get back your lease if you do not produce the volume of sales projected. If your percentage payments do not meet expectations, the landlord can buy, or have, you out.

There are two sides to this issue. It is a kind of threat over your head, but if your business goes sour, it can also provide an means of retreat. The people who like these clauses least are the ones doing a large, unreported, cash business.

Your version of this is called an *escape clause,* and allows you out of your lease, generally upon three months' notice. Landlords, as you would expect, are reluctant to grant these.

Estoppel. A landlord planning to borrow money against the property may be required to show that he has good and valid leases on all of it, and so may demand from you a letter showing that you still consider the lease to bind you.

If you read these clauses carelessly, you may later be shocked to discover that they also allow the landlord to demand copies of your personal financial statements for the last three years. These he will be entitled to give to potential lenders or buyers to show that the tenants are all people of substance. Personally, I'd dislike the idea of a crew of strangers perusing my financial statements, and would resist agreeing to this part of an estoppel clause.

Those are some of the terms for which you want to be alert. Understanding them will give you a much clearer idea of what your lease is about. Still, I cannot overemphasize the idea of using a lawyer to check out *any* lease before signing it.

Fair Rent.

The only reasonable generalization here is that a rent is fair if 1) you can afford it, and 2) it accords well with the rents of comparable buildings in the immediate area. The only way to learn that, is to get out and do the comparison shopping yourself—or to find a real estate agent you trust.

Be careful about percentage-of-sales clauses in retail locations. Not too many years ago, 2 or 3% of sales (plus, or against, a minimum fixed rent) was common. Then it became 4 or 5%, and now, more and more often, we're seeing leases calling for 10% of the gross—and we're also seeing more and more stores under such leases going belly-up. Remember that if your gross margin before the rent percentage is 30%, you're suddenly giving up one-third of that margin to your landlord. Unless you're catering to the carriage trade—and can ratchet up prices as you like—that's a lot to surrender. Think carefully before signing away that 10%, no matter how attractive the center seems.

In sum, then, your plan for siting real estate should go something like this:

1. *Determine* your needs as precisely as possible, including price, location, size, services, energy use, and so on.
2. *Evaluate* as many properties as possible, according to those needs.
3. *Decide* whether purchase or lease offers best.
4. *Negotiate* the sale or lease with the help of legal opinion.

Real estate is a complicated field, and this chapter covers only the basics. For more details, you might well consider books like Diane C. Thomas's *How To Save Money On Your Business Rent,* or Kinnard and Messner's (rather technical) *Industrial Real Estate.* Remember, though, that even the finest book knowledge must be supplemented with practical knowledge of your local real estate markets. If that means a few Saturdays a year spent scouting shopping centers or working with brokers, well, so be it. There's really no substitute.

One last cautionary tale: most first-time business people don't really believe that excessive rent can do them much harm, but people with experience know better. Consider the case of Gordon Mathews, a currently chairman of ECS Telecommunications in Dallas. Mathews, a former Texas Instruments engineer, is a big success today, but the first company he started to market his innovative products was "a total failure." The main reason?

"I made every mistake in the book. We were terribly undercapitalized —$80,000, mostly people's savings. But we still had eleven employees and we rented the most beautiful suite of offices in the Expressway

Tower so we could ride in the elevator with [Dallas Cowboys coach] Tom Landry."*

That first company was installing computer switching systems at $200,000 a pop, but—because it went too fancy too soon—was burning up every cent office overhead. By the end of its first full year, the company had lost one million dollars.

So when it comes to real estate, think lean and bargain tough, and let the other guy go riding around with football coaches. Put your money into *your* pocket instead of some landlord's, and before long you'll own the whole blinking team.

*"Three's the Charm," *Forbes,* 29 March, 1982, p. 58

17
BUILDING YOUR WORKFORCE

SITUATION:
Finding hard-working, honest, and creative employees may be the single most difficult job for a small business owner
OBJECTIVE:
To build a staff which will work for the company, instead of against it

---

Employees: The Scope of the Problem.

Not long ago, Walter E. Heller, the giant capital-lending firm, commissioned a study to discover the biggest worries of American small business owners. The worst single problem, it turned out, was not energy, not interest rates, but rather employees.

In some ways, that is not surprising. Labor costs comprise anywhere from 40 to 65% of the overhead of the average small business—by far the largest single item. Add to that our well-publicized problems with employee theft, drugs in the workplace, and declining craftsmanship, and it's easy to see why small business owners lose sleep over employees.

Still, let's not oversimplify. There's a huge difference between the well-run company paying 40% for labor, and the ill-run one paying 65%. Often, too, the difference has an emotional cast. It does not take long as a business broker to realize that companies differ hugely in their abilities to make employees work together as a team. You walk into one firm, and the mood is like a happy family at home; you walk into another down the street, and it's more like taking a gunboat up the Yangtse River. You expect the riots and the shooting to break out any moment.

Thinking Intelligently about Workers.

OK—your labor force, rather than being a niggling detail best left to others, is the ultimate key to your success as a business owner. But how do you achieve those seemingly incompatible goals of low labor costs and a happy workforce?

The best single first step may be to head down to your local library and check out a copy of *Forbes* magazine for July 5, 1982, and read the article called, "This is The Answer" by William Baldwin. It's the story of Lincoln Electric Co., a Cleveland firm. Lincoln does a lot right—including leading the world in production of arc-welding equipment—but the main point is that over its sixty-seven years, Lincoln has cut the cost of its basic product from $1500 to $996 while increasing its wages *one-hundred fold.* In 1981, the average Lincoln worker took home about $44,000 a year, but the company earned an astounding $28.95 per share. Worker turnover is a miniscule 6% a year, and there hasn't been a lay-off in three decades.

Now, the Lincoln plan, which rewards workers strictly according to productivity by paying piece rates plus bonuses for innovations and production increases, may not work for everyone. Yet the point should be clear. When you think about wages, it's naive to spend much time worrying about the hourly rate. Instead, think about how much is being *produced* for every dollar you pay out. That's productivity, and it's the only thing that matters.

In the three chapters following this one, we'll discuss some practical methods—automation, quality circles, and just-in-time inventories—for increasing the productivity of your workers. Before that, let's cover the most effective ways of hiring and training people in the first place.

Defining Your Needs.

Intelligent hiring begins with a clear knowledge of your needs. Otherwise, you'll slaughter productivity by hiring people with vague duties, and paying them for too much busy-, or even non-work. That will happen even when it *seems* you have a clear need. Consider this case:

You have a travel agency with six salespeople and one secretary. As business grows, so does the pile of work in the secretary's in-basket. Soon, the top of his or her head disappears behind the mounds of untyped correspondence, unanswered queries. One day, he or she tells you in desperation that without help, he or she'll have to quit. So you run an ad, and hire a second secretary, boosting payroll by, say, $12,000 a year—and perhaps forcing you into larger offices with higher rent. Inevitable?

Well, perhaps, but let's consider some alternatives.

Before doing any hiring, ask your secretary to keep a work log for a week. Explain that you only want to know where the slow-downs are occuring; you're not accusing anyone of laziness.

The log will tell you 1. how much of each day goes to each particular task—answering phones, typing, greeting clients, etc., 2. what parts of each day, and which days of the week, are busiest, and 3. which of your salespeople are demanding most of the secretary's time—and especially whether any are asking help with personal business. (The log will also show specific advertising responses, which, though not a personnel issue, are worth studying.)

Sometimes the log will tell you that your secretary is working steadily throughout the week, is dividing time equally among all tasks, and is aiding the salespeople in a fashion roughly proportional to their sales volumes. If so, then probably you do need to hire another secretary to assist.

More probably, the log will tip you to economies that will let you at least delay hiring. Perhaps one or more salesmen is having the secretary type records he ought to be keeping by himself. You can buy him a good used portable typewriter for around four days' secretarial pay—or simply tell him to bring a typewriter of his own. Maybe someone is taking too many personal calls, or arriving late for office appointments, leaving the secretary to entertain the unhappy clients. Maybe an hour of secretarial time is lost each day to brewing coffee or other nonessential tasks. Jobs like making coffee belong to the salespeople who drink it.

Again, perhaps your secretary is only overwhelmed on Monday mornings, but then labors the rest of the week to catch up. Simply hire a temp to work that extra half-day once or twice a week. Maybe twenty minutes of each secretarial hour go to answering the phone. In that case, consider hiring someone with a pleasant voice to sit in the back room and knit while answering the phones for $3.35 an hour—under half what you'd pay a second secretary.

In short, don't commit to an employee until you know exactly what you want that employee to do. Once you *do* know, don't pay for more time or skill than you actually need. The same principle —including the work-day log—applies to any job from line worker to executive. Analyze carefully—even the difference between one temp and one full-timer can send $10,000 straight to your bottom line.

Automation, Contract Services, and Independent Contractors.

Remember that, before hiring a full-timer, you have several options:

1. *Automation.* This is covered more fully in the next chapter, UPPING PRODUCTIVITY THROUGH AUTOMATION. Meanwhile, let's just note that you can nearly always boost productivity in every part of your operations by use of computers or microprocessor controlled-machinery. Portable computers will nearly double the ground a single salesman can cover. You can unfrazzle a secretary's nerves (and postpone hiring a receptionist or phone-answering back-room person) by a modern phone answering machine. If you mail out 100 envelopes a day, you can free one-half hour of secretarial time daily by going to an electronic postal metering machine. They rent for around $30 a month, and save about $3000 yearly in lost postage and secretarial time—much more if they keep you from adding an extra person. And so on.

2. *Contract Services.* Often, especially where you lack enough work to justify hiring a full-time person, you may want to shift to contract services. Answering services—which offer a human touch lacking in the machines—are one example, but so are contract payroll, janitorial, and general bookkeeping firms. Contract ser-vices charge a high hourly rate in order to cover both the worker's wage and the contractor's profit. They still make sense whenever the savings in hours exceeds the hourly overpayment total. A good firm will also save you hassles with hiring, firing, and sudden resignations. Just watch out for efforts to sell you extra services— that's how they grow fat and you lose money.

3. *Freelancers and Independent Contractors.* Both of these can be a lively play for some small firms, but they must be used with caution.

A freelancer or independent contractor saves your paying any fringe benefits, Social Security, or unemployment compensation. He also provides the flexibility of a person who works by the task, not by the hour—and so, is only paid when there's specific work to be done.

The IRS considers someone to be your employee if you control the use of his or her time. That's a loose definition, but probably you are risking trouble if you try to claim as a freelancer anyone who works for you more than about fifteen hours a week. As usual, the IRS will provide a free opinion in advance, which makes more sense than trying to trick them and then getting nailed for all the money due, plus penalties and interest.

Used properly, a freelancer can save you 10–20% on hourly costs, reduce the total hours worked, and lessen your office over-head, since he or she only visits your property to deliver the finished product.

It is also possible to have workers who are full-time and gener-ally on-premises, but still not paid as employees. In the "Indepen-dent Contractor" arrangements favored by, for example, real es-tate offices, the salesman is paid purely on a commission basis, and agrees that, while the firm has no control over his time or efforts, he will still labor in its best interests. As the name suggest, these contracts really only succeed with independent, highly motivated people; otherwise, you'll only acquire a bunch of idlers. With self-starters, though, the productivity can be tremendous.

Finding a New Worker.

When none of these methods will serve, it's time to add permanent staff. From your job-log analysis, you know exactly what the job will entail; you also know what training and experience you consider important, and approximately what you want to pay. The next step is to find candidates, by advertisements, agencies, enlistment bonuses, personal recruiting, or use of headhunting or executive recruiting firms.

ADVERTISEMENTS will draw the largest pool of applicants—including, unfortunately, a large number of completely unqualified people. You can trim the number of unsuitables by 1) being as specific about the job requirements as possible, 2) pegging the requirements a notch higher than what you actually need (if you want someone who types 70 wpm, ask for 80; that'll at least reduce the number of applicants who really type about 55), and 3) giving a phone number instead of an address and then doing some quick screening during the first call. The phone interviewer might, for example, stress the strictness of the requirements, and add that at least two strong personal recommendations will be required at the first interview—anything to trim the number of flakes you have to meet.

Still, before running your own "help wanted" ads, consider how much time and money you will spend just in preparing your "short list" of desirable candidates. Unless your firm is big enough to support a full-time personnel director, direct ads are perhaps a doubtful approach.

EMPLOYMENT AGENCIES will, in theory, do the preliminary screening for you, and only send along candidates meeting your exact specifications. They are especially good at locating office, clerical, and secretarial personnel. Remember, though, that some agencies bill only the employee, while others will also collect a fee from the employer. It pays, therefore, to shop for an agency. If you do go with a firm that bills you, see that they have a refund procedure for employees who don't stick a specified period of time —say, four months.

ENLISTMENT BONUSES, useful for finding people with scarce skills, turn your own staff into recruiters. It's perfectly legal to pay a bonus—$25 to $1000 or more—to employees who persuade others to join the firm. The practice was widespread during the super-boom years of Silicon Valley, where, in a few cases, employees earned more in a year on bonuses than on their salaries. Just remember to make the bonuses payable after a new employee has been with the firm at least six months.

ACTIVE RECRUITING. You can also quietly recruit skilled people while addressing professional groups or, even better, college or university classes. Business classes are often glad to have small business owners explain how actual firms operate. You may not only receive useful feedback, but are always entitled to make a brief employment pitch—it's your compensation, in a way. Even better, you can frequently arrange to let a business graduate student aid you as part of his coursework—a good one can do the work of a true management consultant for free, and thank you for the chance. Simply call a school nearby and ask what's available.

Smart firms also mine college classrooms for promising technical talent. Some years ago, Ampex was wise enough to design custom work hours for a Stanford undergraduate with some clever notions about sound. His name was Ray Dolby, and he went ahead to invent the world's most widely-used recording noise reduction systems. Remember that, especially in technical fields, "experienced" may be just another word for "obsolete". Give young people a shot.

You can do more formal recruiting by arranging with local schools to be on-campus for their recruitment- or employment-day activities. On the bigger campuses you'll be competing against flashy operations from major companies, but you can still make a strong presentation. Stress the advantages of working for a small company—the independence; the chance to stay at home near friends and family; and the prospects of quick growth and promotion.

It's definitely worth your time to compete for this talent. We once had a client who, over a period of years, built himself a kind of mini-conglomerate. Starting with a single large gun shop, he used the profits to buy a series of retailers and manufacturers, each doing about $1,000,000 in sales and having good growth potential. Instead of running them himself, he turned each one over to a newly-minted Stanford MBA, offering a mediocre salary but a generous profit-participation. Then—except for occasional advice —he just stepped aside and let those Stanford stars make him rich.

Going after young talent may be the only affordable approach for small businesses. The fact is that major corporations' salaries rapidly escalate beyond the matching power of small firms. If you *can* afford those salaries, though, you are ready for:

RECRUITING FIRMS AND HEADHUNTERS. True recruiting firms ("head-hunters" is a slang term for those which recruit top- and middle-management personnel), will simply go out and acquire the person you want, sometimes by advertising, but more often by making direct approaches. For that reason, they are generally about as welcome as medflies around most corporate headquarters. They can lure key people away from major firms because they offer fat raises and bonuses of every sort. Of course, *you* are going to have to deliver whatever the recruiter promises, and will moreover be liable for some very hefty fees. During the peak of headhunter madness in the late '70s, some firms began asking as much as one year's salary for their work. If they brought in a $60,000-a-year executive, you owed a them a $60,000 fee. At that point, many companies drew the line, and began in-house recruiting operations. What's sensible for the big guys is probably sensible for you; open checkbook recruiting is a very expensive way to proceed, and better avoided by the cautious small firm.

Fitting the Employee In: The Kirsten Flagstad Syndrome.

Once likely candidates have been located, the next tasks are to 1) choose the best candidate(s), and 2) train them for the job.

It's not a bad idea to have each candidate interviewed by at least two people, one to do preliminary screening for attitude and general competence and the other to give final approval. You are probably wise to ask for at least two recommendations from each candidate, and to check them carefully. Remember that sometimes you have to probe politely before a recommender will give you an honest opinion. Lastly, it helps if you can devise a short (under thirty minute) test for any finalists—just to make sure they really *can* type 90 wpm, or use a DisplayWriter, or whatever. If you still have doubts, you might suggest they try a three-or-four day trial run, paid on a freelance basis. But no matter how superb a candidate appears, don't expect too much from the early days of any career.

When the great soprano Kirsten Flagstad auditioned at the Met in 1935, she walked onto the stage an unknown, but her first few notes (the story goes) sent enraptured performers, critics, and even stagehands, hastening in every direction to drag others in the building to hear her most marvelous of voices. Before she had finished singing, the formerly empty rehearsal hall was packed with cheering admirers.

It's a nice story, but unfortunately, it also suggests the instant wonders too many small business people expect from new employees. In fact, most quickly discover that training a new employee is tiring and expensive. Good employees—especially these days—are more often made than found. As far as I can tell, the main reason small business owners have such miseries with employees is that not one in a hundred knows how to train them.

Long ago, of course, the guilds trained employees, and apprenticeships were long and rigorous. Something of that still exists in Europe. Porsche, for example, takes most of its line workers straight out of high-school, and puts them through a three-and-a-half-year trainee's school. It's an expensive program, but it guarantees that Porsche craftsmanship will be second to none in the world.

Unless you are building $50,000 sports cars, you may not be able to justify anything like the Porsche plan. But even a modest business needs a careful training program—one combining a psychological process of enspiriting workers, with a purely technical training to teach the job.

Surveys have shown that small business owners tend to skimp on training largely because they consider too much of the job to be obvious. Employees, meanwhile, almost always say that their training was hasty and superficial, and left them confused about what their bosses actually expected. The problem isn't lack of native intelligence, but—especially with young and under-privileged workers—an unfamiliarity with both general, and particular company, business practices. You have to start with the basics—with the special language of your line of work.

Our company used to screen secretaries rigorously, pay them top dollar—and then put them through a whirlwind "training program" which included such gems as: "Now, when someone pulls a customer card, you just green-slip it, enter it on the customer lists for the renewal mail-out, and post it in the blue-book. Right?"

Well, right—except that no one had explained what green slips, blue books, customer cards, or anything else were. Inevitably, such efforts at time-saving meant that new secretaries spent weeks in confusion, and often quit, leaving records chaotic. Only when we completely reworked our training process, including writing a secretaries' reference manual (under twenty pages, plus examples), did we begin producing employees who could contribute from the first to the full extent of their talents.

Big firms nearly always provide elaborate employee handbooks, which outline everything from the company history to its policies on benefits and promotions. With little trouble, you might well create a pamphlet for new employees containing:

1. *Company name and purpose.* What the company does, and how long it has been at it. Why an employee should be proud to work there.

2. *Company policies.* What you expect from employees in the way of dress and demeanor. Your policies on employee theft, benefits, overtime, sick-leave, and anything else you think appropriate.

3. *Specific work methods.* Anything you need to say about specific company practices, from standard letter forms to be sent in specific

situations, to company policy on refunds for defective merchandise.

4. *Complaint and suggestion procedures.* The ways in which complaints will be heard, and productive suggestions will be tested and, if workable, adopted. Anything to show employees they have a voice in the company.

Again, you can't train by simply handing out the pamphlet and sending people home to read it. Many of them won't and (sadly), these days, many of them can't. You have to teach the job, and when you do, go slowly and ask frequently for questions: try to let a person attempt each step of the process after you. Give steady encouragement, remembering that (especially young) employees are usually extremely nervous about failure.

Encouragement for workers remains important long after initial training is completed. How far you go depends upon you. You may never adopt the Japanese habits of company songs and morning calisthenics, but you still want to foster achievement. One fine technique is the worker's quality circle—for details, please see USING QUALITY CIRCLES. Even before that, you can promote enthusiasm by such traditional means as banners carrying company goals, departmental picnics, and seasonal incentives like Christmas bonuses and even Thanksgiving turkeys. The experience of firms like Lincoln Electric suggests that cold cash is probably the best of all incentives, but don't underestimate the impact of smaller touches.

A stable and productive workforce is at least as crucial a measure of success as market share, profit margins, or gross sales, because, without a stable workforce, it's unlikely you'll achieve any of your other goals. So you must carefully track changes in 1) the number of dollars' worth of goods produced for every dollar in labor costs, and 2) the average time an employee stays with you. If either of those fall over an extended period, you need to change your incentives, your recruiting, or your training and employee relations—perhaps all three areas at once.

Exit Interviews.

One way to discover the kinds of changes needed, is to conduct what are known as "exit interviews," in which you sit down with an employee and ask 1) why he is leaving, and 2) whether there were any changes at the company which would have encouraged him to stay. If you make it clear that you really are seeking honest answers, usually you'll get them.

Sometimes the answer will be beyond your control—a spouse moving out of the state, for example. Other times, there will be a lesson—the guys down the street are paying more, or the advertisement for the job misrepresented what was involved. Changes are required.

Occasionally the answer will be problematical. Suppose a good employee is leaving to start a family. Is there a way around the problem? Could you start a work-at-home program? Are there enough people in that situation to justify a company day-care program, or are working conditions flexible enough that an infant could be brought to work every day? (A few companies have in recent years begun permitting infants on the grounds, with some success.)

Pay attention to these exit interviews—and also to your general employment statistics. If one department's rate of turnover is consistently higher than the rest (and especially if its supervisor files a lot of bum reports on his employees), it may well be the supervisor himself who is causing the problem. Find out whether departing workers found him difficult—and be alert for phrases like "personality conflict," which polite workers will usually favor over calling their ex-supervisor a jerk. By the same token, be ready to respond immediately to accusations of discrimination or sexual harassment. These are not only repugnant in themselves, but destructive of the work environment and extremely likely to lead to litigation. You need a quick investigation and a solution with teeth in it—which means that a supervisor guilty of such actions must either reform or be let go. You really have no other choices.

The Other Side of the Picture.

With all the (largely undeserved) bad press the American worker has received in recent years, it seems only fair to end this section with an example of how extremely well labor and management can sometimes combine in a small business.

In fact, it sometimes happens that in an employee will help you solve one of the toughest of all small-business problems—finding a trustworthy person to whom you can finally sell the business. Most people who work for you will probably be honest and reasonably competent; a few will fail you badly for one reason or another. But now and again you will find that rare person whose passion for the work matches your own. Such a person can become a cornerstone of your organization, and even, someday, your replacement in the firm.

Some years ago, we tried to sell a chocolate company owned by a man who insisted upon making his chocolates to old-world standards of quality. It was a profitable company—we had it pretty reasonably priced at about $450,000, as I remember—but we got nowhere with it because prospective owners would consider the desirability of rising every morning well before dawn to start hand-dipping hazelnuts, and decide they were going on a diet.

As it happened, though, this owner had among his employees one of those ghetto youths we're sometimes told compose the "hard-core unemployable." This young man had no claim on the old-world tradition of chocolate making, but he did have a passion for the craft, and a willingness to learn. When chocolate had to be poured at 6:00 AM, he was there; when you stopped by the plant late on Saturday afternoons, you nearly always found only the owner and this young man there working together.

Some years went by—while we tried off and on again to make the sale—and gradually this young assistant (no longer quite so young, of course) became a master *chocolatier* himself. One day, the owner, having decided it really was time for him to retire from management, announced that he would sell the company to the best-qualified person he knew—his assistant. The deal they designed required only a small down payment, after which the balance was to be paid from company earnings over the next five years. For five years, that meant the former apprentice would take home less than he had as a straight employee. At the end of the term, though, he would be sole owner of the firm.

The owner by himself had done what we could not—found a competent and eager buyer for the company. He, meanwhile, would stay on as the chief chocolate maker, an ordinary employee. If you stop by the plant today, you'll see an owner and an employee who have recently exchanged roles. But for customers, suppliers, and casual lookers-on, nothing significant has changed at all.

Postscript: About Unions.

I've said very little so far in this book about unions. The reason is that, except in a few fields (such as construction), unions are not a major problem for small business. Of the firms we have sold over the years, I doubt that one in a hundred has been unionized.

First of all, small firms rarely employ enough people to justify a union's costs for an organizing drive. Secondly, there are strong human bonds in many small firms, where the owner and employees are in daily contact, and often upon a first-name basis. These bonds encourage both fair play by management and reasonable demands by labor—the two sides tend to see each other as human beings, not economic abstractions.

So (except in those few heavily unionized industries), you are probably wrong to spend a great deal of time worrying about unions. Stick to the strategies listed in the book for improving the quality of working life in your company, and you will probably do well. Here are a few other general suggestions:

1. If you absolutely refuse to deal with unions, avoid those industries (construction, automotive parts manufacturing, etc.) which are highly unionized. If you're really adamant, consider a region of the country which tends to favor nonunion operations —the South and the Southwest are traditional choices.

2. As suggested in FOUR FINAL QUESTIONS, be sure to ask whether any business you are considering buying has been the target of organizing efforts or a strike notification. (Remember, though, that a union contract can often be a plus, guaranteeing stable labor costs and—often—a stable work force. Indeed, unionized labor costs are not automatically higher than non-union costs. In the steel industry, for example, the independent manufacturers have often paid higher wages than the unionized firms just to keep the unions out. So don't panic when you hear a firm's unionized—it may even be to your advantage.)

3. In any case, to avoid unionization or other labor troubles, be *sensitive to complaints.* Quality of working life matters as much as wages. The owners I've seen nailed by the unions are usually those who ignored their workers for ten years or more, and then, the day the labor organizers appeared, suddenly upped the wages to union scale. They're always shocked when the workers vote for the union—as if money were the only thing human beings wanted out of life. Decent wages are important, but they're not everything.

4. Recognize that, in the majority of cases, peaceful labor organization is a legal right. Make it clear from the outset that you will observe the law—and that you expect any labor organizers to do the same. If, subsequently, you find force or intimidation is being used to promote the union, you haven't got a labor problem, you've got a crime problem—and you need to bring in the police.

Above all, remember that when you have a good relationship with your workers, you can survive even very rough times without labor troubles. A friend of mine owned a good-sized building and engineering firm, which had been unionized since 1946. When the housing market collapsed in the early '80s, he decided he had to deunionize to survive. Just before the wage contract expired, he announced he wouldn't be renewing—that he would be hiring nonunion personnel.

Though his know-it-all friends predicted labor violence, there wasn't a single rock thrown or a tire slashed. In fact, there were only a series of rather sad farewells. He lost a few fine workers, who couldn't afford to abandon their union pensions, but most stayed on willingly. For the thirty-five years he'd been in business, he'd always played fair with his workers, and kept them posted on the general state of the business. Now they knew as well as he did that, unless he left the union with its wage scales and work rules, the company they had helped to build would go bust. Nobody wanted that and so they wrote the union off, and stayed together (very successfully, as it happens) to solve their problems as a team.

18

THE PLAGUE OF HOSPITALITY

SITUATION:
Employees are wined and dined into signing unreasonable contracts
OBJECTIVE:
Keeping distinct business and pleasure

This is a topic so decidedly awkward I have never known it mentioned in any business lecture or text. Since, however, the effects can be ruinous, and the prevention should only be a matter of a word to the wise, I'll make a try at it.

The situation recently hit a friend of ours like this:

This friend had a growing business retailing expensive add-ons for pleasure boats. In particular, he was selling about $70,000 a year worth of short-wave radios. He also had a young manager who was beginning to show definite ability. As a sort of a bonus, the young manager was chosen to make the trip back to Chicago to place the next year's order for those $70,000 worth of transceivers. He came back after four days—he had bought $165,000 worth of gear. He also had one tremendous headache.

What that means is that our friend was stuck with $95,000 worth of electronics he won't be able to sell for at least a year, by which time, they'll be last year's model. Even assuming he can then unload them at full price, the year's financing (at, say, 20%) will mean the big weekend will have ended up costing around $19,000.

Now, without going into *precisely* what happened to the young manager, the general situation is this: companies which want to sell you goods and services hire salesmen. Most of these salesmen will confine themselves to presentations, plus, perhaps, a certain discreet amount of wining and dining, with tickets to a play or golf at the country club included. A few, however, will stage the sort of bachanalian excess which has not really been popular since the Roman empire collapsed. If your negotiator is male (as is still most common these days), the scene will likely feature ladies of the evening—a circumstance long-honored for its tendency to lessen one's judgment.

Under those conditions, almost no one—certainly few beginners —would be able to bargain for a desirable contract, and yet contracts are written under those conditions every day. Keeping your company out of these ambushes requires only a minimal amount of planning and preparation—but you must make the effort.

If you have an employee you trust, then probably only a short discussion of these facts of business life will suffice. If you sound to yourself like *Hamlet*'s Polonius preparing his son for that trip to France, well, so be it. If you have an employee whose judgement is for some reason suspect—who has, perhaps, a drinking problem but is otherwise your best negotiator—either send someone else, provide a chaperone, or write an advance letter (sent certified mail, with return receipt) stipulating the limits of the contract he may negotiate for you. This may crimp your employee's style, but that's a lot better than letting him crimp your bank account—perhaps all the way into bankruptcy.

If you *are* suckered into one of these deals, your options are limited. Contracts, of course, can be voided because of duress—here meaning diminished capacity—but it is unlikely your young manager will want to appear in court and explain he was swinging from a chandelier when he signed the contract—leaving aside the fact that you will need several years before your case gets to court (See Chapter Fifteen). You might simply try to have the contract rewritten, but the kinds of firms which encourage these tactics in the first place aren't likely to let you off the hook. Basically, you've bought yourself those transceivers.

Before leaving this awkward aspect of personal relations, I probably ought to mention another situation famous for sinking otherwise successful businesses, namely, the practice of fooling around with the help. Probably the most notorious arenas for this are restaurants, and perhaps a quarter of the restaurants we offer for sale are otherwise successful institutions which the owner has ruined by launching one or more affairs with the employees. Between risking divorce and stirring up animosities among the other workers (which, after hepatitis, may be the two fastest ways to sink a restaurant), these affairs are infinitely more trouble than they are worth. Avoid them. Life abounds with other opportunities. In this case at least, observe the old axiom, and keep business and pleasure separate.

19

UPPING PRODUCTIVITY THROUGH AUTOMATION

SITUATION:
Modern business virtually demands the use of office or production automation
OBJECTIVE:
Introducing automation (especially office automation) rapidly and safely

Introduction: Automation, Computers, and "Cyberphobia."

It's hardly news that computerized automation—from computers in small business to robots on assembly lines—will be an essential part of economic life from the 1980s onward. When the national robotics show was held early in 1982, the sponsors had to close the doors temporarily on opening day—they couldn't let any more people in safely. GM alone is committed to installing some 10,000 robots before 1990; in just the last year or two, not only GM, but GE, IBM, United Technologies, and Cincinnati Milacron (to name only a few heavy hitters) have announced they're getting into robot manufacture. Add that to the explosive growth of the small computer market—with unit shipments heading up into the hundreds of thousands monthly—and it's clear that anyone who refuses categorically to get involved with these evolving technologies is going to be left far behind.

In spite of that, many small businesses—even those sinking under a flood of paperwork, or trapped by log-jammed production

—resist turning to either computers or computer-controlled machines (robots). They suffer, in short, from "cyberphobia." As a result, they not only throw away their chance to grow from small firms to bigger ones, but they tie their owners to a life of paperwork slavery, their workers to boring and repetitive jobs, and their customers to lower levels of product quality. Sooner, or later, they are going to lose out to more modern competitors—either that, or overcome their fears and start joining the move to computerization.

OK—ninety-nine out of 100 small businesses are going to have to either accept computers in the office and robots on the shop floor, or go slowly out of business. But how do we go about adopting these machines, assuming we are either nervous or uninformed at the start?

Well, since small computers are far more widespread and—at this stage, at least—affordable, I'll use them as my example (small computers usable in an office can be had at less than $1,000, while an inexpensive true robot—say, a Unimation Apprentice—will run nearer to $40,000.) But the basic principles for familiarization are the same.

Simple Automated Products.

One way to begin is simply to recognize that you have microprocessor-controlled products around you all the time, from modern automobile engines to programmable microwave ovens. If you want to start introducing these into your office, you can start with something as simple as a first-rate phone answering machine. You'll quickly see why these products are considered cost-effective. The average phone-answering service will charge you around $35–50 a month, *plus* a charge of 10¢ a call above a certain minimum. Call it $60 a month. These services work fairly well when they are not busy, but when demand picks up, they can let your line ring six or seven times without answering. A microprocessor-controlled answering machine, meanwhile, will answer every time on the ring of your choice, record every message accurately, and even let you screen calls as they come in. It'll run you about $300 *total,* which means (tax credits aside) that after six months the thing has paid for itself. From then until it wears out (some years down the road), that $720 a year you had been paying an answering service goes straight onto your bottom line. Welcome to the world of office automation!

Dedicated Machinery.

Of course, an answering machine with a low-capacity microprocessor is a long way from a computer, which is a device which 1) manipulates large quantities of data at high speed and 2) can be programmed by the user for a wide variety of operations.

One way by which small businesses edge toward computer ownership is through the use of dedicated machinery, which is any sort of computer which has been specially confined (dedicated) to a few particular functions. Probably the best-known of these are *word processors,* which have been placed in offices by the hundreds of thousands in the last few years.

A word processor will allow you electronically to: create several hundred pages of text, use a dictionary to correct spelling automatically, and manipulate a relatively small data base of names and addresses. Word processors have two main applications. First, for large-scale mailing of "personalized" correspondence the processor will turn out individually-typed letters and envelopes for every name on a list, and even make point-substitutions of names within the text ("the reason I'm writing you, Bob, is . . ."). Second, the processor will *edit texts,* allowing you to store long reports (even books) on diskettes, and to rearrange the text electronically, moving words, lines, even whole chapters freely about while watching a screen and without waiting for the copy to be laboriously printed.

Most word processors cost between $5,000 and $15,000, with much going for the *printer,* which is also the component most likely to need servicing and repairs. If you need only a few of the functions of a word processor (if, say, you send letters which repeat phrases or paragraphs frequently) consider an *electronic typewriter,* which lacks the video display and most text-editing functions, but which does have some memory capacity. Electronic typewriters start at around $1500, and recently several companies have begun marketing up-grade kits (at around $3000) to convert them into true word processors.

Obviously, word processors have many applications, especially for companies or departments which deal with long reports (such as law firms). Because they have only one function, they are extremely "user-friendly"; that is, they are set up to require as little knowledge of computers as possible. That's one reason why they were among the first machines to appear in offices.

Unfortunately, such dedicated machines make you pay nearly the full price of a good small business microcomputer, but then give you only *one* of the functions. If you think you want to do more than that, consider going whole-hog and looking at real microcomputers.

MICROCOMPUTERS AND DATA-BASE MANAGEMENT. What other functions will a small business computer handle? Well, to name a few:

Accounts Payable and
    Receivable
Detailed Clients Lists
Engineering Calculations
Forecasting
General Ledgers
Graphs and Tables (Any
    sort)
Order Processing
Payroll
Remote Database Access
Spread Sheet Analysis

And on, and on. Plus, of course, word processing and (dare one mention it) computer games. The essence of each of these functions, of course, is software—and there are endless alternate programs at, usually, between $300 and $500 a pop—which probably explains why the program dubbing and trading underground is so active. You should never consider any computer without first trying a range of its proprietary programs, or buy any program without trying several of its competitors. Most computer retailing stores will allow you this privilege. Make sure, too, any computer you use employs a widely-used *operating system* (master software).

All right; most of the small business computers on the market can handle a wide range of accounting, record-keeping, and (within limits) number-crunching functions. How do you find the right one for you, and how much should you pay? What, in short, are you buying?

CPUs. The first thing you are buying is a central processing unit, or CPU. All fancy rhetoric aside, this is the electronic heart of your system. It is usually ranked two ways—by its *random access memory* (RAM), and the speed of its *microprocessor* (the device which actually does the calculations or data manipulations)—in short, by the capacity of a handful of its integrated circuits.

RAM capacity is an indication of how much information can be put into the computer for use at one time; in other words, how complicated a problem it can handle. Low-end, start-up models usually have about *8–16*K (that is, 8,000–16,000 electronic pieces) of RAM—about four pages' worth of typewritten text. For general business, you probably want at least *64–128*K. The more you have, the more sophisticated will be the programs you can use— which (surprisingly) usually means the easier they will be for the nonspecialist to run. Memories are on simple circuit-boards, and most computers can be expanded (within limits) on a plug-in basis. Whatever system you consider, find out not only its delivered capability, but how far it can be expanded. You should be able to *quadruple* the capacity of most systems.

Microprocessor speed is measured in the number of bits of information which the system can handle at one time. Most early (mid/-late '70s) small business machines were *8-bit* microprocessors; newer machines such as the TRS-16 and the IBM Personal Computer use *16-bit* processors, and some advanced systems are now moving into 32-bit processors. For most small businesses, microprocessor speed is less important than RAM capacity, but the higher-speed machines do usually represent newer machines which have *other* advantages: 1) they are more reliable in general and 2) they are generally less temperature-sensitive. (Early small computers tended to shut down if the temperature dropped into the low '60s or rose into the high '80s).

Generally sold along with the CPU are the *keyboard* for entering data, and the *display screen* (a cathode ray tube, or CRT) for observing results or checking text before having a hard copy printed. The *display screen* should be high-resolution, easy on your eyes (watch it for an hour or so at least), and have a full, *80-character display, 25-line capacity.* You don't want the people using the machine to start developing headaches, or even phoning in sick just to avoid working with it.

The *keyboard* should have a feel as near to that of a real typewriter as possible (tactile feedback), with *full keyboard,* including a separate *numeric pad* and at least six to ten *function keys.*

DISC DRIVES. Since even a relatively large CPU can only hold the equivalent of a few dozen pages of information—and since a growing small business may want to keep lists of, say, many hundreds or thousands of clients, with names, addresses, and needs—you will certainly need some *peripheral* storage units. In the past, this has generally meant *floppy disks.*

Unfortunately, floppy disks have had problems. The *are* reliable and cheap (about $5 apiece), but their capacity (around 250K, or 125 pages) is simply too small. With the usual complement of two disk drives (at around $800 each), the average small business computer *still* does not have enough capacity. That means your operator is constantly shifting from one floppy to another, burning up time and losing much of a computer's efficiency. This failure of capacity for what is known as *database management* led a fair number of small businesses to abandon their computer efforts early on.

To remedy the problem, the best product currently on the market is the *Winchester Disk System.* Invented by IBM, the Winchester is a sealed, hard-disk system with a minimum capacity of about 5*M* or 5,000,000 bytes of information—about 2500 pages. The units aren't cheap—around $3500 a crack—but if you want database management at its best, this is what you need.

The last of the standard computer peripherals is a *printer.* There are two general types, dot-matrix, and daisy-wheel. *Dot-matrix,* or "draft-quality" printers produce characters from a set of dots. The resulting printing is readable but clearly inferior to regular typescript. They're fine for rough drafts; hence the name. *Daisy-wheel* printers use regular typeface mounted on a wheel which spins at high-speed. The result is "letter quality" work. Dot matrix printers are fast (around 120 characters per second) and reliable. Daisy wheel printers are slow (basic models run around 30 CPS) and tend to break fairly frequently. But, of course, the daisy's quality of final copy is far superior. If you go for the daisy wheel printer, don't omit the service contract—it won't be cheap.

There are any number of other peripherals available for computers, but two are especially worth mentioning. If you want to tap remote data-bases—which can provide your computer with anything from medical bibliographies to the latest Dow-Jones averages—you need a phone/computer interface called a *modem.* And whatever computer you pick, be sure to spend the extra hundred bucks or so for a *line voltage* regulator; the variations and surges in ordinary current can do your system in.

Choosing a System.

You now know at least the terms so you can talk intelligently when you go to shop. But the truth is that—despite the dozens of people out in the marketplace trying to sell you a system—the hardware is basically going to be that of a very few chip suppliers (like Intel and Motorola) wrapped in a whole slew of different packages. You need to know that you want 64K/8-bit, say, but 64K/8-bit from Apple really isn't any different from 64K/8-bit from Radio Shack. How do you chose one over the other?

PRICE. Too obvious to mention? Not really. Remember that computer prices, driven downward by competition and the learning curve, are almost unbelieveably deflationary. Early in 1981, DEC introduced a small business system at around $9,500. One year later, responding to the competition, they slashed the price by 40%, to under $6000. Whenever you've got a market where a top-grade, nondiscontinued product can drop 40% in price in one day, you've got to buy tough—or you're going to be hung out to dry. With small business computers, you've got to watch packages, promotions, and model introductions, and shop price as much as features.

SERVICE AND RELIABILITY. Small computers are rapidly getting more reliable, but they are still a long way from being table radios. A service contract for, say, an average Apple III will probably run you around $400 a year—which means the company expects it will need to do nearly that much work on it annually. That in turn means you will gain by shopping for reliability (follow the popular computer magazines for surveys), and also for service availability. If there's an Apple—or a Tandy, or Wang—service center three blocks from your office, that ought to be a major factor in your choice. There are still quite a few companies around which try to make repairs by flying out their one repairman from the office in Duluth, or else ask you to ship them the computer—and they'll get to it "right away." That's just not good enough.

SUPPORT. Support in computer terms means both assistance in getting your system—and each new program, if necessary—running, and also the availability of instruction for your people in computer skills. Nearly every computer retailer promises courses, but some of these prove to be a couple of hours after closing with you, a bored salesman, and a dog-eared manual. The big companies still have a big edge here.

One excellent way to get an idea of the quality of a company's support, in fact, is simply to sign up for some of its computer orientation or instruction courses; the big firms run these on regular monthly schedules. The courses are cheap—many are free if you come across as a serious buyer—and they do several things simultaneously. First, they let you wander around inside the company's offices (where the classes are held) and meet people in a nonsales situation. Too, they let you gauge the quality of support (these class teachers will be the same one who later help you on-site), and they let you get your mitts on the hardware, to really work with it for several hours in a relatively low-pressure situation.

That last is probably the most important point of all. You can read this chapter several times over—you can read half a dozen books or magazines devoted to nothing but computers—but with *any* type of hardware, you'll never know which one is right for you until you actually get out and work with it. So that leads to the last tip of all—*get out and get hands-on experience.* It's true even if you're not ever going to be the one to run the computer once it's installed. You may want to bring along your designated computer operator, but *you take the course too.* Remember that computerized executive workstations are now standard-issue in many big corporations, and that the newest generation of high-performance personal computers (like Apple's Lisa models) will help popularize them for small businesses as well. If you don't get in, you'll get left behind. *Now's the time to get started.*

You can find these courses at:

1. Major small computer vendors—IBM, DEC, etc.
2. Many retail computer outlets
3. Some night schools
4. Most junior or community colleges, nearly all universities

Starting Up.

The systems I've described are all entry-level business units, or a bit beyond. It may well be, if you've waited a fair while before committing to computers, that you'll decide on a far more complex system. In any case, your next task is getting it into operation. What's involved, and how long will it take?

Partly, of course, that depends upon the complexity of the system. If you are going for a fully-interactive office (with word processors, executive workstations, photocopiers, etc., all tied together,) then you have to wait first of all to have coaxial cables pulled through all your office walls. Count on a period of some months at least. But if you are starting with a more modest system, the hardware and all standard software should come straight off the shelf. Depending upon your basic aptitude for the machines, you should have a working system within a couple of weeks.

Remember that simply having a running machine won't mean

much, until all your company records have been *loaded onto storage disks.* To get a rough idea of how long that will take, ask your secretary(s) how long it would take to *retype* those records. Loading them for the computer will take about as long.

One cautionary note: even though the whole idea of office computing is to get your paper blizzard under control, *make the changeover slowly.* In spite of computer company warnings, too many companies start tossing away hard (paper) copies as soon as they make disc entries. Then, a few days later, they discover an inexperienced operator has accidentally erased all the accounts receivable. For the first few months at least, make hard copies of everything, and keep them. A reasonable shakedown period is essential, and even afterwards, all computer records should be routinely duplicated—put on spare discs or floppies—and stored in a safe place far from the computer center.

Security. That in turn raises a last concern about computers. Because they concentrate all your business paperwork—from payroll to accounts payable—they are the natural targets of sabotage, and the natural tools of fraud. Anyone out to hurt the company has only to erase or destroy a box or two of floppy disks—or smash a couple of Winchester units—to do you the worst harm he can short of burning down your building. Similarly, a computer offers unequalled opportunities for subtle, hard-to-uncover frauds.

So let's repeat the warnings given in the chapter on Security. First, if you set out to harden against crime any part of your operation, give the computer system priority second only to cash-carrying points-of-sale. Second, see that any employee with access to the computer who has to be fired is fired without advance warning, ordered to turn in any keys immediately, and escorted from the building. If you can, have the locks changed.

Third, to protect against computer fraud, use *divided responsibility* precautions. Make anything involving computer-accessed funds (payrolls, accounts payable, refunds, etc.) a *two-person* (at least) job. If one person opens the envelopes and reads off names and amounts, another should do the computer entering. Now, 1) it takes the collusion of two people to perpetrate a fraud and 2) the

reading position is so entirely low-skill that you can rotate personnel almost daily.

Computer auditing programs are being developed by many accounting firms, but until they become generally available, keep to
these basic precautions, and you'll be able to make the move into
office automation swiftly, smoothly, and—above all—safely.

20
USING "JUST IN TIME" DELIVERIES

SITUATION:
Japanese-style just-in-time delivery systems can mean big savings in costs and big gains in quality
OBJECTIVE:
Adapting a large-scale technique to small businesses. Enlisting the support of suppliers and workers

Just in Time: Not Sexy, but Smart.

Since even a great business can always use lower costs and higher quality, you should at least consider a stalling a "just-in-time" inventory system. These systems may not sound especially exciting; they simply mean that inventory arrives just as it is needed, as closely as possible to the day—or even minute—when it is going to be used. Yet some firms—GM for one—are already using JIT to save tens of millions of dollars annually. Just in time may not be sexy, but it sure is smart.

How Inventory Hurts.

"Just in Time" (the Japanese call it *kanban*) works because inventory is expensive. In the first place, all inventory is negative cash flow. In the time between your buying something from a supplier and selling it to a customer, the cash has all travelled in the wrong direction. Even worse, that inventory on the shelf is costing you money in interest charges. If you've got $100,000 in inventory (which isn't much), and you're borrowing at 20%, that's a cool $20,000 a year you're kissing off. When you add in the cost of inventory insurance, the real estate costs of a place for inventory storage, and the likelihood of losses to pilferage, you can see the fiscal logic of leaning your inventory.

Those are the immediate financial costs of inventory, but lately another kind of cost has become apparent, what you might call the "plenty more where that came from" syndrome. Large and loosely-controlled inventories seem to promote waste and poor quality of work, partly because they make supplies seem cheap, and partly because they let people mask their mistakes. If you've got 10,000 widgets sitting in a bin, the guy who's breaking two out of every three he picks up will probably go unnoticed for a long time, but if those widgets are only arriving at the rate of forty a day, he's going to be caught short pretty fast.

Against these incentives to shrink inventory, of course, you have the problem that, without inventory, you haven't got anything to sell. So far, the best compromise anyone has found is to shrink the time goods sit in inventory—in other words, just in time delivery.

WATCHING JIT WORK. Most of the people who talk about JIT, treat it as a Japanese invention. Certainly the Japanese deserve credit for refining and spreading it, but in fact the first practitioners were probably American supermarket chains, who (along with all the other incentives) needed to keep inventory spinning because so much of it spoiled so quickly. If you want to get a glimpse of JIT in action, just wander down to your local Safeway. If they kept inventories the way most companies do (given their selling rate), the average supermarket would be about a block long and four stories high. Instead, you'll see remarkably little on-site warehouse space, with round-the-clock restocking and reshelving. That's home-grown JIT in action.

MAKING JIT WORK FOR YOU. Obviously, not every kind of business can make use of JIT (it's hard to see how it would help a law firm, for example). Still, if you intend to make use of it, you need to pay attention to the following:

1. Inventory control
2. Demand forecasting
3. Distance from suppliers
4. Statistical tracking/Quality control
5. Floor supervision

Most of these would matter to you in any case, but become even more important with the narrower margins of JIT planning.

INVENTORY CONTROL AND DEMAND FORECASTING. Simply put, this means that, because JIT requires giving up the buffer effect of a large inventory, you have to be very quick to adjust for any changes in demand, and very quick to catch any discrepancies between what you're supposed to have in inventory, and what's actually there. If you're supposed to have 10,000 widgets in a bin, but there are actually only 9500, that's probably OK. But if you need forty a day, and only thirty-seven came in last night, you're going to lose production. Similarly, you've got to make sure that any new orders which are going to affect production are passed along *immediately* to your suppliers, so that they'll be able to ship you what's needed right away. This in turn means, for all but the very smallest businesses, that you'll need to go to computer-control to see that inventory and demand are accurately correlated.

KEEPING CLOSE TO SUPPLIERS. One reason the Japanese can use JIT so effectively is that their industrial centers all cluster suppliers immediately around the big manufacturers. Those short lines of communication mean that supplies are almost never lost or delayed in shipment. If your only possible supplier is 1,000 miles away and notoriously unreliable, forget about JIT—you can't make it work unless you install a production line of your own.

STATISTICAL TRACKING FOR QUALITY CONTROL. This is one of the by-products of JIT, and one reason the Japanese have consistently bettered us in Quality Control in recent years. Obviously, if you are cutting inventories thin, you can tolerate only a very few parts failures. The usual American policy with suppliers has been simply to return defective parts for credits and rarely to say much about them unless or until the supplier began to balk at giving full credit (or, rarely, the failure rate became so absurdly high that somebody *had* to complain).

Long ago, the Japanese began keeping meticulous computer records of the rate of failure of industrial supplies. Not only did they actively reward the highest-quality suppliers, but they programmed the computers to kick out a warning *whenever the rate-of-failure turned upward.* This careful statistical tracking lets Japanese manufacturers catch slipping quality control long before it affects production. As soon as there's a hint of trouble—long before the JIT system is threatened—they call a meeting with the suppliers to find out what's causing the slippage. They work together to solve the problem—and suppliers who won't cooperate are dropped *pronto.*

FLOOR SUPERVISION. To make JIT work effectively, you similarly have to cut your production waste to the bare bone, and that means making sure your employees understand how and why the system works. An excellent time to introduce the system is along with the "quality circles" discussed in the Chapter following this. Once people are actively involved in improving the way the plant runs, they'll naturally favor anything which so greatly improves plant efficiency without in any way worsening the quality of their own situation.

The one exception to this is the loss of that protective screen which a large inventory provides. Under JIT, mistakes are going to stand out much more clearly.

The solution is simply to attack the problem as one of techniques or procedure, rather than personal failure. Instead of telling Walter what a clumsy jerk he is, supervisors simply get the group to search collectively for ways to reduce losses. Often the solution will prove to be a new tool or piece of machinery—or simply a reorganizing of the work area. If you do prove to have an incompetent employee, you can deal with that in standard manner. At least the inventory method won't be shielding him from detection.

Just-in-time may turn out to be an unachievable ideal for many small businesses, but you will still gain by coming as close to it as possible:

1. If the situation permits, try to locate as near as possible to your suppliers.

2. Keep inventories as lean as possible, even without going to JIT. Hold periodic reviews of your needs.

3. Track failure rates any way you can. If you can't afford computers, then have the people on the floor keep you posted on any change in the quality of what you are receiving from suppliers.

4. Make sure your suppliers hear from you regularly—even when things are going well—about your degree of satisfaction with their product. Give them your ideas about ways to improve their offerings—and get rid of any who refuse to listen. (Remember, though, that JIT is a new idea to many Americans. Take time to explain to your suppliers what you're attempting. Perhaps you can even show them this chapter. Most people are eager to learn ways to make this country more competitive.)

3. Don't let inventory—whatever its level—mask problems or inefficiencies in your own ways of doing business. Keep a sharp eye on what's going into the waste bin.

21
USING QUALITY CIRCLES

SITUATION:
As small businesses grow, they tend to lose most of the "family feeling" binding owners and employees
OBJECTIVE:
Optimizing quality and productivity by use of Japanese-style quality circles

Quality and Productivity: Beyond JIT.

Few Americans object to "just-in-time" inventories. After all, they are only a mechanical innovation, equivalent to a new tool. Adopting other Japanese methods—especially those involving personnel —however, raises problems. It's hard to know which methods will survive the transition between two quite different cultures.

For example, some large Japanese companies use "consensus management," in which a major policy move can require the (literal) stamp of approval from 100 or more executives. Not only would most Americans balk at such procedures, but recent results have shown that consensus management simply performs poorly in fast-changing markets. It is superb at building momentum, but poor at changing direction. Thus, in their efforts to capture the rapidly evolving American small computer market, the Japanese have mostly been too late with too little.

That is not to detract from the Japanese achievement, or to deny that we can learn much from their experience. The point is rather that we want to pick and choose, and only assume techniques which are 1) sound in themselves and 2) adaptable to American manners.

One Japanese idea which does seem to work with Americans—and which is being applied by American giants like Lockheed, Ford, and General Electric—is the quality circle. There are any number of variations on the concept, so rather than defining them exactly, let's first consider what they are meant to accomplish, and how they work in general.

QUALITY CIRCLES: WHAT ARE THEY? Basically, quality circles are groups of about six to ten people who meet on company time to discuss specific ways their jobs can be more effectively done. That's a simple idea, but it accomplishes much, through two different channels. First, it has a strong moral or emotional effect on workers, who can feel they are contributing to the company with their minds as well as their hands, and who have the satisfaction of seeing their ideas tested, and, often, adopted. This psychological gratification almost always produces people who want to work harder because they believe they have a real stake in the company's success.

The second advantage is simply that many of those ideas are extremely sound. The Cadillac engine plant in Livonia, Mich., saved over $1.2 *million* based on circles' suggestions during 1982 alone. (*Business Week,* May 16, 1983). As a key executive of Sony once put the matter, in a plant without quality circles you have 100 heads working to solve problems; in a company with them, you have 10,000 heads doing the same thing.

Some people have claimed that the gains from the circles are really only part of the "Hawthorne Effect," which says that any show of interest in employee welfare—from a new health plan to a company dance—will temporarily boost productivity. Maybe so, but gains from quality circles are proving more profound and more durable. They appear to have a far greater impact on people's sense of self-worth and personal responsibility.

Maybe a personal reminiscence will help. One summer I worked as a busboy in the San Diego Zoo restaurant. We had a problem in the kitchen, where the busboys' leather-soled shoes were slipping on the often-slick floor. The possibility of a serious accident provoked a management meeting, involving half a dozen people who knew nothing about the problem, and who decided that a new floor was the only answer. Meanwhile, one of the busboys had done a little afterhours experimenting, and discovered that deck shoes (standard gear for young California males in those days) effectively solved the problem. I was delegated to convey this information to the head of the restaurant, who listened absent-mindedly for about ten seconds, said, "thank you for the suggestion, Bob," and then went off to order the new floor. The idea wasn't even mine, but I was stung by the feeling that busboys were only mindless bodies, and for the short remainder of my stay, I was as lumpish and unhelpful a worker as I could manage to be.

Quality circles are meant to prevent disappointments like that. In some ways, they may seem like elaborations of the old suggestion box, but in fact they achieve far more, and must be far more carefully organized to work. Oddly, what they really do is to preserve the spirit of mutual dependence and cooperation common in very small companies but usually lost as those companies grow.

Making Quality Circle Work. Here are some guidelines for your your own quality circles:

1. *They have to be formalized.* You have to set a fixed size (usually, again, six to ten members). The meetings should be weekly, though they need not be long—a half hour may be all that's needed—and should occur the same time each week. Some small firms even close down operations during the meetings, and use the fact as a promotional gimmick: "We're closing early every Friday to plan how to serve you better the rest of the week." Meetings must be on paid company time—otherwise even those workers who later will be spending their own weekends preparing reports for the Monday circle meeting will balk at the outset.

2. *They must be civilized.* All members have to agree at the outset to a "pact of mutual respect" which specifies that the group will discuss procedures, not personalities. Where the two areas blur, the group leader has to clarify the issue. If someone criticizes the way Charlie trims the flash off extruded casings, it's the trimming method, *not Charlie,* which is being criticized.

By the same token, all ideas should be treated with respect, and all contributions encouraged. As any teacher can tell you, it's usually the quiet ones who have the right answers.

3. *They must protect jobs.* Members have to be assured that even if —as often happens—a group improvement leads to the elimination of a particular job, the people affected will be given comparably rewarding work elsewhere in the firm. As the Japanese have shown, higher productivity means more, not fewer jobs (compare the US and Japanese auto industries), but you must make this formal policy. Otherwise, your people (to say nothing of the unions) will never cooperate.

4. *They should refund part of any savings.* Since many American firms have long paid bonuses for usable suggestion-box ideas, this should not prove difficult. A reasonable rule might be that any bonuses are to be shared among the circle members, with a larger share going to the person(s) who made the actual suggestion.

(Payment or nonpayment of bonuses is rarely a sticking point, because most employees realize that the circles exist to help the company compete in a tough world, and for themselves are far more concerned about job security.)

5. *They should work systematically, and train workers to think like managers.* Circles are not just forums for conversation; they are tools for dealing in hard dollars and cents. That's why the circles in big companies include not only workers, but management representatives, *and* specialists to train workers in the basics of data collection and presentation—flow charts, chi-squares, and so on. The idea is to help workers move beyond the realm of speculation, and into the kind of cost-and-effect analysis which justifies change. You may not be able to manage anything so elaborate, but at least stress presentation of facts instead of opinions—and remember that for many young graduates of the American educational system, you will first have to explain the difference between the two.

SETTING UP. One reason that quality circles have thus far been largely the province of large companies in America is that small companies seem to accomplish many of the functions of a quality circle almost unconsciously. In a small firm, after all, the owner and his or her few employees usually work quite closely together, so there is no deep labor/management division. At the same time, operations usually are simple enough that an employee suggestion can be adopted without any elaborate studies or management run-around. Lastly, because the owner is often a worker as well, many of the improvement ideas which occur to people "on the floor" will occur to him just as quickly.

Eventually, though, most small business owners find themselves shunted off into a purely managerial role. That strange day comes when they discover someone they don't know actually working in the business. By then, if not sooner, it's probably time for a formal quality circle.

Setting up need not be complicated, especially if you have prepared the ground from your first day in business by stressing to each employee that the company is a team and that you actively seek their ideas to make the team more effective. That early feeling of openness is essential.

When the day arrives that you sense the early team spirit is beginning to fade, you can shift into formal quality circles. It's important from the first that you solicit ideas. Even though *you* decide that circles are needed, let the circles themselves decide, for example, when they are to meet. They might suggest that because their big shipments always go out Wednesday morning, they can best spare half an hour on Wednesday afternoon. Let them practice decision making on small matters first.

Stress, too, that quality circles are part of an on-going program to improve the firm. Try to see that information flows two ways. Even as the circles are sending the company profitable suggestions, the company should be sending back information on its competitive position. You may not want to go as far as red-hot Tandem Computers, which flashes updated reports on its stock trading price three times daily to every company computer terminal. Do remember, though, that the companies which have done best with

Quality Circles are those which use information to help heighten the workers' sense of being part of an on-going, struggling organization.

The best plans will establish quality circles early on, allowing them to improve with time—and without the interference of inflexible unions. The final scope of your program will be up to you; some owners resist sharing control, or even information, with employees. I don't pretend that a full-blown plan is needed in every firm, but I do know this: no major company which has adopted circles has yet dropped them. You may have to experiment with yours before it works entirely to your liking, but without a quality circle system of some sort, it's unlikely you are going to be competitive in the late '8os and beyond.

22
UPTRACKING SALES VOLUME

SITUATION:
Rapid expansion of business volume is essential, and requires both adding and keeping customers

OBJECTIVE:
Discovering, reaching, and convincing the greatest number of customers at the lowest possible cost

Even while you are instituting the refinements in operating procedures we've already discussed, you're going to want to start building sales volume—which, aside from acquisitions, is the only way in which your business grows. To do that, you have to take on a big domain, marketing. If you've got twenty million dollars a year or so to invest in the problem, it's simple: you just announce a competition, and let the country's biggest advertising firms beat each other's brains out designing a campaign for you. If you don't have that much loose change, then consider the following.

The First Quick Shots.

Experts will tell you to attack your market planning with long-range goals in mind. In the abstract, that's perfectly true. Unfortunately, most small business owners are operating under the gun, and a superb ten-year plan won't do you much good if you go broke around the fourth month. What you need right at the start is quick-response advertising—something to make the competition duck and let the folks know you've come to town—and advertising that doesn't cost much. That means mostly do-it-yourself stuff. What's available?

Well, first of all, remember that you have two choices, since efforts to market generally are divided into *promotions* and *advertisements*. *Promotions* are temporary monetary or quasimonetary incentives to buy your products; *advertisements* are simply ways of drawing attention to your products or your firm. The general rule is that in good times you advertise; in hard times, you promote. When money is easy, the average person probably won't look twice at your 50¢ discount on a sandwich—he or she'll go to the place with the fancier decor, or the livelier advertisements on the radio. When things get hard, though—when lay-offs are spreading and people are thinking about building the six-months' nest egg most experts recommend having during tough times, you'll start bringing the customers in.

Some industries live off of promotions, and vary them with surpassing skill. Gillette, for example, has the lowest manufacturing costs of any maker of razor blades. Instead of steadily underpricing the competition (which might give it the reputation of building a lower-grade product), though, Gillette keeps list prices fairly high, but then unleashes an endless stream of refunds, two-for-ones, instant winner games, and so on—one promotion after another.

Since most experts (for what they're worth) are predicting a lean era for the 1980s, keep promotions in mind—and pay special attention to them if you're operating in a region, or an industry, facing especially hard times.

One thing to note about these promotions: they should only run for a fixed, prespecified length of time. For most retail sales, a period of a couple of weeks or less is optimum. If you run the discount too long, or too often, you effectively create an new price for the item, and you also create a fair amount of buyer apathy—consider what happened to automobile rebates during the early '80s. Note that Gillette, for example, always shifts the terms of its discounts: "buy two, get one free;" then, "get two free blades;" then, "mail in ten labels and get a dollar back." The variety not only keeps up a measure of excitement, but keeps anyone short of a financial wizard from figuring out what the heck the effective list price really is.

A fast-growing San Diego shoe chain runs an interesting variation on cost-cutting promotions. Instead of taking anything off the price of running shoes, they charge full retail, but include a coupon good for a free resoling. The customer is happy—the coupon is worth a good $15 to him or her—and the store is happy, because it has deferred the cost of its promotion. It doesn't pay up until the customer brings the shoe back in, some six months or more after the original purchase. As an added bonus, of course, the store owes nothing to those customers who, for whatever reasons, neglect to return for their free resoling. Delayed promotions make great sense. See if they'll work for you.

A WARNING ABOUT PROMOTIONS: With customers or clients flocking in the door, your cash flow is going to shoot way up. That's fine, but remember you're selling at below your usual margin. Make sure there's still a *real* profit there, or else cut off when you've used up the promotion budget. Otherwise, you'll wind up like those skydivers who get so fascinated by the ground rush that they forget to open their chutes. (One natural way to control promotions, of course it to tie them to either major holidays, or the anniversary date of your having started business.)

Advertising.

Advertising is simply the collected ways of drawing favorable attention to yourself or your products. Since the various tactics are as limitless as the human imagination (to coin a phrase), I'll only suggest some general ways of accomplishing it on the cheap.

First of all, recognize that a neighborhood operation should begin with a neighborhood campaign, and that can mean something as simple as door-to-door leafletting (with mimeographed leaflets and some neighborhood kids paid a minimum wage) or even signs up in the neighborhood. Early on, those signs will work better if they offer mystery rather than a bunch of information—just use something like an arrow and the words, "Three blocks to the opening." Get people curious enough to swing by.

If you're not too egotistical about your ads, and are willing to plug products you carry as well as your own store, you can often get aid—from support money to camera ready copy—from manufacturers. That's why some upper-class retail outlets (gourmet and audio shops, for example) often take to putting out their own newsletters, describing their latest product additions. Be sure you get copies, too, of any posters or displays tied to your manufacturers' own promotional drives.

Yellow page advertisements are a standby, but don't underestimate the cost. If you have to cover a fairly wide area (say, two or three county regions), a medium-sized ad can cost you $1000–$1500 a month. You also have to deal with long lead-times and relatively long-term contracts. Still, they can't be overlooked.

Television and radio are, naturally, prestige media, but even the smallest areas they target are quite large. Costs vary hugely, from as low as $5 for a thirty-second spot on early-morning (i.e., 3 AM) radio or second-market TV, up to the roughly $1,000,000 a minute which ABC is tentatively estimating it will charge on the 1985 Superbowl. One possibility, if regulations and your needs permit, is the low-power FM transmitters some colleges operate. Some of these only reach the college dorms, but if those form a part of your market, this can be a dirt-cheap way of approaching them.

Print media are far older, but, obviously, you've got to decide whether your buyers are readers. Classified ads run around $2.50 per line per day in a medium-large-sized city; you get around a 30% discount if you become a contract advertiser. Classifieds have two pluses: 1) anyone can draw them up—you just ask the paper for a form sheet and instructions, and 2) they can be in the paper and running within a day or so of your turning them in. Regular ads catch more readers, but are costly, running up to $15–20,000 for a full page in a major newspaper. Lastly, don't overlook those small "neighborhood" papers which are really only glorified advertising circulars.

For both radio and newspapers, consider joining in those collective ads run for, say, all the area's independent bookstores or automotive repair shops. They can multiply your clout when money's tight, and give you a scrappy-underdog image as well.

All that's fine, but relatively obvious. The real gravy comes with your ability to get press for free. You can always simply put out a press release saying that you've opened for business, but that will normally get you about one line on page six of the business section, if you're lucky. Anything better than that is going to require imagination, or money. I can't give you imagination (or money, for that matter), but here's an example of what I mean:

Video arcades have been a hot commercial product for some time now, but like almost any activity which draws the unbroken attention of young people, they've also attracted a lot of bad press from adults. They waste time, they waste money, they turn young brains into tapioca. Still, the money rolls in; by one estimate, the PAC-MAN game will ultimately make more money for Warner Brothers (which owns Atari) than *Star Wars* made for Twentieth Century Fox (about *one billion* dollars.)

In the first flush of their success, video arcades did not seem to need any promotion whatsoever. The customers were literally lining up. But the owner of a San Diego arcade was astute enough to know that anyone's image can be improved. Early on, to counteract the idea the video games are vaguely sinister places (like pool halls) which also destroy creativity, he hired some local artists to decorate his (relatively well-lit) place with amusing giant murals on the themes of the games. In an industry which was mostly bare walls and dim lights, this aura of culture automatically guaranteed him some free publicity. He quickly got a few brief special interest items on local TV news, which let people see he was a nice, clean-cut fellow instead of a sleazy promoter. He made plenty of points, and all for free.

As the video craze took off so did the pressure to license or even close down the arcades. This particular parlor, which was near to both a high school and a community college, faced its share of the pressure. But here the owner struck back in the best, most creative possible way—he ran a promotion which made him a hero. With the help of the local high school, he announced a program to give $4s' worth of free video play to any student showing a specified improvement in his grades.

The program was a hit, and everyone involved came out a winner. The schools got a set of better-motivated, more enthusiastic students. The students themselves showed demonstrable improvement, some formerly failing students moving up into the B+ range for the first time in their lives. And the arcade had increased floor traffic, better relations with its community, and more free television and print publicity—all at no real expense to the business, since the free games were good only in the arcade, thus allowing recovery of nearly all costs.

Now that's creativity, and perhaps you'll see why it can't be taught. Still, a while back, Compton Advertising devised a fine list of 10 tactics for promoting tired products. Here, with modifications, are some which work for small business (The 10 tactics for big business appeared in the Wall Street Journal, 18 Feb., 1982)

1. Can you turn a minus into a plus, as the video arcade did? Humor often works here—consider those Midas ads which play off of the general mistrust of auto repair shops, or the Smucker's ads which declare, "With a name like Smucker's, it has to be good." There's supposed to be a restaurant in Oregon which got a lot of complaints about its food. Now they bill themselves as "The Worst Food in the World," and people come from miles around to see whether they're right!

2. Can you inexpensively repackage or newly display an existing product? Fortunes have been made repackaging and remarketing goods which other people thought were useless: Army surplus after World War Two was a dramatic example, but even today there are firms which specialize in the repackaging of unsuccessful products. Usually they pick bright colors and a lively, fashionable (even gimmicky) name, and fiddle with the price—raising it as often as they lower it.

Sometimes you can leave the products the same, but repackage the business. In many areas, people have done extremely well by persuading their neighbors to join in theme remodellings. Thus, Leavenworth, Washington seemed to be a only a tiny mountain town without much future until the merchants got together to remodel it as a Bavarian village. Today, sometimes known informally as "Germantown," Leavenworth does a land-office business, spurred by its uncommon style, its ethnic promotions, and a goodly amount of free publicity from human-interest reporters. I'm thinking, too of the booming gaslamp districts in places like San Diego, and Vancouver, British Columbia. Perhaps best of all, in some areas (depressed inner cities, for example), you can sometimes arrange for governmental redevelopment funds to underwrite part of your costs. If you can persuade your neighbors to cooperate, the potential here's tremendous. Sometimes, of course, even product repackaging is too expensive for very small businesses, but you can nearly always afford to brighten your display areas. At the very least, if you're taking over an unsuccessful firm, see that the windows are washed and the immediate display areas are freshened up. A bright, attractive place of business is the best of visual advertisements.

3. Can you find a new attribute to promote? Consider Philip Morris's campaign for 7-Up as the "no caffeine" drink. 7-Up *never* had caffeine.

4. Can you talk to an entirely new audience? Sometimes professional-grade products can be sold to general consumers. it seemed unlikely that average stereo owners would spend $1,000 or more for professional record-washing machines, until an English manufacturer proved that some of them, at least, would pay out eagerly.

5. Can you build high recognition around a clever or attractive name, or a personification? Sunkist, for example, used to be a plain generic, the output of a citrus co-op. Chiquita bananas were United Fruit. Consider Mr. Goodwrench (GM), or Brother Dominic (Xerox). The low-ball way of doing this, of course, is to build around a real person—yourself. But you need a certain measure of charisma to pull it off.

6. If you *have* a high-recognition trade-name or character, have you tied it to all possible products? During the '70s, Binney and Smith, with one of the world's best-loved tradenames (Crayola) manufactured several dozen products under various other names

—and with dubious success. Beginning at the end of the decade, they began slapping the Crayola name on everything in sight— and sales began to take off, with gains of up to 20% in short order. (from *Forbes,* 12 April 1982)

7. Again, use humor freely. Year after year, some of the best-remembered campaigns feature humor, often aimed at some attribute of the company itself. Small companies, especially, cannot afford much stuffy vanity.

8. Only one negative. Never let your advertising become so charming, or so amusing, that people remember it but not your product. According to the *Wall Street Journal,* one of the best-rated campaigns of 1981 featured Marriette Hartley and James Garner. Consumers rated it extremely highly. Many people surveyed thought it was among the best Kodak campaigns ever. The only problem is that the ads were for Polaroid.

Direct Sales.

Direct sales can and should be key adjuncts to any ad or promotional campaigns you might run. For a small business, and especially one in a hurry, direct sales are intensely important, because they can bring quick results with *minimal* outlay.

In direct selling, you or your hired salespeople aggressively approach clients on a one-to-one basis. You can hire salespeople on a commission or a salary basis, or offer a combination of both— which is why they are cost-effective. They can go to work without waiting for an ad agency to devise a campaign, or for a magazine ad to appear—which is why they get into action quickly.

You will have either inside salespeople (who work within the store or from the plant), outside salespeople (who spend their days calling on clients), or sales representatives (or "reps"), who may carry several other lines than yours, and generally work on a strictly commission basis. The commission schedule is something you have to work out according to industry norms. commissions range from a fraction of 1% (for, say, travel agency salespeople working against a salary) to as high as 20% for outside salesmen of high-ticket items which move very slowly (say, certain large manufacturing tools).

In many ways, you seek from your salespeople the same personal traits you wish in any employee: honesty, intelligence, neatness, and an enthusiasm for the company and its products. Indeed, it is standard in most companies to remind all employees that they are potential salespeople every time they come in contract with someone from outside the firm. More particularly, in salespeople you *must* have self-starters, people who create their own goals. Since they do most of their work outside the office, they need self-reliance and a clear sense of personal responsibility. I recently met a gentleman who is a partner in a chain of men's up-market clothing stores. In 1946, when he first came west, he got his first job selling expensive clothing by showing up three times a week for eight months at the sales manager's office asking whether there were any openings in sales. When the manager finally came out to see him in person and asked, "You really think you're going to work here, don't you?" he responded, "No, you've got it wrong. Sooner or later, I *am* going to work here." He got the job that day, and stayed with the firm for thirty-five years. That's the kind of salesman you're looking to find.

At times you'll need to be your own salesman. That may not be exactly your strongpoint, but you must do what you can. One trick I've seen work for relatively shy professionals going into business for themselves is simply to hold to a brief, informational approach. Let's say you've spent five years with Price-Waterhouse or Touche Ross, and now you're opening your own accounting firm. Simply get yourself some honeyed tea and a box of throat lozenges, sit down in front of the phone, and start calling anyone who might be, or know of, a potential client. Just say something like:

Hello, Walter? This is Bob Jones. (I used to handle your books for Price-Waterhouse a few years back). I won't take much of your time, but I wanted you to know I'm in business for myself now and I'll be sending you a packet of information in a few days. I hope you'll look it over and give me a call if I can answer any questions.

If it's someone you know well, you can drop the line in parenthesis. As you get more experienced, you can make the approach into more of a salespitch if you like. The main thing is to blend personal contact with whatever literature you send out: after all, the whole point of your business is *personal* service. You won't face any sales resistance because you aren't trying to make a sale, but your packet will get the attention it deserves.

Stress favorable impressions: anyone who might answer a phone or greet people at the door should be 1) *positively* friendly (not just smile or say "hello," but offer to help), and 2) usefully informative. Customers should never hear a flat "No" for an answer. If they want a product you can't provide, suggest the alternatives you do carry, or even another firm to try. Remember that *partings* (on the phone or in person) matter even more than greetings: salespeople who are friendly only while they expect to make a sale are death to your reputation.

Especially with new, or unusually costly, products, it may be a long time before you make *any* sales on first contact. Be patiently friendly, and remember the role of education. Recently, an extremely pricey French bakery opened in my neighborhood. The owner told me she had opened the month before the start of the Christmas season because she planned to use the month to teach customers why her sweets were worth four times the going rate. During that month, she faced mostly timid or shocked customers, unaccustomed to paying $60 a dozen for chocolate eclairs. But each customer got a tour of the shop and a brief discourse on the art of fine baking, and most left on a first-name basis with the owner—even if they didn't buy a thing.

The education program worked. People came once by accident, a second time from curiosity, and a third time to buy. By Christmas, sales were exploding, and two months later, she took over the place next door to start a coffee-and-dessert shop for the evening trade, again at absolutely premium prices. So think of selling as the process of educating as much as motivating. What's true of a relatively simple field like baked goods, is infinitely truer of high-tech, or informational fields: take the time to educate yourself and your employees about the merits and uses of your field and your products, and you'll be able to sell effectively. And then you'll do very well indeed.

Equally important, you must aim your educational efforts *at your audience.* Time and again I see businesspeople who cannot produce sales because they cannot communicate with clients. Technical people are especially prone to this problem. Not long ago, while looking into office automation software, I had lunch with a gentleman who had enjoyed a brilliant career as an engineer with NASA and a private aerospace company, and was now running his own computer consulting firm. I had a series of very naive questions to ask—but questions which mattered to me. Our conversation went something like this:

> "Now, how many pages of business letters can we expect to get on one of these diskettes?"
> "Well, there are 1000 bits to a kilobit, and of course 8 bits make a byte. So four bytes equal one character, and there are six characters to a word, meaning you need twenty-four times three hundred, thirty words to the page, divided into. . . ."

By that time, I had forgotten my question. The gentleman later hinted that his business wasn't growing as fast as he had hoped, and I was able to suggest a reason why. If you're going to deal with a particular set of people, learn to convert your knowledge into their terms. If, for example, my friend had remembered that a computer needs about 2K's worth of storage for one page of text, he could have smoothly calculated that a 250K diskette held roughly 125 pages' worth of documents. I'd have had my answer while I still cared about it.

Now, absolute professionalism comes only slowly to a sales force, but from the day you open your doors, your people should be able to:

1. Take an active, polite, and friendly interest in their potential customers. Make sure that all inquiries are directed at once to the person qualified to answer them.

2. Talk knowledgeably and intelligibly about their products. They should have the key facts, dates, and prices clearly in mind, and should be able to put them *into* terms their *customers can follow.* If they can't meet a specific request, they should be ready to suggest alternatives.

3. Follow up on all inquiries, and especially, on all sales. At the least, get back to anyone who asks for specific information, and make follow-up calls to all major customers to make sure they are satisfied with the product. Remember, people dealing with small businesses are often trading best price for personal attention. See that they get it.

4. Pass along information to management. If you carry only Ajax brand video disks, and you're getting nine calls a day for Bojax brand, someone had better get word to your buyers. And if eight of ten Ajaxes are falling apart, someone had better get word to Ajax.

This amounts to a fair list of skills to teach quickly to new salespeople. You'll improve your chances if you 1) choose only experienced (or very highly motivated) personnel at the beginning, and 2) run an intensive but brief formal introduction. A good short training program will have at least two parts—a formal introduction to your company and its products, stressing selling points and allowing for plenty of question-and answer and exchange of ideas, and a multi-hour stretch devoted to mock sales calls.

Mock sales calls—where your salespeople approach "clients" from your own staff—provide "live ammo" training at a minimum cost in money and time, and are far cheaper than having unqualified people out on the streets losing sales and tarnishing your reputation. See that your people face hostile and evasive "clients," as well as those who let them make their pitch smoothly. There really are no surefire ways of handling clients who become abusive, or who stretch out conversations pointlessly, but you want your salespeople to keep their composure in the first case, and to use their time productively in the second. This is your best chance to weed out the ones who aren't going to make it. Be sure the ones you keep are those who will represent you fairly and effectively.

A last general word. Remember that you make your reputation in your early days, and live on it for a long time after. If you are ever going to honor disputed claims, or offer generous promotions, now is the time to do it. The best efforts of advertising, promoting, and selling all serve the future as well as the present.

Recently I met a former college teacher who now owns a truck and auto reconditioner which sells to the construction industry. He follows up every sale, regardless of size, with a personal phone call to check customer satisfaction. Many of his customers cross over the border from Mexico; he sees each of them receives a call in Spanish. Not only that, but he sends all the women customers flowers as well. He receives in turn a steady stream of letters and calls of thanks, and more to the point, during the construction slump of 1980–82, while his competitors were going bankrupt left and right, he showed unbroken growth in volume and profits. Even lady truckers, after all, like to feel their business is appreciated. And advertising, remember, is the art of making people *want* to do business with you.

Those are some ways to get business volume quickly a-building. Once the business is throwing off large amounts of cash, you may want to invest in a professionally-mounted campaign. In your early days your goal is to build volume without blowing your capital. So bear in mind two things: advertising agencies come extremely dear, and (if they're realistic), they'll start by telling you most of the same things I already have. It's always best to carry yourself as far as you can before asking others to help you on. Give the ideas in this chapter a try first.

23
LONG-RANGE PLANNING

SITUATION:
Running a business without a long-range plan is a recipe for disaster
OBJECTIVE:
A systematic approach to your long range goals and prospects, producing a workable plan for the future

Introduction: The Trap of Stability.

At some point—a few weeks, a few months—after you begin a new business venture, your day-to-day operations are going to become routine. You will be paying creditors regularly, tracking accounts carefully, running ads in the right places, and having salesmen bringing in steadily more business. There will still be— heaven knows—enough daily disruption to keep you active and involved, but basically you will seem safely established.

You're not. The problem is that those daily crises and opportunities—which small businesspeople traditionally handle extremely well—too often disguise more subtle problems like demographic shifts, aging technologies, stale products, faulty management, and the like. The bold entrepreneural spirit which so adeptly seizes fast-moving chances often misses the dangers and the possibilities which arrive more slowly. It's fine that you're a gambler and an improviser, but if you only respond to situations when they stare you in the face, then one day you'll find yourself —as hard-charging as ever—running a company that simply cannot do the job.

The answer is long-range planning. Long-range planning is *not* a matter of chaining your company (and yourself) to inflexible plans. Instead it's the process of analyzing what your company is, what it does, and how its prospects will develop over the next several (at least three) years, and what steps will help strengthen your situation over that time.

How to Start.

Start early in your career,—and recognize that you can plan long range without a research staff or an advanced degree from Harvard School of Business. Realize that a plan begins with information— that in fact the constant collecting of information about your business may prove just as useful as any formal plan you finally produce. Finally, remember that information has about the same shelf-life as raw milk; you need to keep it turning over.

What kind of information do you want? Here are some areas for collecting:

1. What business am I in?
2. What are my five biggest expenses, and how can I bring them down?
3. Who are my customers; how can I best reach them, and how are they changing?
4. What market segment do I want?
5. What new products, or manufacturing techniques, or suppliers are available in the near-term? Within a year? Within three to five years?
6. How well is my management system functioning? How well can it cope with growth?
7. What major investments of mine are most nearly obsolete? Machinery? Buildings? Key personnel?

WHAT BUSINESS AM I IN? Not a trivial question—here's why:
When Peter Schutz was appointed president of Porsche in December 1980, his first official project was a study of the company's actual line of business. Given Porsche's rank among the world's great sports cars, it might seem that Schutz—an American—was asking who was buried in Grant's Tomb. In fact, the study showed

that Porsche was in the leisure time, not the car, business. People who buy Porsches do so because they haven't the time (or the interest) for world cruises or expensive yachts. (*Fortune*, 5 April 1982)

What did that mean to Porsche? In the first place, it meant that Porsche wasn't competing with General Motors; it was competing with Cunard Lines and Hatteras Yachts. It should spend more of its advertising budget in *New Yorker* and *Forbes* than in *Motor Trend*. Most importantly, it meant that the company should drop efforts —such as the Volkwagen-powered 924 model—to build popularly priced cars to compete with the Japanese. Not long after the study was completed, Porsche replaced the 924 with a more expensive variant, the extremely successful Porsche-powered 944.

Use this question to keep clearly in mind the main purpose of your firm—and to help you spot and trim marginal operations.

MY FIVE BIGGEST EXPENSES? It's an ongoing theme of this book that you can never get your costs down too low. This question is simply a way of keeping those costs at all times closely in mind. When you prepare your plan, then, you'll want not only to list those five major expenses, but to seek every possible way to reduce them. Is energy a big cost? If so, has the power company done a use-audit? Have you priced insulation? Cogeneration? Figure out the return on conservation measures. Factor in something for protecting the firm from possible shortages, and if the numbers are right, budget for it in the coming year or two. And so on, down the list of your main expenses.

This will force you to look for new yields in unlikely places. During the '60s and '70s, the US shoe industry was supposedly being swamped by "irresistibly" cheap shoes from Asia. But in 1981 good old American Buster Brown shoes made $55,000,000 in profits ($1.5 billion in sales), and was *the* low-cost producer of medium-priced shoes.

So what was the Buster Brown plan for 1982? Slash corporate expenses *another* $18 million a year by "cutting back on everything from pencils to executive travel." (*Forbes*, July 19, 1982). You can't cut costs if you aren't aware of them—that's why cost recognition is essential for long-range planning.

WHO ARE MY CUSTOMERS? HOW ARE THEY CHANGING? WHAT MARKET SEGMENT DO I WANT? Even in a seemingly bland business there is always market segmentation—and separate segments need separate treatments.

Take travel. Are you serving business or pleasure travellers? If business, you don't need a fancy, accessible office, you just want to be sure you can find the cheapest tickets to Milwaukee, and have them on your client's desk two hours after he or she has ordered them.

Even within the pleasure/vacation segment, there are subsegments. Do you want to custom-design packages for up-market clients (which takes time and expertise, but should mean higher margins)? Or do you want to go after the high-volume package tours? Do you want to lead tours (good profit, lots of hassles), or not?

Markets get finer still. We once sold a travel agency which dealt almost exclusively in trips for Japanese/Americans wanting to visit the Islands. It wasn't a huge market, obviously, but it was stable, and they had almost 100% of the regional business. The owner wasn't getting rich, but he was dealing with people he liked, and had frequent chances to visit a country he favored.

Companies nearly always do better when they focus clearly on a particular market segment or two. Not only do they gain economies of scale, but they climb the learning curve; by concentrating on a specific area, they eventually learn the most efficient approach to every part of it. Even if you can potentially handle effectively every part of a market, you'll still suffer from an image problem; the people who can afford ninety days cruising the Orient won't want to share your services with the people who can barely afford a three-day package tour of Las Vegas.

More generally, you need to watch how your customers and your markets are shifting. Americans are getting older—do you still want to specialize in disco tours of the Riviera? What about the tendency toward complete vacation centers like Club Med— is it going to hurt your market five years down the road? If so, start planning now to get a place in the field. You deal with businesses? Then how will you answer the growing trend towards in-house travel specialists for companies? And so on. Raise the questions, and then find the answers. The more you know about the kind of customers you want, the better job you'll do of keeping them.

WHAT DO MY CUSTOMERS WANT? WHAT NEW PRODUCTS, TECHNIQUES, OR SUPPLIERS ARE NOW AVAILABLE OR ON THE HORIZON? One big part of keeping customers, of course, is giving them the products they want—especially those they can't find elsewhere.

Formal market research is expensive, and most small businesses need an alternative. I've already suggested you should have a feedback system which lets you hear about customer requests or complaints, but it doesn't hurt to get a tad more aggressive:

Some years ago a struggling little manufacturer appeared to be on the verge of ruin when the mine it bought turned out to produce only a low grade of corundum suitable only for sandpaper. In desperation, the little company did go into the sandpaper business, but it sent out its salesmen with a specific instruction. After they were through selling sandpaper to the purchasing agent of each firm they visited, they were to walk around to the back of the plant and talk with the workmen eating lunch. They were to ask each workman what new product he'd like to see on the market. As soon as a product was requested often enough, the little company would try to build it.

Things worked out pretty well. One product followed another, and today the little company—now known as 3M—puts out some 45,000 different items, from sandpaper and Scotch brand tape, to computer disks and photocopying machines. So informal research will work—if you get out and hustle. Try it. (From *Fortune*, 20 October 1980).

Sometimes you need to know about products long before your customers recognize their own needs. This is the question that keeps you studying trade and technical journals, scouting the competition, and contacting suppliers' representatives. It may also keep you in the classroom a certain percentage of the time. You may not find that your favorite activity, but the alternative is falling far behind your competition, and (probably) going quickly down the tubes.

If you can't fit all this reading and learning into your work day, make it one of your leisure activities. You've *got* to know the field. If time's short, hire a clipping service, or at least join a trade or professional association which publishes a newletter or bulletin. If technical details are over your head, aim for the more popular journals, or hire a graduate student to write summaries or precis for you. Don't overlook the speaker's sessions at trade fairs and conferences. If need be, you can subsequently hire one of the better speakers to consult for an hour or so with some of your top people. When you get big enough, you can appoint a full-time Director of Research.

How suitable is my management team? That last point suggests yet another area to watch—the presence of a management team which, while lean, still provides needed expertise. You need to watch for signs of insufficiency—unsuccessful product introductions, production logjams, undue personnel turnover (or an inability to get workers you need), rising bad debts, or cash-flow problems in a profitable company. Any of these are signs that your management team is malfunctioning.

Better than waiting for problems to surface is anticipating them. Some things you can expect; once sales rise above, say, two to three million dollars a year, you're probably going to need a full-time financial officer, usually called a *comptroller.* Any unit which grows above about $20,000,000 in annual sales will probably need its own complete *management unit*—that is, a staff whose manager reports to corporate headquarters only periodically, but otherwise has day-to-day control. Planned new offices will need experienced *office managers*—plan early to train them from within. And so on. Prepare early, so that you only have to shop outside the company for the expertise you cannot find at home.

Above all, recognize when *you yourself* need a good dose of expertise training. Management courses are in limitless supply, but investigate carefully any which either 1) take place in resort locations (they're often nothing more than tax-free vacation dodges), or 2) blow into your city as one stop on a wide-swinging tour (if you're not happy with them, how are you going to find them?)

Probably your best bet is to stick with well-recognized college or university programs, which, thankfully, are increasingly common. One frequently praised by the media is the Harvard Business School Smaller Company Management Program. It's open to owners and CEOs of companies with at least forty employees and sales volumes between 3 and 75 million dollars per year. You'll work from case studies, and learn the kinds of fiscal-control, business planning, production organization, and other skills which tend to be fatally absent in small business. The work's extremely hard, but most people who have been through it consider the program invaluable. It's certainly not cheap. The program comes in 3 units, each lasting 3 weeks (most owners stretch the program out over several years), and costs are going up fast. In 1983, each unit cost $4500; for 1984, $5200, and for 1985, Harvard is projecting around $6000. You need to triple that for the full program, but remember that one management miscue can cost you a lot more than $18,000, and that job-related education is, after all, tax deductible.

Harvard's SCM Program is the Rolls Royce of its field, but most universities and colleges offer courses (sometimes through inexpensive "extension" programs) that will help you. Nearly 400 schools, moreover, belong to the Small Business Institute, an SBA-backed coalition to help small businesses by providing, free of charge, advanced graduate students in business to act as advisors. Similarly, the Department of Commerce runs a Business Development Centers program which will put you in touch with a college-based consultant, often a full professor. For the BDC program, you'll be asked to pay 10% of the normal consulting fee—as little as $2.50 an hour for expert advice. All these programs are bargains, and you'd be well advised to consider them. They're a fast track to management expertise.

WHAT MAJOR INVESTMENTS—MACHINERY, BUILDINGS, PERSONNEL—ARE MOST NEARLY OBSOLETE? Never wait until the last minute to make large-scale changes: you'll have too little time to consider options; completion will probably take longer than expected; and you'll almost certainly overpay for hastily-arranged financing. By planning ahead, you can shop carefully, build smoothly, and finance wisely by moving when the price of money is low.

Don't wait until the presses stop, the roof falls in, or old Harrington the head of research drops dead on the laboratory floor. Act upon the natural life expectancies of things, and assume they will need replacing within a predictable length of time.

One of San Diego's best and oldest Asian restaurants—a real landmark—had leased the same building for decades. With three years remaining on their latest lease, they were told there would be no more renewals—but that they could buy the building if they chose. They were a prosperous firm, with three years to raise the money. We urged them to act, but they procrastinated and procrastinated, always assuming that yet another lease extension would be forthcoming. Suddenly one morning the lease expired, and, as promised, they were out on the street. It took them two full years to find, buy, and equip a (less satisfactory) new location. Meanwhile, somebody else ended up owning "their" landmark, and used it to anchor a state-wide chain.

That's an extreme case, but it typifies the kinds of problems you face if your long-range planning does not allow for the protection and updating of your major assets.

It may seem heartless to include people in that category, but your normal human regard and affection for your employees should be complemented by an awareness of their value to the firm. The company needs to be prepared for the loss of key personnel, both by insurance (see INSURANCE) and by the presence of suitable replacements. Every manager (yourself included) should spend at least some time preparing his or her stand-in. Young trainees not only add enthusiasm to the operation, but provide a crucial degree of continuity for the firm.

HOW ARE MY KEY FINANCIAL INDICATORS VARYING FROM MONTH TO MONTH? The point of this chapter is to get you to think long-range, but it often happens that these short-term results will play an important role. In the first place, they can motivate you, because any persistent drops in sales, profits, etc., usually indicate failures of long-range planning. These figures probably won't contain answers, but they will bring the key questions loudly to your attention. Conversely, your need for useful data will likely force you to refine your short-term figures to include data about equipment downtime, delinquent accounts, and so on.

Long-Range Moves: What to Look For.

Again, the actual design of a long-range plan is your responsibility. But here are the kinds of things for which to plan:

1. Major Capital Expenditures
2. New Products
3. Dropping Lines
4. Market Repositioning
5. Expanding Management
6. Making Acquisitions
7. Selling Out

MAJOR CAPITAL EXPENDITURES. Do you need a new plant? Big firms might give a plant-siting team six months or more to scout locations, work up plant specifications, and take bids. Allow another six months to a year before the site is actually built, and you have a minimum lead-time of a year. So watch sales growth as well as asset aging in order to anticipate your needs. It's never too soon to begin scouting locations, monitoring interest costs, and so on. Once you have a clear capital need in mind, you have to allocate specific tasks to ensure that things are getting done.

Sufficient lead-time will also let you seek alternatives to capital spending. For example, if you know expansion is approaching for your retail business, you might consider franchising. Selling franchises, you add locations with other people's money, and grow without having to build a large, centralized management team: each franchisee, for example, will do his/her own hiring and training. Before pouring in the money to build new outlets for a successful operation, at least investigate franchising by talking with 1) whatever agency in your state regulates franchisers, and 2) a business broker specializing in the field.

CREATING NEW PRODUCTS—DIVERSIFYING. When a product begins to go flat, a competitor develops a better version, or you just want to expand your sales base, it's time to begin diversifying.

Whether you intend to broaden an existing line, add complementary lines, or launch an entirely new venture, early planning of new products offers two big pluses. First, it allows time to discover the very cheapest way to produce the goods—to seek suppliers, test alternate designs, and (especially) work out the bugs. Second, it lets you *test-market* before you launch full-scale production.

Hasty introductions can damage even the finest reputations. Consider the Oldsmobile diesel V-8 or the Cadillac V-8-6-4, two products which combined to sully the GM reputation for first-rate engineering. Both were made necessary by GM's race to improve its fuel economy, and both were introduced prematurely. Even Apple Computers'—for all its expertise and experience with the Apple II—stumbled badly with the Apple III, which had to be withdrawn from the market and then redesigned before succeeding. Apple's momentum was sufficient to survive the blunder, but no company can live through many such miscues.

More successful—because better planned—was IBM's introduction of its Personal Computer. It came on the market a little later, but worked well from day one. IBM, moreover, cut its risks by producing its first units in small batches in Japan, waiting until the system proved itself before starting large-scale production in the US.

It's almost a proverb among investors in small corporations that anybody can build one successful product. The real test comes with product number two or three. The pressure's especially high on small firms, because they haven't got the capital to absorb many flops. So if you've got a first hot product going, start now preparing to develop and test-market its replacement.

DROPPING LINES—SPECIALIZING. Sometimes it will become clear that certain products have to go, because they are aging, or the market has shrunk, or even because they are overtaxing your managment. Try to identify 1) those products with the lowest profit margins

2) those with contracting markets 3) those which will least productively absorb new capital. It's expensive to carry a lot of lines —and often you'll do better as a specialized, high-volume, low-cost producer.

Don't get stuck by sticking with a failing product. Once a product starts downward, you should try 1) a fixed amount of advertising and 2) if margins permit, a price cut. Note that a price-cut is not a sale—you're setting a new, permanently lower price. Sometimes—as with the Apple II computer—a price cut will revitalize sales and add years to a product's life. If the price cut doesn't work, then it's time to phase out production—as soon as possible, sell off existing stocks (at close-out prices, if necessary), and devote the shelf or manufacturing space to something better.

MARKET REPOSITIONING. Sometimes you need something more dramatic than simply adding or dropping a product or two. Sometimes you need to entirely remake the company.

Consider the case of the Swartz Brothers, who inherited a troubled private label firm called Abington Shoes. Like most American shoe manufacturers, Abington was saddled with old plants, unhelpful workers, and crushing foreign competition. The brothers saw that no possible refinements of their existing operation could save the company—there was simply not enough money in making shoes for other peoples' brand-names. The profit margins lay in owning the brand names themselves.

So the Swartz brothers decided to invent a high-margin, high-recognition shoe of their own. Aiming for hikers and backpackers, they persuaded their father (an immigrant shoemaker) to fashion a shoe which could be built on their existing equipment. They hired an advertising agency, and brought on board an experienced marketing man. The agency named the product, and built a campaign around a folksy, woodsy theme, while the marketing man sold it to the stores.

Between 1973 and 1978, the company's sales rose from 500,000 to 625,000—but most importantly, the number of shoes bearing the high-margin new trade name rose from 0.6% to a burly 75% of total production. The company marketed hard, but shifted production gradually—it wasn't until 1978 that their first new factory opened. Debt remained manageable, and the product, high-quality. With careful planning, the floundering Abington Shoe Co. became the highly successful Timberland. As the *Wall Street Journal* says:

> Getting the Timberland boot established involved borrowing millions of dollars, doing some astute forecasting, and developing a bold strategy for marketing and advertising. It also involved a bit of luck.
>
> (August 24, 1981)

A bit of luck, perhaps—but mostly a willingness to face facts and to develop a long-range plan sweeping enough to do the job.

REFINING THE MANAGEMENT TEAM. As the Timberland case suggests, growth often depends upon locating new talent—for Timberland, a good marketing man to engineer the shift from private label manufacturer to promoter of a brand-name product. Sometimes, though, the problem is not the lack of any particular talent, but simply company growth making single, centralized management impractical.

Take the story of Mark Controls, the precision-valve maker which boosted its sales from $17 million to $264 million in just twelve years. Another company might have reacted by adding layer-upon-layer of centralized management. Mark Controls kept itself lean and limber by breaking off new operating subunits every time a division's sales passed $30 million per year. Each division manager has a free hand for any expenditure under $200,000, and a salary heavily dependent upon his division's performance. The result is that a large, fiscally-sophisticated firm still has the entrepreneural spirit of a small operation. Division managers meet together just four times each year. (*Business Week*, 31 August 1981)

You do need to plan for new management skills as your company grows, but aim to preserve the traditional "risk and reward" system which motivates the private entrepreneur even as you evolve into a stable corporation. The best way to do it is to allow managers wide latitude within a certain financial limit. It might be

$200,000 as with Mark Controls, or it might be just $2,000. In either case, don't let the company choke in its managerial effluvia —keep staffs small and let your managers manage.

MAKING ACQUISITIONS. Sometimes—as with Timberland and Mark Controls—your best prospects for growth will come directly from expanding your existing business. Often, though, you will do better by buying someone else's ongoing operations—that is, by making acquisitions.

Acquisitions make particular sense where you cannot see a cost-effective way to generate growth internally. Wherever a realistically priced going business offers useful market share, assets, technology, or managerial strength, you may well be wiser making an acquisition than trying to build a new operation from scratch. It's also often the only practicable way to do what too many people try to do by using headhunters—acquire another company's secrets. When the acquisition can be made for stock instead of cash, it's a doubly sound investment—you can build your company without going farther into debt.

Sometimes only a single available firm will fit your requirements; other times, you'll consider any proposition which makes general business sense. In either case, remember that a major corporation might check a hundred or more offered businesses before acquiring one. You probably can't match that, but do allow yourself time to comparison shop—if possible, examine at least half a dozen likely candidates before acting.

It's entirely possible to assemble even a medium-sized conglomerate using only acquisitions. Consider CML Group—a good example both because it was created entirely by acquisitions, and because it illustrates other principles of this chapter, from lean management to a clearly-focused market goal.

CML was started in 1969 by a former Harvard B-School professor named Charlie Leighton, and raised its initial capital solely on the strength of its business plan, which was to acquire small-to-medium sized companies specializing in "ego-intensive" leisure-time products. It acquires about one company a year, and currently owns, among other firms, Boston Whaler, Sierra Designs, and

Carrol Reed Ski Shops. Total sales exceed $100 million a year. As specified in its initial plan, CML allows its held companies wide operating freedom. It teaches modern management techniques, but otherwise avoid interference in daily operations; it trusts the entrepeneurs who built the companies to keep them growing.

CML itself runs extremely lean. The home office employs exactly nine people, including three secretaries. In 1981, it netted $2.7 million, and annual profits have been growing at an average rate of over 18% a year. Not bad for a company started with $2 million in total venture capital—the capitalists and foundations (including the Ford foundation) who backed Charlie Leighton and his long-range plan have all done exceedingly well. (From *Wall Street Journal,* 12 July 1982)

Long-range planning for acquisitions should begin with the careful study of your requirements—annual sales volume, return on investment, types of products, and so on—and by socking away cash and/or negotiable securities. It's important that your directors' minutes specifically state that you are seeking an acquisition; otherwise, the IRS may assume you're stalling the shareholder's taxes and hit you with a special corporate "retained earnings" tax of almost 40%. Also plan ahead to get your books in order and your debt as low as possible—banks loaning you money for acquisitions are really loaning on the strength of *your* balance sheet.

SELLING OUT. Sometimes but not often, the information you gather will tell you that there's simply no future in the business —at least for you. Perhaps the market is decaying; perhaps it is becoming too capital-intensive for your means. Maybe the company is simply growing beyond your ability to manage. Whatever the cause, the key point is to notice the tendency soon enough that you can still sell it at a high price. If you see a severe problem coming, don't ignore it; either solve it quickly, or get out while the getting's good. For more details on this, please see ROUGH WEATHER and SELLING OUT—but above all, remember to take the results of your long-range planning seriously.

Summing Up.

The point of this chapter is simply that you must avoid becoming so involved in day-to-day concerns that you neglect to plan long-range. Long-range planning is not daydreaming. It's the process of looking closely at your situation today in order to prepare yourself to do well tomorrow. A well-run business will grow, and growth (just as much as stagnation) will produce problems. Your goals in planning should be:

1. To anticipate future needs, hazards, and opportunities
2. To prepare a management structure which keeps a growing company under control without crushing its original, small-company inventiveness and flexibility.

Since I've been trying throughout this chapter to encourage you to think (at least part-time) like a big-company director, it may be only fair to mention that in recent years some of the world's biggest companies have been working to make themselves behave more like littler firms. One of the best-run of the giants is General Electric, but in a 1982 interview, the company's chairman proudly told the *Wall Street Journal:*

> We're trying to reshape GE in the minds of its employees as a band of small businesses . . . to take the strength of a large company and act with the agility of a small company.

If you've got a growing small firm, you've got a very valuable possession. Plan long to protect it both from external troubles, and from the corporate dangers of size.

24
ROUGH WEATHER

SITUATION:
Either from miscalculation or a general business slump, a small company gets into trouble
OBJECTIVE:
A quick response to circumstances, making it possible to weather rough times without damaging the future of the firm

Expecting Trouble.

Here's something most businesses don't like discussing: if you plan on staying in business more than about six weeks—no matter what your field—you had better be prepared to face troubled times. From innumerable causes, nearly every business will face periodic woes, even disasters. If it can happen to Westinghouse, Lockheed, and Chrysler, then, brother (or sister), it can happen to you. When it does, survival depends upon recognizing and responding to the problem quickly and coherently. That last thing you can afford is the "birthday party" response, where you close your eyes and make a wish. Most likely, when you open them again, someone will have swiped the cake.

RECOGNIZING TROUBLE. The easiest thing to say would be that you should always be alert for trouble. Certainly that's true as far as it goes; as I've mentioned before, you should always follow any general or financial news likely to affect your business. You should minimize dependence upon any single customer or type of customer. You should study your month-to-month and year-previous sales comparisons, to see whether you are slipping or gaining ground—and whether you need to alter your tactics. You should budget for equipment failures and replacements, carry adequate insurance, and not expand too rapidly. In short, you should take all the reasonable precautions and have all the foresight in the world.

And yet, you can still find trouble upon you in very short order. A business downturn can hit in a matter of weeks or even—as with the loss of a key client, or rights to a key product—in a matter of minutes. When it happens, what do you do?

THE RIGHT PSYCHOLOGY COMES FIRST. Above all, avoid either panic or unreasonable guilt. Finding yourself suddenly owning a losing business is a lonely feeling. It hurts your self-respect (as a manager, perhaps as a provider), your vanity (for all the possessions you'll have to sacrifice temporarily), and even your sense of the world's orderliness. How could anything so sudden and unfair ever happen?

Remember that 1) much of it was likely beyond your control 2) it has happened before to better managers than you or I will ever be 3) you are so highly paid as boss because it's your responsibility to handle crises like this 4) nearly any problem can be reversed with luck and effort, and 5) even if it can't, the world has not ended.

Time and again, panic or discouragement wreck businesses which should have been saved. Hang tough; the odds are you'll get through it. Here's a possible graduated plan of response:

GET YOUR FAMILY ON YOUR SIDE. Almost inevitably, your first crisis will be admitting to the family that you're in trouble. Your notions of your personal worth probably rely (perhaps too heavily) on your financial contributions, so it will hurt to confess. Yet little will be possible until you feel secure at home. Beyond moral support, the family can help by cutting expenses, postponing vacations, even assisting with the business. Explaining the situation is far wiser than turning mean-spirited and quarrelsome, and creating domestic troubles to equal your financial ones. Put family support first; after that, consider:

TRIAGE: In battlefield parlance, "Triage" is the sorting of the wounded, deciding which can be treated in the field, which should be evacuated, and which are goners. In this case, you need to determine which parts of your business are still sound, which are breaking even, and which are losing. It will take some months to complete the evaluation and design a plan for changes. Meanwhile:

STOP THE HEMORRHAGING: Work immediately to stop the flow of red ink. Your first-stage responses can include the following:

1. *Cut Down Cash Outlays.* Pick up all the loose change you can. Cancel waiting-area magazines, and request refunds. Reduce business lunches, or suggest breakfast meetings and cut your average check by half. If the annual Christmas party is approaching, consider holding an open house at home instead of a fancy, costly restaurant party. Make all the small economies you can.

Continue all necessary maintenance as long as possible: deferred maintenance costs in the long run. But such items as interior painting can be done on extended schedules. Advertising can usually be trimmed; start omitting ads on the days that you know draw the worst response. (Don't try advertising your way out of a slump. Until you know what's wrong with your products or your pricing, an ad blitz is premature.)

2. *Cut Out Free Services.* Stress paying items for paying customers. This means, for example, optometrists ought to think twice about doing free minor eyeglass repairs for customers off the street, and consultants ought to consider sending bills to "buddies" who call during business hours for a word of free advice.

3. *Consider Sales Bonuses.* Offer incentives (such as commissions) to employees who drum up business. (Few people know this, but Toyo Kogyo [Mazda] nearly went belly up in the mid-'70s. Instead of laying off workers, management simply put them through a sales course, and sent them out *door to door* all over Japan to drum up sales for their unpopular rotary cars. They saved the company.)

4. *Stretch Payment Schedules.* Without causing trouble for yourself, hold payment until the last due-date, or a bit past.

5. *Press for Collections.* See that people who owe you money hear about it *frequently.* Turn accounts over for collection earlier, or (since collection agencies often keep half of whatever they collect), start taking settlement payments on weak accounts. Tell them they can settle up for 65¢ on the dollar if they act within the current day.

6. *Reduce Inventories.* This will both bring down carrying costs in line with sales, and reduce cash outlays. If you've already adopted just-in-time methods, then you've already taken most of the possible gains here.

7. *Sell Nonproductive Assets.* A minor-scale version of what you will do in your long-range plan. Here you only want to unload any spare office or plant machinery. Even a small professional office will have, say, a couple of old typewriters, an extra desk and chair, and so on, somewhere in a back room. You can liquidate this without raising suspicions; you're just clearing out the clutter. A quick Saturday sale can net you, say, $1,500 without much trouble.

Selling off more than that requires care. Don't handicap future operations. But wherever you can consolidate and sell off *unnecessary* equipment, do it.

If those adjustment are not enough to refloat the business, then *Stage Two* offers three additional options:

1. *Cut Prices.* Of all the moves with long-range implications (including firing personnel, closing offices, dropping product lines), this is the easiest to execute and, if needed, to reverse. Often a price cut—not selling at a loss—will be enough to turn sales around. At the least, it will quickly get inventory under control.

2. *Reschedule Debts.* This is an informal, case-by-case, arrangement with all the people to whom you owe money—not the formal rescheduling of Chapter 11 bankruptcy.

Approach your suppliers fairly early on. Say that you are having a problem—be as specific as possible, so they won't think the roof's fallen in—and want to continue paying them, but at the temporary rate of so much a month or week. Remember: People you owe money know it's in their interest *not* to force you into bankruptcy, as long as you are working to set affairs right. Also remember, that the people who extend your payments are helping you, and deserve to be treated politely. Try to be neither hostile nor aloof—just explain the situation fully, and ask for their cooperation.

3. *Talk with Your Employees.* Japanese competition and the recent recession have forced American workers and managers into gradually closer cooperation. More workers are recognizing how closely their fates are tied with their companies'.

It's hard to generalize about what you can fairly request from employees, but here are a few points to keep in mind:

A. From the first, make it *clear* that the company is not in, or near bankruptcy. (See Chapter 25)
B. Employees are generally more willing to give up perks and personal holidays—or even donate time on weekends—than to take a pay cut. If you need pay cuts, aim for temporary ones.

   Sometimes you'll be asked to trade profit sharing for wage concessions. This is not a point to concede quickly.
C. You can ask employees to loan money to the company. They are often willing to accept very low interest rates in order to save their jobs. The loans can come in the form of pay-check reductions.

As a last option, consider selling a part interest to your employees.

Stages one and two, even if they do not solve your problems, should give you time enough to develop a long-range plan. In fact, usually these simple tactics for generating cash and cutting or deferring expenses will suffice to get you through any temporary storms. But if several months have passed without a return to health, then you have to consider two tougher choices. You should prepare for these well in advance:

1. *Will you put in money of your own to keep the business alive?* You should have a clear idea of 1) how much money it is costing you each month to keep the doors open, and how much more you need to draw to live on, and 2) how many months you can or will carry the business on that basis. If you haven't got any savings, of course, the issue's quite simple. If you do have savings, you must decide if the business can be turned around within an *affordable* period of time. Once again, no "birthday party" economics. Unless you have a clear idea of when and how the market's going to turn —indeed, unless there is already evidence of a turnaround underway—you may well be better off shutting down entirely and then starting up again later afresh.

2. *Can you execute a major restructuring?* From the start of your crisis program—the "triage" stage—you should have been calculating the relative worth of every part of the business, deciding what might be liquidated. Are there too many employees? Is there real estate you can sell? Should one branch or another be closed? Don't act hastily—take as much time as possible to confirm your judgements, and to see whether milder measures will serve.

But *do* make the judgements in advance, and *do* act quickly if the situation continues critical. Sometimes—usually—these moves will cost money, but they can also prove to be the only way to save the firm.

Here's the *simplest* example in my recent experience. A couple opened a tiny retail shop which, considering the product line— ornate gift plates—did very well, netting about $3000 a month within a few months of opening. Almost immediately, they decided to double their income by opening a second shop. So they took a ten year lease in another, more fashionable spot—at $2000 per month, plus percentage. This shop had nothing but troubles, and was soon *losing* $4000 a month. The couple had been self-employed less than a year, and soon they were sinking the last of their savings, plus everything the first store made, into that hopeless second location.

The only answer they could contrive was to hold on until the second place turned profitable. Given their past record, there was an outside chance they could do it, but the numbers showed they would never come *close* to matching the record of location one.

The solution? We told them to bite the bullet—to close the doors, let the employees go, and then open up the place by themselves only on weekends to sell off whatever stock they could not transfer back to the first store. Before this, of course, they had to deal with their one long-term committment—the lease. But as is usually the case, their landlord was willing to let them escape for six months' rent—about $12,000. That's a stiff bite, of course, but it takes off the books a far worse obligation for $240,000 or more —ten years at $2000 a month plus Cost-Of-Living Adjustment. With luck, they may negotiate the payment down to as little as six or eight thousand dollars, and with their full attention devoted to location number one, they can pay that off in less than six months —without major belt-tightening at home. Next time, they can expand slowly and more carefully. It's a shame that anyone has to be laid off, but if the *company* had failed, then *everyone* would have lost.

Again, that's a very simple example of restructuring, but the principles remain the same for any business. Those high-priced corporate rescue artists and turnaround specialists do nothing more than:

1. Cut outlays and free all possible cash
2. Scrutinize operations and prepare turnaround plan
3. Negotiate concessions from creditors, suppliers, and employees
4. (If necessary) sell nonproductive assets and close down losing operations.

Remember, too, that because tax losses can be carried forward, they can even rank as an asset if your corporation is acquired by another. So there is a silver lining to even these darkest of clouds. The best ending of all, though, is to keep control of the company yourself, and use those losses to shelter your *own* earnings in the months and years to come.

25
BAILING OUT

SITUATION:
Sometimes, normal measures to restore profitability fail
OBJECTIVE:
Saving your personal stake by selling out, closing the doors, or engineering voluntary bankruptcy

---

Insoluble Troubles.

Sometimes it happens that you have not made one mistake, but many, or that the general business climate is so bad that your company may not survive it. The products you have are simply not selling fast enough for you to earn a living from the business, or even to meet expenses. You take the steps outlined in ROUGH WEATHER, but the situation only worsens. When that happens, you still have several options—*if* you act quickly enough. You can 1) raise more money, 2) close the doors, 3) sell out, 4) hire a turn-around specialist, or 5) file for voluntary bankruptcy. If you fail to pursue one or more of these options, then your creditors may combine to force you into involuntary bankruptcy.

RAISING MORE MONEY. It's by no means impossible to raise new capital for a troubled business. Just don't assume it will be as easy as it was before, or that you'll be catching your older creditors unawares.

One early-warning system you will have already triggered comes from the early-payment discounts many suppliers offer. People who pay their bills upon receipt are often granted small price reductions. Especially during good times, businesses in sound condition usually take advantage of this bonus. When business slumps, slow payment conserves cash, but one of the fastest rumors to circulate is that "so-and-so isn't picking up his discounts." When that happens, your efforts to raise money will be hindered by hints that your credit is already shakey—even before anyone has seen your books.

That doesn't mean more credit can't be arranged. In the first place, banks realize that the most common error of beginning businesspeople is to take out loans too small for their needs. In the second place, banks have a vested interest in not recording any bad debts. If they think a second loan will guarantee your repaying a first loan, they'll very likely grant it.

In any of these cases, though, you have to be prepared, now more than at any other time, to convince lenders that more money will solve your problems. Doing that will require some real work, including:

1. *Making Sure Your Act Is Clean.* You've got to convince them that you have taken steps to run the organization as leanly as possible —that you have moderated salaries, cut extra personnel, trimmed inventories, and so on. Bloated inventories are worst of all, because they not only cost money, but suggest your product line is bad.

With the business in trouble, lenders will be banking more than ever on you personally. You'd better not seem a spendthrift, so ditch the Cadillac and the company boat, and, even better, take a paycut a month or so before you walk in looking for the loan. The one thing lenders most dread is loaning to support an owner's lifestyle.

2. *Developing a Clear Plan.* This time, your plan has to demonstrate that lack of capital is the firm's only major problem. Remember that anyone seeking a loan under these circumstances is automatically suspected of managerial incompetence. You will need plausible explanations of how the company got into trouble (lack of capital is always your basic claim, but have the specific examples), and details of how every new loan dollar is going to be spent.

3. *Being Ready to Accept a Lot of Advice.* We've already covered the ownership positions sought by some types of lenders, and in a moment we'll talk about the similar demands of turnaround specialists. Even where you can avoid those kinds of impositions, though, you had better realize that loans made to troubled firms usually contain both preconditions and restrictions (on the uses of the loan and the actions management can take in other areas), and are subject to frequent review. Few lenders are going to just hand you the money to do with as you like.

With those provisos, you can can often secure loans to keep a troubled business afloat. Just remember never to try deceiving a lender into making further loans when you know (or even strongly suspect) that lack of capital is not the problem. If the business simply isn't competitive, why squander the bank's money, and your time and reputation? Instead, consider closing down.

CLOSING THE DOORS. Closing the doors has nothing at all in common with bankruptcy. When you shut the doors on a firm, you simply decide that its prospects are poor, so you pay off your debts (sometimes at a negotiated rate, more often dollar-for-dollar), sell off your assets, relinquish your lease, and walk away. Your credit rating remains intact, you keep the money made in more profitable days, and you can start anew in the morning.

In fact, closing the doors is often the tactic of entrepreneurs who follows fads—hot tubs, video arcades, or whatever. The ideal approach in any such fad, of course, is to get in at the start, ride the boom to its peak, then sell out to someone else for a big price, and let him ride it down into the ground. If your timing is slightly awry, though, and the market slumps suddenly, then closing the doors makes perfect sense.

Closing the doors also applies in certain highly cyclical businesses. Suppose, for example, you owned a real estate office in Southern California. During the boom years of the mid- and late '70s, it was common for a small real estate office (or, indeed, an individual salesperson) to net $100,000 to $200,000 a year. When interest rates soared, though, the market went dead, and suddenly those small offices with fancy floorspace and ads to run were often *losing* $6000 or 7000 a month. The folks who could not see the handwriting kept doggedly on, gradually putting back into the business everything they had earned. The smart operators—who had hung onto a good chunk of those easy dollars—simply said, "thank you, and goodnight," and closed their doors. Even if they only went home and put their feet up, they were $6000 a month or more ahead of their brethren who kept on slugging. And most of them instead tended their own investments or went to work for one of the hardy perennials. When the market revived, they could always reopen for themselves.

I've suggested that one way to endure rough times is to reduce your overhead—well, often closing the doors is the very wisest form of that.

SELLING OUT. Closing the doors works so well for a service business like real estate because such firms have little invested in valuable fixtures and equipment. If your company is less liquid— if it owns expensive machinery or valuable patents—closing the doors may offer fewer pluses. Then you probably want to try selling out, especially where your financial strength is sufficient to support the period of waiting necessary to complete the sale.

There can be tremendous value in many unprofitable businesses, especially those whose potential profits have all been reinvested in business expansion. By the middle of 1982, for example, Ted Turner's Cable News Network had yet to show real profit, yet industry sources were saying that he could sell it "in the morning" for $200,000,000. The same was true of some of the genetic engineering companies. Investors lined up to put money into firms lacking even any products to sell.

Less, dramatically, we once helped a growing air-purification company sell franchised dealerships for its innovative electrostatic equipment. The franchises sold very well, but after a fair number had been sold, it became clear that the parent company was in serious trouble. High development costs and a weak pricing structure were creating operating losses, and the company was only living on the proceeds from franchise sales. When those were subtracted, the company—for all its growth and technical expertise—was a money-loser headed for trouble.

On a strict financial basis, the firm was a basket case, but there was real value in its technology and its market position, and we were able to convince a national corporation to buy out the whole company. The new corporate owner not only had the management skill to turn the business truly profitable, but thought well enough of its potential to assume all outstanding debt, and pay the old owners $250,000 besides. Not a bad resolution to a financial crunch which otherwise would have ended in bankruptcy and litigation.

In selling a troubled business, then, the trick is in locating the items of value not apparent on the balance sheet. For that, you will often need the help of a broker with experience in the field. No matter what credentials such a broker may offer, it's essential that you request the names of three or four distressed firms he has recently sold, and then contact at least two or three of the sellers to ask for a personal recommendation.

A troubled business can contain hidden value in its equipment, leases, real estate, technologies, even (for corporations) adoptable market share. Unless these are unusually large or rare though, a realistic broker will price price them at only a fraction of their maximum worth. The exact discount will depend upon how desperate you are to sell, but the first thing you seek in a distressedbusiness broker is the ability to identify every source of value within your firm. You cannot judge the appropriateness of the price he sets unless you demand a clear explanation of what he believes to be your assets. Do not let him set an unjustifiably high price. Remember, you want a quick sale—not a lovely but unattainable figure.

Whatever price is set, be prepared for some hard negotiating. *Everyone* sharpshoots the price of a distressed firm, and even your broker will be of two minds because he knows how much it is costing you to stay in business every month. Since the last thing he wants is to have you slip into bankruptcy while a deal is pending, he too will likely be pressuring you to accept whatever is offered. Often, in fact, he will be quite right in his approach—

but the decision must still be yours. Base your response not on your natural resentment of a hard-dealing buyer, but on the strict likelihood that a better offer will appear soon enough to justify the intervening operating losses.

Your agreement with your broker should grant him only an exclusive agency listing, which reserves your right to find a buyer on your own without paying commission. Don't agree to a long listing. You may be willing to bind a profitable business for 90 or 120 days, but a distressed firm demands optimum flexibility. Give the broker thirty days to accomplish something. If appropriate, you can always renew. After all, (not to offer false hope), a sudden improvement in a firm's situation is hardly unknown. When that happens, an authorization to sell becomes merely an inconvenience.

BRINGING IN NEW MANAGEMENT. Whether or not conditions improve, one possibility short of an outright sale, is surrendering a measure of control by bringing in someone to help you manage more effectively. If your broker can find one, a partner willing to commit expertise as well as capital may represent an ideal solution.

Unfortunately, most people with management skill and money are likely to be more interested in buying a prime business or even starting one of their own, unless they can buy in at a truly bargain rate. That makes these partnership much the business equivalents of shotgun marriages—which is to say, difficult propositions. I can think of only a very few we've put together during our time in business.

Far more common is management brought in on a consulting basis. Business consultants are plentiful; an average big city will offer several hundred people claiming the ability. Turnaround specialists are scarcer, and competent ones are scarcer still. For the names of these, you can either watch the local financial papers (people who pull off successful turnarounds get a great deal of publicity), or ask your banker or accountant for recommendations.

Remember that these specialists are expensive, with fees starting around $100 an hour, and rising swiftly. It is quite possible to spend $25,000, or even much more, on a single case. Since most troubled companies (which, by definition, are already strapped for cash) cannot afford these kinds of fees directly, they often are forced to surrender either the chief executive's chair, or even an equity position in the firm. That's not necessarily bad. It can mean your consultant thinks you have potential. Since he *may* only mean "potential" for liquidation, though, *any* consultant's contract *must* give you final veto over major moves. Remember: some lawyer/consultants love pushing clients into early bankruptcy. They get big fees; the clients lose everything. Keep that veto!

The qualifications of good turnaround specialists vary greatly. Some are CPAs, some are lawyers with background in bankruptcy law, and some are simply former corporate executives or even middle-managers. Beyond the evidence of previous successes, you want to check for personal compatibility. Otherwise, you may end up like the head of a certain family-held German automobile company, who was literally forced from the corporate grounds by endless disputes with the man he had chosen to run the firm. More cheerfully, it sometimes happens that a consultant is so taken with a firm's owners and prospects that he or she wants to come aboard as an investing partner. That's a valuable opportunity, which can grant you the most desirable of partners—consider it closely.

Before hiring any paid consultants, though, at least attempt to get what help you can for free. I've already mentioned several government sources, including the SBA's Service Corps of Retired Executives. In this case, you might find stronger support from your suppliers, especially any major corporations. During the mid-'70s, many majors began establishing programs to help their small-business partners. Along with special pools of contracts reserved solely for small businesses, these companies offer free consulting services, usually subsidizing their own retired workers for the help they provide. Most of these programs, frankly, were prompted by a 1978 law requiring any company holding more than $500,000 in government contracts to make a "good faith" effort to secure minority subcontractors. If you qualify as a minority, be sure to ask help of every big firm with which you might even potentially do business. If you don't qualify, but do have contacts with one of the major firms, try to borrow their advisors anyway. If they refuse, you can easily mention your intention to go to the press and the courts with a charge of reverse discrimination, but given the strong interest of suppliers and contractors in keeping their customers and subcontractors afloat, that's not likely to be needed.

Seeking Court Protection.

Sometimes none of these actions will suffice. Either your problems are too great, or your time is too short, for you to work out an adequate compromise. Perhaps the crisis simply comes upon you too quickly, and is too complex—too many stores opened too soon, or a bad product introduction, or any other set of complex and costly mistakes which require time to analyze properly. Then you face a true crisis, because your creditors can forestall the recovery by combining to force you into involuntary bankruptcy. When that happens, you lose everything. Court-appointed representatives of the creditors will simply sell off whatever the company owns and divide it up among the people holding paper. That leaves you with nothing—and even worse, if you've personally signed any of the notes or other obligations, people are going to be coming after your personal assets. Just for safety's sake, you'd be advised to homestead your house. This simple filing can provide bankruptcy protection for your primary family residence. Ask your lawyer for details. Give any assets you can to family members—through work contracts, if possible. There are legal limits to what is permissable in this regard (your attorney can advise you) but you must do whatever you legally can.

If you are moderately alert, though, your creditors will never have the chance to force you into bankruptcy, because you will beat them to the punch by taking shelter under Chapter 11 of the Federal bankruptcy laws. Before they can act, you will already have filed for a court-protected reorganization of your debt.

Filing for Chapter 11 bankruptcy no longer carries nearly the stigma it once did. Some critics have blamed that lessened stigma on a fading of American pride in self-reliance, but a truer reason may simply be that in recent years, a number of important firms have managed to emerge from voluntary bankruptcy successfully.

Penn Central and Toys 'R' Us are two of the better known, but some of the less famous cases are more spectacular. In 1957, an obscure little glassmaker called Guardian Industries filed for Chapter 11 after its owner died. A nephew of his, named William Davidson, assumed the presidency, and worked to turn matters around. A year later, a strike at a major rival manufacturer gave him his chance. Guardian picked up momentum, and within two years it was out of bankruptcy. Within a few years more, it had paid back every creditor 100¢ on the dollar. Today, Guardian—with Bill Davidson still at the helm—is the fourth largest American firm in its field, and in 1981 it netted better than $31 million on sales of about $365 million. So comebacks do happen, and they show that voluntary bankruptcy, far from being weak-minded or cowardly, can often be simply the most appropriate business tactic. (*Fortune*, 5 April 1982)

Obviously, you want to avoid filing for as long as possible, since it not only damages your credit, but turns your private problems into a public affair (which hardly builds customer or consumer confidence), and costs you a large measure of control over your own fate. Still, don't let a false sense of pride deter from filing, if you believe you have a salvageable business.

When your attorney files (in Federal Court) for Chapter 11 protection, he will append to the filing a list of known creditors. Within a few days he will be expected to add a statement of your affairs and a schedule of your assets and liabilities. You will be allowed 120 days from first filing to present to the court a plan acceptible to your creditors for repaying them; after that time, they will be allowed to present a plan of their own. In most areas of the country, a federal trustee will be appointed to oversee the plan's execution. The system's been in turmoil recently, but that's how it works in theory.

Once your first paperwork is submitted, in other words, you have a grace period of four months to persuade your creditors to agree to your proposals for settling accounts. During this period you must prepare yourself for dealing with some very unhappy people, in an atmosphere slightly more tense than the clubhouse of a baseball team about to lose the World Series in four straight games. It isn't very pleasant, but you can come through it if you remember a few rules.

1. *Don't act like a loser.* You've got to convince them you still have the right stuff to turn the company around. You need to be positive and firm, while never denying the problems. Your situation will be much enhanced if you have been frank and forward with your problems from the earliest days.

2. *Remember your common interests.* Never let your creditors forget that they lose if you lose. Especially for bank loan officers, the loss can be as personal as your own; they stake their futures with the banks on their ability to judge borrowers, and a sufficiently large bad debt can blight their careers.

3. *Line up the big guys first.* This is standard advice, but true. The major creditors, especially the banks, can usually put pressure on the little ones to play ball. That's why you're in the best shape if your biggest debts are to the biggest banks. If most of your money is owed to some other poor yokel of a small manufacturer, the big creditors may be just as well satisfied to let you both go down rather than gamble more of their own money. Sorry, but this is a rough game.

You'll probably need the help of a bankruptcy attorney to achieve the best possible deal, but there are a few general guidelines to bear in mind. First of all, as a rule, banks would much rather get paid in full, no matter how long it takes them to get paid. Your best bet with them is probably to try to *reschedule* the debt— that is, reduce or delay the payments, so that you pay in full but over a longer time.

Your suppliers, on the other hand, generally feel pressure to get at least *some* money in hand, and will likely favor a *settlement* over a relatively short period of time. They will probably settle for much less than you might expect if they believe it will keep you alive as a viable source of future business. Bankruptcy attorneys often persuade suppliers to accept only half of what they would have gotten by forcing you to cash in your chips. They're gambling that, in time, you'll again be a valuable customer. With a potential buyer for your company waiting in the wings, you can often do still better: we recently helped a Chapter 11 client negotiate a $46,000 debt down to $11,500 in one day.

Above all, remember that this is a negotiating process, not a law court. Once the papers are filed, is the emphasis shifts from litigation to old-fashioned wheeling and dealing. Much of what you achieve will depend not only on the clarity and completeness of your rescue plan, but on the kind of rapport you have built up with your lenders and suppliers over the years—and on the native force of your personality in tight negotiations.

Building Credit Anew.

Theoretically, any final plan you achieve should (after concessions) leave you with an immediately positive—or at least even—cash flow. That does not mean, however, that you are precluded from trying to borrow more money at once. The practice is in fact surprisingly common, mostly because the court will automatically subordinate your old (unsecured) debt to any new obligations you might assume. As a debtor in possession (your technical designation), you are hardly a prime loan candidate, but some money will likely be available.

Your suppliers, meanwhile (except for a rare few who may be asleep at the switch) will immediately put you on a COD basis, but if you can cover these purchases from cash flow for a matter of a few months, you may soon find a certain amount of credit extended to you here, as well. Surprisingly, even early on you may be able to find new suppliers willing to gamble on a shakey situation and let you have goods on account. It does no harm to look around, and if the credit's available, fine. Just don't misrepresent your situation to obtain it—you can go to jail for that.

The main thing in the months after filing for Chapter 11 is to keep her slow and steady. Make progress in increments, and look for opportunities as you recover strength. Sometimes these will fall into your lap; remember Guardian Industries and the heaven-sent strike. Still, you want to move cautiously from chicken soup to solid food.

Other Considerations: Taxes. In the interim, you may even be able to work out a compromise on what most people think of as the most inexorable of financial obligations—federal income tax. The stated goal of the IRS is recovery in full of all taxes owed, but it does have a system for dealing with troubled taxpayers. Simply arrange early on to speak with someone in the collection department, and bring your financial documents to the meeting. Tell them you are in trouble, and want to file for a compromised tax offering. You will be assigned to a revenue officer who will help to determine—based upon factors ranging from your age to your financial prospects—the likelihood that you will be able to make a full repayment. The IRS is probably the toughest of all creditors, but it has been forced by recent court decisions to drop some of its former rough stuff, and it will try to work out something if you start early and are completely honest.

Employee Response. A Chapter 11 filing can be peacefully handled by you and your attorney, and once the papers are in, most of your creditors will—however grudgingly—cooperate. Still, you had better be ready for one episode about which few lawyers will warn you:

One of our clients, a very successful restauranteur, found out about the phenomenon when he arrived for work at one of his bayfront locations about eight o'clock one morning only to discover his employees stripping the tables and packing every movable piece of kitchen hardware away in the trunks of their cars. It seemed that the land developing company which owned restaurant's waterfront property had filed for bankruptcy the afternoon before. The morning paper had unintentionally implied that the restaurant itself (which was in fact so popular that three more on the same plan were under construction elsewhere) had gone belly up. So the employees had been there since dawn, carting off whatever they could hammer loose, assuming it was their due, since they would not be getting paychecks or severance money.

The mutiny our friend faced was accidental, but, unfortunately, many businesspeople *design* the same problems for themselves. Afraid that news of their troubles will cost them valuable workers

—the proverbial rats leaving the sinking ship—they keep everything a secret until the day the bankruptcy papers are filed. When that happens, their people feel betrayed, and react strongly.

One solution, of course, is simply to have guards at the door the day you make the announcement—and if you want to play it this way, then guards are essential. The alternative is to try keeping your employees informed from the beginning. You may have defections (especially if the job market is solid elsewhere), but on the other hand, people working hard to stave off crisis are a tremendous asset. You should not entirely neglect the human capacity for self-sacrifice. Still, the choice to confide in your employees must depend on your judgement of their basic quality. Whatever you decide, a financial crisis is going to provide you with an education in human nature.

The Hopeful Side. Much of that education—the friends who turn you down, the silence when you enter a room—will be disheartening. Still, no emotional hardships should distract you from the task at hand. Above all, remember that with work and a measure of luck, even a very dismal situation can be turned into a triumph.

My father still likes to tell the story of a near-bankrupt firm which he sold not long after starting business in 1946. The company made field radio parts, for which the wartime market had just vanished. The buyer and my father were both fresh out of the military, and between them probably had about enough cash for a good dinner out. Our commission was $500, and money was so scarce that we had to loan it back to the buyer so he could complete the deal. It was, all in all, the poor leading the impoverished. Still, the buyer would not be deterred, because in that homely little business he saw something invisible to others. Over the next year or so—usually barely ducking insolvency—he repaid our $500, and most of the business's other debts. Then we gradually lost touch with him.

More than twenty years later, we received a call from the head office of one of the larger manufacturers of medical electronics gear in the Western U.S. The president of the company was going to be flying into town (in the company's executive turboprop), and wanted to stop in to say hello. The privileged executive was, of course, Dad's old friend, meaning to talk over selling out his multimillion dollar firm and retiring, a very rich man.

So, you see, a business in trouble isn't always the end of the world. Often, it's the beginning.

26
SELLING THE BUSINESS

SITUATION:
Selling the business is a time of equally great risk and opportunity
OBJECTIVE:
Putting together a deal which is smooth, profitable, and safe

With a Wing and a Prayer.

The day you decide to sell your profitable business should be a day both for celebration—and for caution. In theory, selling a successful firm is far easier than building one. In practice, too many sellers end up like a scene from a John Wayne air-war-in-the Pacific movie. They come roaring back to base from a successful mission —a bit shot up but still victorious—and then suddenly, in mid-barrel roll, they slam into the palm trees at the end of the runway.

Of course, I'm kidding—but not entirely. Although it's often the hot-shots who score the early victories at business, selling a profitable firm is more like landing a 747 with a Space Shuttle on top. Slow and steady does her. It's no time to play fighter pilot.

This chapter covers the basic precautions for safely selling off a business. Above all, remember that, as the owner of a desirable going concern, *you* should be in the driver's seat. Just stick to your plan, and act in good time, and you'll do very well indeed.

Prelude: State of Mind.

One prime reason so many people make bad deals when selling out is simply that they have never planned for the day. When a situation forcing a sale arises unexpectedly, they have to take the first offer made. It's surprisingly common for business brokers to get phone calls from small business owners who say, "The doctor just told me to get my affairs in order. I'll take whatever you can get me." These requests lead to those unfortunate classified ads about "Illness forcing sale," and "Sacrifice for emergency" businesses—bargains for astute buyers, but tragedies for the sellers.

Clearly, none of us can foresee every emergency which will befall, but some general preparations are still possible. At the very least, you should periodically review what your business is worth, for both its tangible and intangible assets, and see that some family member is apprised of the figure. Even better, see whether some family member is willing to take a short course in the running of the firm, even if he or she has no interest in ultimately taking over. A short holding action can make all the difference between a liquidation at auction, and a successful sale. Lastly, consider one of the buy/sell arrangements mentioned in INSURANCE, whereby a policy is written on your life to provide some valued employee with the money to buy the business from your estate. These are not pleasant things to anticipate, but you must be prepared.

Less dramatic, but far more common, are owners who stick with a business long after they've lost enthusiasm for it—in fact, until long after they've come to loathe it. Not long ago, I was talking with the owner of a successful direct mailing company, a fellow who had worked long and hard to build the plant to where it was netting around $120,000 a year, and was poised to grow much larger. As we talked, his contempt for his work became apparent, until when I asked him how long he would stay on to train a buyer, he answered vehemently, "Not five minutes. The day I hand him the keys is the last time I look at this damned place." Now, how in the world can such a seller possibly hold out long enough to get his best price?

Often your feelings about a business will have little or nothing to do with the money you're making. A good family friend inherited a large manufacturing concern. He really wanted to go to Europe and be a painter, but from a sense of duty he ran the company for years—until he ran it, and himself, into the ground. By the time he admitted he couldn't stand the firm another day, it was worth less than a *tenth* what it had been the day he took over.

Sometimes people begin enthusiastically and then undergo a change of heart—a "midlife crisis." OK—so after thirty years in the hardware business you decide you want to grow a beard and go save the whales. So what. Why apologize? You've spent thirty years of hard, honest work, and if you want a change, you've earned it. The whole *point* of small business is freedom. Just act while you still have the patience to work methodically, allowing time to set your price, find a buyer, hold an escrow, and train the new owner. Plan intelligently, and you will enjoy the fruits of your labors.

Planning to Sell.

The basic steps of selling a business are simple:

1. Set your price
2. Clean up the deal
3. Choose a broker or advertise yourself
5. Agree to terms
5. Watch for traps
6. Hold escrow
7. Train buyer
8. Sail away!

("Sailing away" can mean either retiring, or taking on another operation. A client of ours supplements his social security by starting and selling off one small office-building coffee shop each year. He's started and sold seven or eight, but in the process he's developed quite a formula—one which his son-in-law has used to build and *keep* more than eighty similar shops throughout California, creating a multimillion dollar company in the process. Practice does make perfect, but whether you are planning to retire, or to launch a new venture in the morning, these are the first steps.)

SET YOUR PRICE. As I tried to show in the early chapters, there are no absolute price formulas, although few people will normally pay more than, say, two and a half times net income plus book value, or perhaps a flat four to five times net earnings. If you *do* have features (copyrights, patents, huge market share, or anything else) of uncommon value, don't be afraid to charge to the hilt for them. A serious buyer who thinks you're being unfair can always counter-offer.

One tip: even if you're in a hurry, don't set your price too ridiculously low, because buyers are always suspicious of an implausible price. A low price will probably be OK if you're selling to someone in the same field, or a friend who knows that you've got a good business, but other buyers are likely to shy away from anything which looks suspiciously cheap. It sounds odd, perhaps, but it's true.

CLEAN UP THE DEAL. As far as possible, you want to present to any buyer a package which is both fiscally and physically clean.

The fiscal improvements can include settling or consolidating any outstanding debts, securing a longer lease (a five-year option with a good transfer clause will do wonders for the saleability of the firm), and acquiring a complete set of up-to-date financial records. Try to settle any significant outstanding litigation. Be ready with frank explanations of any other problems the company might be having. Lastly, decide how long you would be willing to stay on to train a new owner.

Physical Improvements Even though sale of a business—especially a manufacturing concern—is not supposed to depend much upon the firm's aesthetic appeal, a bit of discreet spending on paint, carpeting, or furnishings, may be worthwhile. The more the company depends upon on-site visits by customers, the more important such spending becomes. Sometimes you can benefit from your landlord's efforts. If he happens to paint the lobby, or install new carpeting or elevators, that may be the time to act on a long-pending urge to sell.

Equally important is creating a good spirit among employees. An experienced buyer may ignore new paint in a factory (while still noting broken machines and leaky roofs), but an unhappy workforce will register as a strong negative. Make a few extra friendly gestures abut this time. Remember the Hawthorne effect, which shows that productivity rises even after such simple devices as an extra company picnic, or some free tickets to a ball game. Anyone passing through should gather a favorable impression of your labor relations.

CHOOSING A BROKER OR ADVERTISING YOURSELF. Once you've set a price and made efforts to put a shine on the business, you need to decide whether or not to let a broker handle the sale. A broker will normally charge a 10% commission for smaller businesses; for larger businesses, he will expect either that 10%, or else the "Lehman formula," a descending scale: 5% on the first $1,000,000; 4% on the second million; 3% on the third; 2% on the fourth; 1% on each additional million. Even though the better brokers rarely bend, these fees are negotiable—try for a discount, and be sure to discover which items (e.g., liquor inventories) are exempt from commission.

Since you as seller will be paying the broker's commission, he is expected to represent your interests only. He in turn will expect you to sign a "listing agreement" for anywhere from 1 to 180 days; ninety days is average and reasonable. Listings may be either "exclusive" (only the broker can provide the client); "exclusive agency" (limited to a single broker but allowing you to find a client on your own), or "open" (giving the broker simply one chance among many to find a buyer—you can give out a dozen open listings, if you like). Few brokers will work open listings. If you want to be able to find a buyer on your own, an exclusive agency listing is a fair compromise. Your choice of listing type should not in any way affect the commission rate.

Beware of cancellation clauses. Some listings say you are liable for a commission if you cancel the listing before the expiration date. If your broker won't scratch this out, find another broker. Remember that if you sell to, take as a partner, or hire as a worker anyone introduced to you by the broker, you will be liable for commission—and that this holds for, normally, six months after the expiration date. Since a broker will have earned his commission if he produces a buyer ready, willing, and able to meet your price and terms, don't list until you're absolutely ready to sell. If your business is large enough, a more flexible *letter of intent* can take the place of a formal listing.

Good brokers earn their money by 1) advertising the business, 2) using their files to quickly locate buyers for your type of business, 3) screening clients, making sure anyone inquiring is a sincere, qualified buyer, 4) handling technical details from copying leases to setting up an escrow which protects your interests, and 5) helping you in negotiations with the buyer, landlords, and other interested parties. Often, indeed, a broker helps you most by smoothing your buyer's way, advising him on packaging loans, finding lenders, fast-tracking permits, and so on.

So a good broker certainly earns his or her money—especially since most of them can get you a price high enough to cover most, or all, of their fees. The emphasis, though, should be on the word *"good"* broker. Personally, I wouldn't trust anyone without 1) at least five to ten years in the business 2) recommendations from a bank, CPA, or respected lawyer, or 3) references from recent clients. Remember that your business is probably the most valuable thing you own—take time to protect it.

SCREENING CLIENTS. One unpleasant chore a broker will spare you is screening clients for their financial strength, honesty, and technical competency.

Some idea of the unsavory characters who appear when a good business is offered for sale can be had by considering two who nearly slipped through our net. One was a charming fellow who wanted to buy a liquor store. All went well until just before the close of the ninety-day escrow. Then the mandatory fingerprint check with the FBI revealed the fellow had a Washington State rap-sheet as long as your arm—including a conviction for armed robbery of a liquor store.

More amusing—or at least less dangerous—was the fellow who came in, looked at one or two businesses, and quickly agreed to full price and terms. He left a generous deposit check, shook hands, and left. The next day he called us and said, "My attorney just has one question for you." Then the attorney came on the line to ask, "Say, did Walter mention to you that he filed bankruptcy yesterday?"

Well, those are the sorts of adventures you can expect on a regular basis if you try selling by yourself. In addition, you will have a very hard time concealing the sale from your employees and competitors. You can run a classified ad listing a newspaper box for replies, but frankly, those rarely work for long.

How Long Will It Take?

Given the number of flakes about, and the difficulties even worthy buyers have these days raising money, it's natural to wonder how long it might take to sell an averagely desireable business.

Unfortunately, there's no way to tell. Sometimes it happens so fast that even the broker is amazed. A couple of years ago we got a call from a panicked travel agency owner who had just learned that a key employee had stolen $25,000 from the firm. If we could not find him a cash buyer for at least a half-interest in the company, the air travel conference (afraid he lacked sufficient capital to honor his commitments to customers) was going to yank his certification in five days.

That was a Wednesday midmorning. By that afternoon, we had signed him to the necessary papers, and collected copies of his financial records. The next morning we had found a likely buyer, a doctor with sideline investments in travel, from our files. Friday the doctor saw the physical plant. Saturday he visited our office to review the financial records, phone the man he wanted as manager, and write up an offer to buy the whole operation. When the banks opened on Monday morning, he started the escrow, and on the strength of the money he deposited there, the firm received an operating extension. We had gone from crisis to sale in just under five working days.

That was a textbook case, one I remember because it worked so well—and because it saved a good company from bankruptcy. More realistically, I'd say that you should be able to find a buyer for a reasonably priced business within thirty to sixty days. If nothing has happened by then, a worthy broker will pause to help you determine the problems and possible solutions. Do you need a price cut? A change in financing terms? An inventory reduction, or longer buyer-training? Sometimes, it will be only bad luck that no buyer appears. In that case, all you can do is to keep trying. The longest we ever needed to sell a business was about 12 years, off and on, for a specialty steel manufacturer.

Protecting Yourself in the Escrow.

As discussed back in ESCROWING AND TAKING OVER, there is no way to list all the considerations appropriate for every type of sale. As seller, though, you need to protect yourself on several special points.

1. *Collateral.* It's generally nice if you can get all cash, but in the likely event that you can't, you need to make sure that the money owed to you is secured by *first-rate* collateral. Two items should be viewed with suspicion:

A. *The business itself.* The true mark of the low-ball buyer is a suggestion that he be allowed to use the business itself as collateral for the loan. That means if he misses payments (probably because he's wrecked the business), you can have the business back. Big deal. Thumbs down.

B. *The buyer's home.* In the first place, you probably won't have the heart to throw anybody of his house, and in the second, you may not be able to. Quite likely, either it will have been homesteaded, or other creditors will be there before you. Add those points to the fact that residential housing markets periodically go flat as a pancake, and you've got dubious security. Better to let a home mortgage firm loan your buyer the money. If the title's basically clear, okay. Otherwise, go slow.

That leaves as suitable collateral other real and personal property, stocks, bonds, and the like. Just make sure you get an independent appraisal of their worth.

2. *Insurance.* If the buyer owes you money, you want him and the business both around for a long while. That means insurance on both the business and the buyer's life. Most brokers will recommend this, but there are still hazards for which to be alert.

The worst situation is where the buyer agrees to take out a life-insurance policy payable to you, then dies—leaving you to learn that he had long before stopped paying premiums. Since the insurance company was not obliged to notify you, the policy simply lapsed—and so, now you get nothing.

The problem can be circumvented two ways. Either have the buyer deposit the money in a trust account which will pay for the policy (and notify you if payment stops), or buy the insurance and make the payments yourself. (Naturally, you will adjust the selling price to compensate for your expense. What you are looking for is control over the paperwork.)

Another, rarer situation, perhaps bears mentioning. At least once we sold a business to two people who made payments for a single month, lost the place to what was (it now appears) almost certainly arson, collected the insurance money—and disappeared. The old owner got his down payment, one monthly check, and that was all.

The trick here is that if you help the insurers prove arson, the buyers don't get paid—but neither do you. Neither does double insurance make much sense. Probably your best bet is to check out any potential buyer very carefully—and then, in case the business does catch fire, to camp out on his doorstep until you're paid in full.

3. *Approval of Your Attorney and CPA.* As with any other major transaction, you want to seek the approval of your business consultants. Remember, though, that this time their natural conservatism may be reinforced by their fear of losing a good client. Whenever possible, brokers like to have the potential buyer announce early that he will be keeping on the old CPA and attorney—it's *amazing* how this tends to quiet their doubts about the wisdom of a sale. Make sure that *you* are the one to finally decide—listen carefully to any arguments, but at last judge for yourself.

4. *Goodwill vs. Noncompete Agreements.* As noted much earlier, when it comes to assigning value to the abstract or "intangible" part of the business, your tax interests are the opposite of the buyer's. The buyer wants the largest part of any payment above book value to be listed as a "covenant not to compete," which offers him clear tax benefits—as a tangible asset, it can be depreciated over the life of the covenant. You, on the other hand, will find such a covenant taxed as ordinary income—while the same abstract value, listed as "goodwill" will be taxed as capital gains. You'll probably have to compromise somewhat, but hold out for the largest chunk of good will that you can.

Training the Buyer.

The normal escrow agreement will call for your training the buyer in your business methods for some period of time. The average buyer quickly realizes that this constitutes getting a prime worker for free. Be reasonable, but don't overdo it. Two weeks for the average business is about right; after that, you want a work contract and a decent wage. On the other hand, it's in your interest that the buyer succeed. If a problem arises later, and he asks for your advice, help him out. Just remember *never* to hand over a key until the escrow closes.

And here's a general suggestion, based on past observation: Don't rush to sign a work contract at the time of the escrow. You'll probably be so glad that someone is buying the place, that your gratitude will transfer to an unrealistic sense of friendship. Most often these hasty agreements end badly. Use the training period for a trial—and then consider a longer pact.

Selling Out for Stock.

When you sell out to another corporation, the first proposal they will normally make is that they buy you out for stock—perhaps by an exchange of shares. There can be tax advantages to this, if properly executed. Assets exchanged "like for like" (land for land, or, here, stock for stock), are entirely tax deferred until the asset is sold. Just remember that taking others' stocks makes you dependent on their management skills, and that you *will* owe the tax once you begin liquidating. (*Note:* if you ever accept stock as *collateral* for a sale, see that it's placed in a bank trust. If the stock turns wobbly, the bank can protect your payments by liquidating the shares and holding the cash.).

GERMANY CALLING. Being acquired also involves possible risk for owners planning to stay on with the firm. No matter what promises a big firm makes at the time of the sale, it can always find a way to bounce you if it chooses.

A friend of ours built a chain of around 70 auto parts discount centers with sales up near a billion dollars a year, and then sold it out to a West German concern which—as he understood it—promised him continued operating control. That was fine, except that every week more people around him were replaced by folks from the home office back in Dusseldorf, until finally whenever he picked up the phone, all he'd get was a hearty, "Ja?" Pretty soon charges were being bandied about that he wasn't cooperating with the management team. Finally, just as the stores were launching their big Oktoberfest promotion (I'm not kidding), they told our friend he was gone—without the expected fat severance package.

He finally had to sue in court for the money due him. He won, but only after considerable loss in time and legal expense. (He did achieve a kind of revenge; the foreign owners ran the company into the ground, and in 1982 it filed bankruptcy. Our friend, meanwhile started another chain on a different formula, and at last count his annual sales were zooming past the quarter-billion mark.

Now, I've probably been unfair to the new corporate owners—no doubt they had reasons which seemed proper to them, and in any case they *were* the corporate owners. I'm simply trying to illustrate a warning: whenever you sell out to a larger firm, you have by definition diluted your control. No matter what assurances you might be given, it's a mistake to think of yourself as an owner, because when the real owners decide you're obsolete, you'll be gone in the morning.

For safety, then, you need two precautions when selling to a larger company for stock. First, sell only to a company with a known reputation, and second (if you plan to stay on with the firm) demand a worthwhile severance package. With those two provisos, you should at least be able to go to sleep each night with confidence that your money (if not your job) will be there in the morning. Even allowing for the periodic troubles of the stock market, I'd certainly rather be out on the streets with 50,000 shares of IBM or Kodak, than with 200,000 shares of the Ajax Weasel Mender Co.

Summing Up.

As always, I fear I've made the situation seem darker than it really is. Every year, owners by the tens of thousands sell their business to people who are competent, trustworthy, and successful, and who meet their obligations cheerfully and fully. We've sometimes taken long-term notes on particular deals. The vast majority of these have been honored without ever a word of prompting—sometimes even when we knew the owners were sacrificing greatly to do so. One or two such notes have been paying faithfully for ten years or more, and I can think of only a single absolute default in the last decade.

Selling out does have its dangers, but if you observe all the precautions—if you screen buyers, set realistic terms, and demand adequate insurance and collateral—the chances of a trouble-free sale are superb. *That's* the main reason for my including, and your studying, the cautionary tales in this chapter.

Selling your business—instead of simply liquidating—is more than a way of profiting from your achievement. It's a way of letting someone else share in that achievement, and even expand it beyond what you accomplished. A competent buyer links you to permanence, and to the satisfaction of knowing you created something that will endure.

Shortly after selling your business, you may well be eager to start over with something newer, bigger, and better. If so, you can turn again to the first chapters of this book. Or you may simply decide that you've taken everything you want or need from the world of business, and are ready for a quieter way of life. If that's the case, then, in the words of Horace, "here ends our voyage, and our story."

A successful end to any business venture is a cause for celebration and good cheer. You've made it safely into the jungle and back out again. Congratulations—and farewell!

Appendix 1

READING BUSINESS
STATEMENTS, OR HOW TO
MAKE $21,500 INTO $310,000

To work through this simple illustration of the kinds of creative paper-work you'll face in the business world, first note the two P and L statements (Figures 1 and 2) of that dull-looking (and mythical) manufacturer of lawn ornaments, Acme Custom Metals.

Now you're sitting in the luxurious main office of Acme. The carpeting's five inches thick, the walls are panelled in Tamo ash at a thousand bucks a panel, and there's a $10,000 custom stero playing softly while one of the owners tells you he's just back from China and leaving tomorrow for three weeks in London. You look again at the tax statement showing Acme made just $21,499.23 last year—and paid just $800 in taxes. (Figure 1) Before you can speak, the owner slides across the desk a "revised" P and L which shows that the company *really* made $311,797.69. (Fig. 2) Who's being kidded—the IRS, or you?

Probably both of you. The revised statement does shift from a calendar year to a more favorable fiscal year (adding $70,000 to the total sales). It also uses the kinds of rounded numbers ($3,600, $2,600, $1,500, etc.) which suggest someone is guessing freely. Still, most of the deductions used to reduce the net to where Acme only owed $800 in taxes are probably legal—at least, they're darned common. Let's consider a few:

· $17,000 extra is figured in the IRS-reported wages and salaries. One of the owners has her boyfriend on the payroll, doing nothing but picking up his paycheck. If that's true, it means another $17,000 (before taxes) you'd take home as owner.

· $56,108 was legitimately deducted from company earnings because the owners took it as their salaries. Perfectly standard, perfectly legal.

· $17,000 the company charged off for advertising and promotion, compared with the $3600 they figure the business actually required. Add to this their $10,006 for travel, $9100 for autos (all for the owners), and $8800 for officer's expenses, and you are well up into realms of legal gravy. The IRS might challenge some of this, but considering that Acme buys most of its product overseas, the deductions may well stand up. That's almost $50,000 worth of perks from a company showing a net of under $22,000.

· $47,231 reported for rent, plus $16,492 for depreciation—against the revised figures of $22,590 for rent, $8200 for depreciation. The extra $34,000 or so they took off their taxes all went for the plush office you're savoring now. They're saying the office can be dispensed with—you can put a desk in the warehouse and do just fine. Maybe so, but keep in mind the difference between $34,000 in tax-free luxury and $34,000 in heavily-taxed cash.

· $24,418 in legal and accounting expenses, against the $2600 they figure you'll have to pay. The owners say they faced some absolutely atypical litigation last year, and that (stictly between you and them), they may have charged off to the business a certain amount of personal legal expense.
Now you have complications. First off all, what about this "atypical litigation"? Remember what we said about extraordinary expenses in Chapter 9. Have all the legal bills been paid, and can you be guaranteed there will be no reoccurrence?
Next, what about that "certain amount" of personal legal expense? If it means one call to a lawyer to ask about a parking ticket, perhaps that's no crisis. But heavy personal expenses run through the company almost certainly mean eventual IRS trouble. Everything may be perfectly legal, but you *must* inquire. It's yet another reason to avoid buying an existing corporation.

And so on. In inventing Acme, I've been trying to walk a thin line, warning about the complexities of financial records without running a short course in tax evasion. The main point is two-fold. First, remember that 99 out of every 100 small business P and Ls carry accountants' disclaimers, saying they were prepared without audit. Financial documents should always be viewed cynically.
Second, recognize that small businesses offer many legal opportunities for tax reduction—but also many temptations to dubious or illegal deductions. Acme as I've invented it is mostly on the legal side—only those personal legal expenses, and perhaps the salary

to the owner's boyfriend are clearly suspect—but it does suggest some of the less savory dodges you may encounter. Many will be *far* worse than these.

Be aware of both your legal responsibilities, *and* the hazards of the marketplace. Buy a business solely by the "bottom line," and you'll likely suffer, either missing choice firms with tons of buried income, or else overpaying to acquire someone else's litigation. To survive, have someone (a CPA or a tax attorney) help you check every deduction for its legality, safety, and applicability to your own situation. Once you take possession, is time enough to pursue all the *true* exemptions our laws allow.

ACME CUSTOM METALS, INC.
TAX BASIS STATEMENT

PROFIT AND LOSS STATEMENT
19 2

	Month of	%	Year to Date	%
Sales-Cash			631,019.55	
Sales-Layaway			33,192.00	
Total Sales			664,211.55	
Cost of Sales-Cash			225,519.75	
" " " Layaway			10,940.50	
Total Cost			236,460.25	
Gross Profit			427,751.13	

Operating Expenses:

	Month of	%	Year to Date	%
Wages and Salaries			90,041.45	
Officer's Salaries			56,108.00	
Accounting & Legal			24,418.91	
Advertising			8,249.16	
Promotion			8,819.82	
Auto Expense			9,100.00	
Cash Over/Short			825.16	

	Month of	%	Year to Date	%
Credit Card Discount			6,525.00	
Burglar Alarm			1,247.51	
Depreciation Expenses			16,492.27	
Donations			6,010.00	
Dues and Subscriptions			684.65	
Entertainment/Travel			11,006.81	
Freight			4,944.03	
Insurance/General			17,920.02	
Insurance/Officers			1,341.11	
Misc. Expense			512.59	
Office Expense			5,833.52	
Officer's Expenses			8,800.00	
Outside Services			4,936.91	
Packaging			3,021.44	
Postage			386.30	
Rent			47,231.72	
Repair & Maint.			3,114.16	
Shop Supplies			4,009.51	
Payroll Tax Expense			13,129.25	
Taxes & Licenses			3,441.28	
Telephone			8,916.36	
Utilities			13,217.77	
Total Expenses			384,894.60	
Net Operating P/L			42,856.53	

Misc. Income/Expense:

Interest Income			65.90	
Interest Expense			(53,175.11)	
Misc. Income			32,351.91	
Net Profit Before Taxes			22,099.23	
Taxes Paid			600.00	
NET PROFIT/LOSS			21,499.23	

ACME CUSTOM METALS, INC.
REVISED STATEMENT

PROFIT AND LOSS STATEMENT
Jan. 19 2-Feb. 19 3

	Month of	%	Year to Date	%
Sales-Cash			701,743.45	
Sales-Layaway			35,333.88	
Total Sales			727,077.33	
Cost of Sales-Cash			234,816.52	
" " " Layaway			13,638.13	
Total Cost			248,454.65	
Gross Profit			478,622.69	

Operating Expenses:

	Month of	%	Year to Date	%
Wages and Salaries			73,516.00	
Officer's Salaries			—	
Accounting & Legal			2,600.00	
Advertising & Prom.			3,600.00	
Auto Expense			1,940.00	
Burglar Alarm			1,500.00	
Cash Over/Short			141.00	
Contributions			—	
Credit Card Disc.			6,525.00	
Depr. Expense			8,200.00	
Donations			—	
Dues & Subs.			—	
Employee Benefits			1,300.00	
Freight			4,942.00	
Insurance-General			6,027.00	
Insurance-Officers			—	
Misc. Expense			250.00	
Office Expense			1,100.00	
Officer's Expenses			—	
Outside Services			—	

	Month of	%	Year to Date	%
Packaging			3,021.00	
Payroll Tax Expense			8,527.00	
Postage			150.00	
Rent			22,590.00	
Repair & Maint.			1,738.00	
Shop Supplies			4,009.00	
Taxes & Licenses			600.00	
Telephone			2,106.00	
Travel & Enter.			800.00	
Utilities			11,643.00	
Total Expenses			166,825.00	
Net Operating P/L			311,797.69	

Misc. Income/Expense:

Interest Income
Interest Expense
Misc. Income
Estimated Income Tax
Net Profit Before Taxes
  Taxes Paid
  Taxes Paid

NET PROFIT/LOSS   311,797.69

Appendix 2
OFFER TO PURCHASE

Figure 3 is a typical Offer to Purchase the assets (but not the corporate shell) of a going business. Whether you buy through a business broker, or make the offer on your own, the form you use should provide at least as much information as this one, and should bind you to no other conditions. Here are some specific points:

1. "Stock" in the first line means inventory. If you are buying a going corporation, the offer should say as much in the title line above, and then specifically mention, "... *Corporate* stocks in _____, a corporation registered in the state of _____."

2. The entire purchase price, including encumbrances to be assumed and the amount of your deposit, must be spelled out in full.

3. "Subject to buyer's approval . . ." is your essential safety clause. Include it no matter what you've been promised or shown. You want the deposit check held uncashed, and the broker's promise to return it if the records or lease don't prove out.

4. "Seller agrees not to compete . . ." The "Noncompete" is one of the primary assets you are buying. Specify it clearly in the offer, and ask for the heftiest one possible—say, five years and 150 miles for retail sales. The value of the noncompete will be set later; right now, concentrate on the terms.

5. Termination hour, day, and date. Seventy-two hours is the longest an offer should stay in effect. Until the seller responds, you're bound, but he's free. You deserve that response.

7. "Receipt of above mentioned . . ." The offer form should double as a written receipt for your deposit.

Some brokers' forms may include space for a counter-offer. Anything more—especially anything binding you to further performance—should probably be struck out and initialled. Reject out-of-hand anything binding you to the payment of a commission—that's the seller's responsibility in every case. If you have any special conditions, see that they are written directly onto the form.

Once everything's to your liking, sign it, have the broker sign, get your copy back, and tell him or her to go get that acceptance. You're on your way!

(Figure 3)

AGREEMENT to PURCHASE PERSONAL PROPERTY and RECEIPT for DEPOSIT

The undersigned hereby offers to purchase from the owner thereof, the following described personal property in   County, California, being sold is, Trade Name, Fixtures, Equipment and Stock of ....

....

....

....

....

....

Entire Purchase Price is $ ...., to be paid as follows:

Cash (Check) delivered to Broker $_____

Cash to be delivered to Escrow Holder on or before .... 19............$_____

By assuming encumbrances ....$_____

   terms: $_____ per month, or more, _____% interest

By new encumbrance ....$_____

   terms: $_____ per month, or more, including _____% interest

....

....

....

....

....

....

....

....

Subject to the buyer's approval of rental arrangements and seller's business records. If either is not satisfactory prior to signing of Escrow instructions, Broker is hereby authorized to refund all funds on deposit immediately. Deposit check will be held uncashed by Broker pending opening of Escrow.

Seller agrees not to compete .... miles for .... years.
PRO RATE TAXES, INSURANCE, RENT-TO POSSESSION: ....
Escrow holder to be ....
Title to said property to be free from all encumbrances, except as above set forth.

This offer shall be binding on the purchaser until 5:00 P.M. on the
.... day of .... , 19....................., unless accepted by seller.

Purchaser

Date... Purchaser

Phone # .... Address

Receipt of above mentioned deposit is herewith acknowledged.

_____, Broker

By...

ACCEPTANCE

The undersigned seller hereby accepts the foregoing offer. I agree to pay the above
named agent the sum of $ .... or 10% of the total
consideration, whichever is greater, as commission for services rendered.

Time ....Seller

Date..Seller

Address

W-Y-P (in triplicate)   2228

Appendix 3
AUTHORIZATION TO SELL

When the time arrives for you to sell, your broker (if you choose to use one) will expect you to sign a "listing" or Authorization to Sell. Figure 4 is a fairly simple example of a listing for an unincorporated business. As with the Offer to Purchase, it represents the most you should agree to—and, as with any important legal document, you should check with your lawyer before signing whatever form your broker uses. Here are a few additional points.

1. Most of the form should be devoted to information about your business—and the more carefully the agent completes it, the more confidence s/he deserves. One tip: a competent agent will examine your business license or articles of incorporation, to ensure having gotten the signatures of every owner.

2. "Does Not Go . . ." Itemize anything valuable a buyer might see at the plant, but which is not included in the sale—you'll avoid later troubles. "A/R" means accounts receivable.

3. "Seller Agrees . . ." These eight points are all fairly standard items of protection for the buyer (except that "send-out slips" are for the broker's convenience). If you insist, a business can be sold "as is . . . where is . . . closed books" which means you guarantee nothing. Most brokers will, however, refuse such listings.

Now, in fact, is the time to raise any problems (say, a landlord who won't give a lease). A good broker can nearly always find solutions.

4. "Exclusive Listing" means you are liable for commission if *anyone* (broker or not) sells the business during the listing period. If you want the right to make a sale on your own, ask for an "Exclusive Agency" form. Note that for 180 days after the expiration date the broker is protected on any clients to whom he introduced you during the listing period.

5. "Agree to pay Broker 10% . . . or the MINIMUM commission. . . ." Though commissions are usually, by law, negotiable, few topline brokers will bend. Try for your best deal, and especially watch that minimum figure. Most brokerages assume they need at least $5,000 to cover their costs. That's OK—but don't let them write in, say, $25,000 on a $250,000 listing. That's 10% alright, but what happens if you ultimately take only $190,000? You get burned.

Ninety days is a fair listing period. Simple listings are best, even for large businesses; beware of any broker whose forms are too elaborate. A form similar to that in Figure 4 will protect you while still giving your broker plenty with which to work. If you have been offered any induce-ments to sign—for example, promises of box ads in the *Wall Street Journal* —this is the time to get them firmly in writing. Lastly, if you've held even informal talks with any potential buyers in the past, be sure to exempt them in writing from the terms of the listing—most brokers will agree gladly to a reasonably short list.

If everything looks fair and clear, if your attorney agrees, and especially if you have confidence in the broker or agent, then go ahead and sign. You will not be obliged to accept any offer unless it meets in full *all* your stated terms. If your broker's on the job, though, such an offer should be swiftly forthcoming. When that happens, go back and reread" SELLING OUT."

(Figure 4)

AUTHORIZATION TO SELL (in Triplicate)

Trade Name: _____   Type _____
Address _____   City _____Zip _____
Owner _____   Consider Partner Yes No   Taxes $__

Bus. Ph. _____   Reason Selling _____
Res. Ph. _____   Does Not Go: Personal Effects A/R $

Price $_____ Including Assumable   _____
Encumb.
Plus Stock $_____ (at assumable   _____
approx. cost)
Total Price $_____ Including Assum-   _____
able Encumb.
                                          Highway Changes Yes No Accu/Sus.
Encumbrance that can be assumed $ Pending __

_____

____@____ Per Mo., Including ____
____% Int.
____@____ Per Mo., Including ____
____% Int. incl.

Cash Down $_____ plus
stock
Total Monthly Payments $_____ inc.
____ Int.

Gross Sales $ _____
Net Profit $ _____
Period of: _____
Verified: Yes No   P&L in file   P&L to
follow
Accountant _____
Employees _____
Owner _____ Spouse ____
_____
Business Hours _____
Closed _____ Holidays ____
_____
Rent $_____ min. ____% Deposit
$_____
Lease until _____ Written Op-
tion _____
Landlord _____
Estab. _____ Pres. Owner
Since ____
Equipment on Rental $_____Mo.

_____
_____

Parking _____ Submit Trade
_____

Bldg. Size _____

Appearance _____ Yellow Page
Adv. Yes No

Call to Show

FIXTURES AND EQUIPMENT IN-
CLUDED IN SALE:
_____
_____
_____

_____
_____
_____

REMARKS: _____

_____

_____

_____

_____

_____

_____

Seller agrees (1) To execute a non-compete agreement in Escrow.
(2) To have all equipment in working condition at time of possession.
(3) All offers to purchase will be subject to buyer's approval of lease
and records.
(4) Possession of deposit check will be held by Broker pending
Escrow or return to buyer.
(5) Seller agrees to train buyer.
(6) Broker is authorized to use "send out slips"
(7) That the premises will pass all existing codes for this type of
business.
(8) To furnish records of Income and Expense to Broker and Buyer.

THIS IS AN EXCLUSIVE LISTING (in Triplicate)
DO NOT CLOSE A SALE, LEASE OR EXCHANGE WITHOUT CONSULTING
THE UNDERSIGNED BROKER

In consideration of the services of the undersigned Broker, I hereby list with said Broker from the date hereof until _____ 19__, at 6 P.M., the business, lease, real and/or personal property described above and I hereby grant said Broker the exclusive and irrevocable right to sell, exchange or lease the same within said time at the price and on the terms herein stated, or at such price and terms which are or may be accepted by me and to accept a deposit thereon. In case of any affiliation, employment, sale, exchange, or lease by the undersigned owner, the undersigned Broker, or any person, during the listing period or within 180 days from termination of this listing, to any party contacted by said Broker during the listing period, I hereby agree to pay

Broker   on demand 10% of the total price received by me or the MINIMUM commission of $_____, whichever is greater.

Seller warrants (a) that he will effect an assignment or transfer of the existing lease and that the terms of the lease are as represented by the Seller to the Broker in the listing of (b) that he will effect an assignment or transfer of the existing lease or the execution of a new lease with the modifications in the terms indicated by the Seller above.

Seller warrants that Seller is the legal owner of the above business, partnership or corporation and that this listing has been signed by person or persons with full legal capacity and authority to do so.

I hereby certify that I have read, supplied, understand and approve the foregoing. All statements contained herein are accurate and correct. I agree to furnish proof of same.

Receipt of a copy of this listing is
hereby acknowledged.   Date _____

By _____(Owner) _____
              Agent   Authorized Signature & Title

                                         (Owner) _____

                                         Authorized Signature & Title

W-Y-P   2228

A STARTER BIBLIOGRAPHY

Before you begin loading your shelves with $60-a-volume business books, consider the following useful but inexpensive sources:

Yellow Pages.

Obvious? OK—but along with the books for your own area, acquire those for the nearest major manufacturing center: Los Angeles, New York, Chicago. . . . You can nearly always save by dealing directly with suppliers rather than with local middlemen. Once you have some likely company names, ask 800-Information (1-800-555-1212) whether they offer a toll-free WATS line. If they do, use it.

To reach customers neighborhood-by-neighborhood, consider a reverse or *Street Directory*, which gives you the name and phone number for anyone at a particular street address. The Bell Companies lease these for six months at a time, at around $50 for six months. They're great for phone canvassers, or for assembling your own personalized direct-mailing lists.

Government Publications.

The Small Business Administration publishes a vast array of free pamphlets. For an order list, either ask at any SBA office, or contact:

The Small Business Administration
2442 L Street, NW
Washington, DC 20230
(202)655-4000

To learn about other government small business publications—from summaries of Labor Department policies to the results of the Census Bureau's very useful Economic Census of American business—request a catalogue called "Publications for Business" from:

US Government Printing Office
Superintendant of Documents
Washington, DC 20402

The listed publications, though reasonably priced, are not free. Before ordering any, try examining them either at a GPO bookstore (in major cities), or at a *Federal Depository Library*—which simply means a public or private library designated to receive such publications. Try the main branch of your public library or any true university library. In fact, many large libraries will have *government document reading rooms*, collections of such documents from here and abroad.

No-Cost Works from Banks and Accounting Firms.

Many truly fine publications are available either free or for nominal charge from major financial and accounting firms. A good start is Bank of America's *Small Business Reporter* series. Between twenty and thirty different titles are usually available at any one time; about half are devoted to general principles ("Cash Flow/Cash Management", etc.), and half to specific businesses ("Restaurants", for example). Copies are free from any Bank of America branch, or available by mail for $2 per copy:

Small Business Reporter
Bank of America
Department 3401
PO Box 37000
San Francisco, CA 94137

If you drop them a line, they'll send you a free list of available reports. Other big banks offer similar services, from pamphlets through full-scale management courses running $200–300—don't hesitate to visit several institutions and ask what's available.

Equally useful are the huge quantities of up-to-date financial (especially tax) information available from the major accounting firms. The seventy-nine-page Price-Waterhouse booklet on the Tax Act of 1981, for example, was the most lucid interpretation I saw, and it was in the hands of P-W clients and other professionals before many people even knew there *was* a 1981 Tax Act. Most of the Big-Eight firms are exceedingly generous with their spare copies—just don't abuse the privilege.

Filling Holes in Your General Background. When it comes to learning the basics of fields like accounting or real estate, your choice of books will depend upon your background, academic self-discipline, and even literary tastes. The following are simply a few books I admire.

If you'd like another general text to supplement this one, there are at least two which I greatly admire. Albert Lowry's *How to Become Financially Successful by Owning Your Own Business* emphasizes traditional issues like insurance, security, office organization: on these topics (and many others), Lowry's book is fine indeed. The same can be said for *How to Run a Small Business* by the J.K. Lasser Tax Institute, which is especially strong on matters of financial infrastructure.

The real estate literature is probably more extensive than that on any other branch of business, but, unfortunately, most of the books are written for investors, developers, or brokers. One book aimed at the business tenant in Diane C. Thomas's *How To Save Money On Your Business Rent: A Tenant's Guide to Office and Retail Leasing,* as good a guide as you'll find.

Perhaps someday Ms. Thomas will write a similar guide to industrial real estate from the businessperson's point of view. Some years ago, I did see such a book briefly, but I've never been able to locate another copy, or even to discover its name. So my best recommendation is a standard text, Kinnard and Messner's *Industrial Real Estate,* published by the Society of Industrial Realtors. It's written for the professional realtor, and the tone is strictly academic, but the information you want is almost certainly there.

In insurance, the situation is much the same: many fine generalist guides to personal insurance, few to business coverage. So I'll just repeat the recommendation I made in Chapter 13: *Risk Management and Insurance* by C. A. Williams and R.M. Heins is both informative and, as textbooks go, quite readable.

I'm reluctant to recommend accounting books, because I think courses, which let you practice doing *corrected* exercises, are a much wiser approach, and because most accounting books are about as stimulating as a case of sleeping sickness. Still, one livelier standout deserves a special mention. With Xerox Learning Systems' *Reading and Evaluating Financial Reports* you'll learn the basics of business finance while working your programmed way through the Annual Report of a fictional company called "Static, Inc." The topics covered include LIFOs, FIFOs, ROIs, etc. Book Two even provides a Dun and Bradstreet ratios table for comparisons. At $29.95, it's pricey for a couple of magazine-sized "books," but you can buy much weightier tomes and leave them unopened on the shelf. Again, if you want to make use of ratios when studying or running a business of your own, you'll likely want either the full Dun and Bradstreet annual tables, or perhaps the *Annual Statement Studies* published by Robert Morris Associates, 1616 Philadelphia National Bank Bldg., Philadelphia, PA. (The *Statement Studies*, as mentioned in Chapter 9, also feature a comprehensive general explanation of ratios).

The most expensive books are reference or resource books, including "guides" or "directories" to buyers, lenders, consultants, and so on. They can be money well spent if you use them often enough, but before plopping down $300 a volume for books which will be obsolete in a year, consider the following. 1) Often you can borrow these volumes from either your bank or a local business- or law-school library. 2) Sometimes the information can be had more cheaply from the federal government, since many of these directories are only elegant repackagings of data available from the GPO. 3) Sometimes nearly the same data is available at nominal cost from *trade* or *professional associations*. For example, you can spend anywhere from $24.95 on up (way up) for a guide to franchise opportunities, or you can send $1.50 to the International Franchise Association for a copy of its annual directory. You'll get details (including entry costs) for nearly 350 types of franchise business, plus advice on avoiding franchising scams. Write the IFA at: 1025 Connecticut Avenue N.W., Washington, D.C., 20036. 4) Increasingly, expensive resource books are being replaced by computerized *data bases*. Specialized data bases are usually listed in big-city yellow pages under the same topic headings (management consultants, marketing analysts) that you would check to find the corresponding resource book. They aren't cheap—up to $150 per inquiry, something less on contract basis—but a good one will be thorough and absolutely up-to-date.

Newspapers and Magazines.

Good as they are, books and pamphlets won't keep you current on fast-breaking business news. Low-cost general information data bases (*The Source, Dow Jones News/Retrieval,* and others) will probably prove the ultimate solution, but for at least a few more years, most of us will continue to depend heavily on newspapers and business publications.

The pre-eminent American business newspaper is, of course, the *Wall Street Journal.* Its fine weekly column on small business appears each Monday—if reading time's scarce, that's your one essential issue.

If you can, supplement the *WSJ* with at least one business magazine. Of the big three—*Forbes, Fortune,* and *Business Week*—only *Forbes* seems to take a consistent interest in small business. In 1982, it began a regular column on venture capital, and its "Up & Comers" section features one or more successful small businesses (or services for small business) each issue. Still, all three are quality journals, and big business ideas are often of use to small firms.

Recent years, moreover, have seen rapid growth of magazines devoted exclusively to small business: *Inc., California Business,* and many others. Some are slickly professional, others, a bit less polished. Nearly all contain valuable information. Check out several to see which is best for you.

And let's re-emphasize an idea from Chapter 12, that major corporations will help small business. The big companies—Xerox, Control Data, and Southland, among many others—which answered my questions during the preparation of this book, all said they'd gladly do as much for any small businessperson. Some majors (like Control Data, through its Small Business Centers) offer low-cost counselling or courses for small business owners. Many others will advise and aid small companies informally. If you have a problem with security, or inventory control, or anything else, don't suffer in silence: either find the nearest counselling center (private, university-sponsored, or SBA-backed), or else just ask help from any major company with which you do business.

So there you have some starting points. For ongoing interests or stubborn problems, you might ask a good local bookstore to call you whenever they get a new title in your field. Certain topics may justify your hiring a part-time researcher to comb the catalogues and library stacks. Be persistent. Amid all the books and pamphlets, newspapers and data bases continually appearing, your answer is almost certainly to be found.

INDEX

accountants:
    approval of, 311–12
    bankruptcy and, 294–95
    corporations and, 51–52, 89, 97
    insurance advice of, 146, 147,
        149, 159
    interpretation of financial
        records by, 43, 104, 109,
        117–18, 128, 317–18
    preparation of financial records
        by, 22, 111, 112
    real estate advice of, 260
accounts receivable, 12, 93, 95, 206
"acid test" ratio, 113–14
acquisitions, *see* taking over
Activision, 174
advertising, 101, 254–61, 266
    displays in, 259–60
    failing businesses and, 277, 284
    humor in, 259, 261
    manufacturers' aid in, 257
    media attention as, 258–60
    newspaper, 257–58
    product recognition in, 260–61,
        277
    promotions vs., 255
    radio and television, 257
    word-of-mouth, 72–73
air conditioning, 202, 203
aircraft, 58, 93, 94
alarm systems, 165–66
alcohol licenses, 34–35, 127–28,
    141

American Arbitration Association,
    130, 184
American Bar Association, 187
amusement licenses, 35
annual reports (corporations), 89,
    91
Annual Statement Studies, 113, 115,
    332
antitrust suits, 96
appeals (litigation), 190–91
Apple Computers, 11, 12, 66, 73,
    178, 276
apprenticeship, 221
arbitration, 130, 184–85, 189, 192
arson, 311
Arthur Treacher's, 96
assets:
    appreciation and depreciation
        of, 107, 111–12, 114, 123,
        137, 196, 312, 317
    bulk purchase of, 95–96, 97
    "dishing off" of, 191–92
    fixed (equity), 23, 41–42, 206
    hard, 93–96, 114, 124
    "like for like" exchanges of,
        313
    liquid, 22–23, 93, 95, 114
    sale of, 88, 114, 124, 131, 148,
        285, 287, 295, 304, 313, 314
"association factor," 195, 200
Atari, 11, 12, 174
attorneys, *see* lawyers
attornment, 207